Praise for

"Rob Halford…is back with another fascinating and insightful book….Rob delivers the scriptures of his life's work with a clever and unique twist….He shares these 'gospel truths' with humor and open candor without leaving out any risqué details….*Biblical*…is told in Rob's relaxed tone, as if he is speaking directly to you one-on-one while mixing serious and in-depth topics with whimsical reflections on life's lessons." —*Sonic Perspectives*

"Fans can rightfully think of [this] as 'The Book of Halford.' A fast and fun read…There are plenty of funny moments." —*Antimusic.com*

"[*Biblical*] is the perfect companion piece [to *Confess*], looser and even more wry and humorous….Halford's 'sermons from the mount of heavy metal' will attract even the non-hardcore Judas Priest fan." —*The Houston Press*

"Halford's honest and warm recollections give the feeling of hanging out with an elder rock statesman who never fails to entertain. He shows the same humility and sensitivity as in his previous book, and readers will find that he is never far from his roots as a kid from Walsall, England. Rock-music readers who enjoyed Halford's first book will enjoy his second just as much, if not more." —*Library Journal*

"Aspiring metal gods…will enjoy these sermons from the mic." —*Kirkus Reviews*

Praise for

Confess

"For nearly half a century, Halford has been the voice of Judas Priest, screaming for vengeance against nonbelievers." —*Rolling Stone*

"Raw and searingly moving, *Confess* will delight metalheads and music fans alike." —*GQ*

"*Confess* can't be reduced to a collection of salacious gay encounters, cocaine binges, or romanticized rock 'n' roll horror stories. It's a cautionary tale that offers redemption through courage and the changing of times. It's a treasure trove of heavy metal nuggets and anecdotes that any rock-blog dork would lose their mind over. But most importantly, it's a beautiful exploration of the human condition and one man's capacity for love and self-love." —*Forbes*

"Salacious revelations....The most hotly anticipated hard-rock autobiography of the year, Rob Halford's *Confess* is gossipy, good natured, and hilarious, often unintentionally. It's also gloriously and relentlessly filthy....With a breezy, down-to-earth frankness...*Confess* is much more personal story than music memoir...Halford is winningly unpretentious and self-deprecating....In its final stretches, *Confess* becomes a moving meditation on family, friendship, personal growth, and social progress...[a] revealing and entertaining book." —*Classic Rock Review*

"Rob Halford led Judas Priest, and heavy metal itself, out of the Midlands and into the big time." —*The Guardian*

"Deliciously readable... *Confess* is a warts-and-all rock 'n' roll confessional."
—*Esquire*

"A unique and deeply revealing insight into the extraordinary life he has led."
—*Metal Talk*

"When it comes to metal memoirs, Judas Priest frontman Rob Halford's aptly titled and long-awaited *Confess: The Autobiography* certainly has enough sex, drugs, and rock 'n' roll to satisfy voracious readers of, say, Motley Crüe's *The Dirt* or Keith Richards's *Life*. But a great deal of sorrow also permeates the just-released page-turner."
—*Yahoo! News*

"A must-read for pop-culture lovers and metalheads alike."
—*The Baltimore Sun*

"His memoir recounts the highs and lows of his history in a medley of comical, candid, and heartbreaking stories about obstacles and experiences... *Confess* is a fascinating portrait, dripping in Halford's polite yet brutally honest demeanor and personal slang: equal parts legendary metal icon and everyday humble Walsall lad."
—*Phoenix New Times*

"Rob tells his story without holding anything back. Some truly incredible accounts."
—NPR's *Bullseye with Jesse Thorn*

"The full, frank, and shocking autobiography of Judas Priest's Metal God.... [T]his book celebrates five decades of the guts and glory of rock 'n' roll."
—*Rough Trade*

"An incredibly candid look at one of the biggest metal vocalists of all time.... Full of great stories and great jokes."
—*Metal Injection*

"The book is well-crafted, detailing Halford's early years and initial forays into the music biz. Fans will love the details of the rise of Priest along with the peaks and valleys along the way... Everything... included helped show a real informative blueprint of [Halford's] background."
—*Anti-Music*

"You can add 'great writer' to [Halford's] resume as well. His story is incredible and his journey is something that reads like a Hollywood script. Albeit a Quentin Tarantino film....The pages are filled [with] so many great stories and memories—both good and bad. But you get the sense that Halford has always been able to persevere and make the best out of whatever situation he found himself in. And he does this by absolutely keeping the reader entertained with anecdotes and an unbelievable sense of humor." —*Sound Vapors*

"What a rock memoir should be—brutally honest and funny as hell....[Rob Halford] has written a rock memoir so full of life, humor, insight, and turmoil that it feels reductive even to assign it to that formulaic genre...complex and richly textured....While much of the book's power derives from Halford's struggle to integrate his public and private lives, there are plenty of beautifully remembered tales of the kind that enliven any rags-to-rock-riches story....A redemptive, funny, honest account....We all carry secrets. The lesson of this unforgettable memoir is not to let those secrets undo what makes each of us uniquely valuable." —RockandRollGlobe.com

"A powerful, often shocking read." —*Vintage Guitar*

"Delivered with refreshing down-to-earth frankness...Simply put, it's a must-read—not only for fans of Halford and Judas Priest, but for all music fans." —*Louder*

"[Halford] didn't pull any punches and he didn't leave anything out. I thought that was very courageous...very heartfelt and very real." —Buzz Osborne, Melvins

Biblical

Rob Halford's
Heavy Metal Scriptures

✝

Rob Halford

with Ian Gittins

BOOKS

New York

Hachette Books
Hachette Book Group
1290 Avenue of the Americas
New York, NY 10104
HachetteBooks.com
Twitter.com/HachetteBooks
Instagram.com/HachetteBooks

First Trade Paperback Edition: November 2023

Published by Hachette Books, an imprint of Hachette Book Group, Inc. The Hachette
Books name and logo is a trademark of the Hachette Book Group.

The Hachette Speakers Bureau provides a wide range of authors for speaking
events. To find out more, go to hachettespeakersbureau.com or email
HachetteSpeakers@hbgusa.com.

The publisher is not responsible for websites (or their content) that are not owned by
the publisher.

Print book interior design by Jeff Williams

Library of Congress Control Number: 2022942565

ISBNs: 978-0-306-82824-9 (hardcover), 978-0-306-83160-7 (B&N Black Friday
Signed Edition), 978-0-306-83159-1 (B&N.com Signed Edition), 978-0-306-83158-4
(Signed Edition), 978-0-306-82826-3 (ebook), 978-0-306-82825-6 (trade paperback)

Printed in the United States of America

LSC-C

Printing 1, 2023

CONTENTS

Contents

The Book of Psalms and Testaments † 43

The Book of Pilgrimages † 97

Contents

THE BOOK OF VESTMENTS † 167

THE BOOK OF DISCIPLES † 183

THE BOOK OF CHRONICLES † 199

THE BOOK OF RITUALS
AND SERVICES † 233

Contents

INTRODUCTION

I believe they call the story of Jesus, and by extension the Bible, "the greatest story ever told." Some people still swear by it (and on it). They pore over its hundreds of thousands of words* seeking the ultimate truth and the meaning of life, and strive to follow its scriptures and strictures to the letter.

I see myself as a spiritual person and yet I must confess (it's a habit!) to you that I've never actually read the Bible all that much. I find it very boring and I can't keep up with the plot: so-and-so begat so-and-so who begat so-and-so . . . *yawn*. It always seems like too much palaver.

I like the idea, though, of a book that compiles all the knowledge that a person has collected through their life and tries to be a definitive guide to what they know about their world. So, I've taken the audacious, you might say presumptuous, step of writing this book called *Biblical*.

What is it? *Biblical* is my book of scriptures. These scriptures are the sacred knowledge, the gospel truths, that I have picked up in the nearly fifty years since I first started fronting a band called Judas Priest. They are my sermons from the mount of heavy metal.

It's been more than two thousand years since a load of ancient wrist merchants cobbled together that first Bible. I reckon we're well overdue

---

*There are 783,137 words in the King James Bible. Not that I've counted them myself, I must admit.

a follow-up. It's definitely time for that difficult second album! And *Biblical* is a follow-up ... but not the follow-up to the Bible.

No, *Biblical* is the follow-up to a book I wrote two years ago that I called *Confess*. It deserved its title. *Confess* was my autobiography, the story of the adventures and misadventures that took me from a Walsall council estate to the (ahem!) venerable Metal God that I am today.

Confess was the story of my personal life in all its devout and debauch detail. *Biblical* is something else: It's the story of a life in music. It's all about the magic and madness of life in a band and of the half a century I have spent religiously worshipping heavy metal.

When I was a kid, I used to wonder what life in a band would be like. It seemed unreachable, unattainable. As I gazed at my heroes in *Melody Maker* or *Sounds*, so many questions bounced around my bonce:

> *How do you write a song? What's it like in a studio? What does it feel like to play a gig? To go on tour? Are bands always best mates? How do they decide what to wear? Do they take drugs and shag groupies every night? Do they always trash every hotel?*

And the biggest, most burning question of all:

> *Being in a band looks like the best life in the world—is it?*

Well, now I know the answers to all those questions, and I want to share them. I have scribed many psalms and testaments, and I've journeyed many times around the world on metal pilgrimages. I've donned my leather vestments, blessed disciples, and succumbed to diabolical temptations.*

You don't go fifty years as a Metal God without getting to know every last thing about what it's like to be in a band. Well, I wanted to collect this divine wisdom into a holy book. I wanted to ascend to

---

*I must admit: I did quite a bit of succumbing to diabolical temptations. I was good at it.

the pulpit (if my dodgy back will let me) and deliver my heavy metal scriptures.

So, take a pew! I don't recommend that you go searching for the ultimate truth or the meaning of life in this book, but there are some cracking stories. Even a few decent parables. And without giving too much away, maybe you'll forgive me a little spoiler:

Being in a band IS the best life in the world.

So, let's get started. It's going to be *Biblical* . . .

THE BOOK OF GENESIS

Whether it's the greatest story ever told or not, *every* tale has to begin somewhere. The Bible opens with the fable of how the world began . . . so let's start our metal scriptures by looking at how groups get started.

What makes anyone want to become a musician and form a band in the first place? What can you learn from the false starts and the flop bands before anything starts happening? And do you need spiritual guidance to see you through the wilderness years of paying your dues?

It's Old Testament time! Let's begin our musical Holy Gospel back in the prehistoric days of the early seventies, when a young Black Country heavy metal band first stalked the earth . . .

ESCAPISM

Why does anyone join a band?

For me, and I suspect countless thousands of others, it all came down to *escapism*.

What do you want to escape? Well, if you're a young person, from a certain background, you want to break free from the life that's been laid out for you: the path you're meant to follow. You want to get out of the routine and transcend the everyday. You want *adventure*.

When I was a kid in Walsall, there was a mundanity to day-to-day life. Everyone stayed where they were put. They'd leave school, get a job in a local factory, and work there until they retired. People talked about "a job for life" like it was a good thing. To me, it sounded bloody terrifying!

I'm not saying that everyone who wants to join a band hates their childhood. That's not it. I was a happy kid. I loved Mom and Dad to bits and I knew they loved me. But the thought of working in my dad's steel factory scared me to death.

I knew that I wanted something else. Something *other*. When I was still little, I would walk to the end of our street, Kelvin Road, on our council estate, and think: *I wonder what's over there? What's out there?* There was just a deep-seated desire to see *more*. *To do more*.

Kids always want to be famous. Today, they want to be on TikTok or to become a YouTuber. An influencer. When I was a kid, the best and most exciting way to get attention was to be in a band.

That was the escape route. In my teens, I'd gawp at the bands on *Top of the Pops* and submerge myself in *Melody Maker* and *NME* every week. I'd see photos of Jimi Hendrix or the Rolling Stones, onstage playing to thousands of people or on their private jets, and that would blow my tiny mind.

What must it be like? What must it . . . feel like?

Rock stars were gods. They didn't seem mortal. I'll never forget seeing Robert Plant propping up the bar at the Grand Hotel in Walsall. I'd never have dared approach him, but I sat on the other side of the bar and I couldn't take my eyes off him.

The biggest rock star in the world! The Golden God! Supping a pint of Banks's Mild in Walsall!

When you're a kid, being in a band seems like something that you could never do. Then, as you get older, you start to dream that maybe, just maybe, you might be able to pull it off.

At sixteen, I saw firsthand what it was like to be on a stage. While working at the Grand Theatre in Wolverhampton, I'd stand at the side of the stage, working the lights, and see the great reactions the actors and comics got from the audience. I envied Tommy Trinder!* It was a life-changing experience, and I knew one thing:

I don't want to be behind this curtain, working the lights. I want to be on the stage. I want to feel what they're feeling.

And, for me, there was only one way to get on that stage. To join a band.

As I said in my autobiography, *Confess*, my first big showbiz break was singing "The Skye Boat Song" ("Speed, bonnie boat, like a bird on the wing...") in class at primary school, and the class clapping me. At that moment, aged ten, I realized how important using my voice and singing is to me.

Even today, I only feel truly alive as a person when I'm singing with Judas Priest. It was always my destiny. There are so many great reasons to join a band—to break free from routine; to have adventures; to be a rock-and-roll outlaw; to see the world. And then there's the most vital of all, without which none of those mean anything:

You have to love, and live for, music.

EARLY BANDS

Bruce Springsteen was in a garage band called the Castiles. David Bowie was in a mod group called the Lower Third. Ronnie James Dio formed a fifties pop group, the Vegas Kings. Billy Joel (!) was in a heavy metal duo named Attila.

It is a rule of musical scripture that virtually every big-name star has a few false starts behind them; flop bands that they formed, full of hopes and dreams, which then got absolutely nowhere. Those groups are vital. They give you something special, something magical.

Your first bands, no matter how basic and primitive, give you the thrill of playing music. They show you how important that is, and

---

*Tommy Trinder was an old-school music-hall star and comedian. Any Brit over sixty will remember his catchphrase: "You lucky people!"

they make you feel more complete. The world may not care—so fucking what? You know: *This is what I should be doing. This is what my life is about.*

They're your first chance to be creative. You're not just being a singer, you're being a lyricist. You're thinking up melodies. You're learning how the bass connects to the drums. That's what first bands give you: building blocks. A musical education.

I had tons of early flop bands. I started off singing covers in a group called Thark, with my old school music teacher. Then I did Abraxis, and then Athens Wood. We played free-form experimental blues and it never seemed quite *serious* enough.

I didn't care. I was just enjoying playing, jamming, and wailing.

I've always been an optimist, especially as a young lad. Even after those groups failed, I thought, *The next band will be the one! The one that will happen!* And I especially thought that when I joined Lord Lucifer.

Lord Lucifer was my first metal band. I was bang into it. I still remember buying red, yellow, and black house paint and painting flames and the band's name on the side of my BSA motorbike. I felt so cool, riding to rehearsals. I'd stop at traffic lights and some bloke driving a car would clock me:

"Eh, pal, what's that mean? Lord Lucifer?"

"It's me band, mate!"

Lord Lucifer never did bugger all, either. But that's how it is. You have to fall down a bunch of times and pick yourself up.

When you're in early bands, you're often doing a day job as well. I was selling clothes in a shop called Harry Fenton's by day. And often, if we got a rare gig, I was playing them in stolen underwear.

I admitted in *Confess* that I used to borrow shirts from the shop, go out drinking in them, then put them back on the shelves. But now I've got a fuller confession. As a young gay man, I was very interested when we went from selling boring old medieval white y-fronts to colorful briefs.

As the shop manager, I'd nick these knickers from Fenton's, wear them when I went out, then stick them back on sale. I'd love to say that I washed them first . . . but I didn't.*

My last early band was Hiroshima. We played blues, and we'd rehearse and rehearse and rehearse, week after week. We'd even get a very occasional gig and I'd think, *Oh, we're getting some traction here!* But we never did. The world wasn't interested. And, thinking back, I can't really blame it.

I learned a lot in my first bands, as I'm sure Ronnie James Dio did in the Vegas Kings (in 1957!), but I only ever had one tipping point, where I knew: *Right! This is a real band with a proper future! THIS IS IT!*

And that came when I joined Judas Priest.

BANDS OF BROTHERS

One of the biggest clichés in music is to say that a band is like a gang. And, like most clichés, there is a lot of truth in it.

The young Mötley Crüe famously lived together in a squalid, filthy hovel within spitting distance of the Whisky a Go Go in LA. Nikki Sixx recalls that, between trying to shag every girl on Sunset Strip, they would plot nonstop about how the Crüe would take over and rule the rock world.

Priest didn't talk like that. The quiet, deadpan West Midlands yam-yam nature is a long way from the brash self-confidence of Southern California hair-rockers.† Yet in our own understated, lugubrious way, we were just as determined to make it.

When you're in a new band that you believe in, you're united by having a shared dream . . . and by poverty. You're committed and

---

*Disgusting, isn't it? Well, I guess it was quite rock and roll. I wonder if Bruce Springsteen wore stolen underpants in the Castiles?

† For those of you who haven't read *Confess* (why not?!): "yam-yam" is a Birmingham nickname for us down-to-earth Black Country folk, and for our accents. Example: "Yam gewin' out?" "I yam! To the pub!"

determined to make it, but you haven't got a pot to piss in. You *are* like a gang in that it feels like it's you against the world.

You really value each other and you know how important each of you is in the makeup of the band. Back in the early seventies, working-class blokes in the West Midlands didn't talk about their feelings—*"Fuck off, you poof!"*—but, unspoken, Priest always knew how close we were.

Today, I'd happily tell Glenn or Ian in conversation that I love them. But fifty years ago, the world was a very different place.

In 1973, we were starving musicians with virtually no money. We'd face hard questions: "Do we buy petrol for the van or can we afford a bag of chips?" The van always won. Every £5 or £10 we earned from a gig went straight back into the band.

Like Mötley Crüe, we often all crashed out together. Our equivalent of their Sunset Strip shitpit was our first manager Corky's one-bedroom flat in Meynell House in Handsworth, Birmingham. Corky, Ken, Ian, and I all squeezed into this tatty crash pad. I usually slept, or rather passed out, on the floor.

You're selling your soul for rock and roll. You're with each other twenty-four hours a day, playing music, eating, drinking, laughing, fighting . . . *everything*. It's a bond, a heavy metal bond that nourishes the band and the music.

In fact, "gang" isn't enough—you become a *family*. You meet as a bunch of strangers and you turn into a family unit; a heavy metal clan; a band of brothers. You stand and fall together; share the same triumphs and defeats.

Of course, the big difference between a band and a family is that sometimes a new member, a new blood brother, can join a band and change the whole chemistry of the unit. It might be great at first, and then . . . go wrong. But that is a *Biblical* topic for us to come to later . . .

REHEARSALS

When you're starting out in a band, there are three things that are so crucial that you do them every single minute that you can: rehearsals, rehearsals, and rehearsals.

It can't be overstated. In the early days, rehearsals are everything. They're where you come to understand the components of the band: the individual characters of the members, and what each of them brings to the table.

You're trying to find a balance, to get a feeling. You don't know what you're looking for until you find it. You're listening to every note, every chord, fine-tuning and searching for that moment when you know: *This is it! Everything feels right! The motor is running!*

As the singer, I've always listened analytically in rehearsal to everything around me: how the drums are working, and the guitars and the bass. I find listening to the music thrilling even before I begin to stick my voice on top of everything else.

It's hard to describe because it's a feeling. All music is feeling. But when you get what you're after, *you know it.*

Priest had that feeling from day one. My very first rehearsal with them made me feel *complete* in a way that Athens Wood or Hiroshima never did. The musicianship and the overall textures felt so strong. I could tell they contained so many possibilities.

Our earliest rehearsals were exciting . . . but basic. Ian would drive us in our van three miles to Holy Joe's, a hall next to St. James Church School in Wednesbury. Over the years, a lot of Midlands bands have rehearsed there: Band of Joy (Robert Plant's first band), Slade, and tons of others.

Holy Joe himself, the vicar, Father Joe Husband, would be waiting. He'd greet us by saying, "Fares, please!" meaning he wanted our three quid to rent the hall for the evening. We'd scrape it together, and Holy Joe would knob off to the pub to spend it. Then we'd set up.

John Hinch would set up his drum kit. Ian had his gigantic bass speaker. At first, Ken didn't have a 100-watt Marshall stack, which was the big thing for guitarists in the seventies—they all used to lose their minds over them. It took him a while to get one of those.

The only equipment I needed was a microphone, and I used to bloody go through the buggers! I craved a Shure mic, but I couldn't afford one so I'd buy cheap ones from the music shop in Stafford Street, Walsall. My voice was so low that they'd break when I screamed into them.

We'd set up and have to get everything *right*. It's like getting a hospital operating theatre ready, or preparing a plane for take-off. The band wouldn't take off until we had the volume levels right, the right tone on the bass, and the mic right, so we didn't get feedback.

Then it was the big moment: *"One-two-three-four!"* And off we'd go, looking for the magic.

We'd start by jamming and playing twelve-bar blues. We never did *loads* of covers, but we'd do a couple to warm up: some Hendrix, John Mayall's Bluesbreakers, a bit of Cream. Just learning whether we had the chops to play these songs by established, virtuoso, genius musicians.

Rehearsals took us where they took us. We didn't have anybody trying to be a band leader and take control. I'd say we got more focused in that way when Glenn joined, because as a musician, he was—he *is*—always formulating plans and ideas.

In their formative years, bands swap out members as they seek the right balance in rehearsals. You know instinctively when you are firing on all cylinders and when a wheel is about to drop off. That was how we knew we needed a new drummer before our second album.

It was all about rehearsal, rehearsal, rehearsal . . . but we didn't mind. In fact, we loved it. Because we knew it was making us a better band; turning us into a metal machine.

Fifty years on, I can't pretend it's the same. There are times that I can hate going to rehearsals. I'll wake up in the morning like a kid who has to go to school: "No! Have I *got* to?" And yet they are still just as crucial.

Playing live is second nature for Priest by now, but we still have to do four or five full-day rehearsals in the fortnight before we go on tour. If we don't, we get sloppy. Even at our great age as a band, we can only stay disciplined through repetition, repetition, repetition.

We need to be able to play without me wondering what I am going to do with my voice on the fourth line of the following song. *You can't be thinking too much.* If you're thinking about the music too much as you play it, it won't be happening. It'll be coming from the wrong place.

Before our *50 Heavy Metal Years* anniversary tour, we knew we'd be doing some old tracks we'd never played live before, so we had to rehearse those. But we also had to run through "Breaking the Law" and "Living After Midnight" and "Turbo Lover" yet again. Or we'd drop the ball.

Rehearsing is still vital. Even now, when Priest are playing a live show and belting it out, it's the result not only of all the miles under our belts but also because of our endless rehearsals and practices. Before we go on, we warm up in a jam room. Because you can never do that enough.

And, you want to know the great thing? Even today, when going to rehearsals can feel like a chore, I still get a frisson of excitement when I'm there and we're ready to play. Because I know how great it's about to sound. Father Joe, bless him, is long gone, but *that* thrill is still the same.

PAYING YOUR DUES

When you've rehearsed and rehearsed until you're properly tight, you embark on the rite of passage that every group since the dawn of rock and roll has gone through. Playing small venues. Working your way up. *Paying your dues.*

Yep, it's the days of living in a rancid Transit van coughing up and down the M6, getting changed in the bogs because the venue has no dressing room, playing to two bored men and their yawning dog, and being paid a tenner for the privilege. There's no shortcut around this character-building experience, and you know what? *I wouldn't want there to be any shortcuts!* It's a huge part of starting out in a band.

Of course, when you play your first few gigs, you don't know it's going to be a slog. You're excited and full of nervous energy. *This is it! Will there be anyone there? Will they like us?* The ref's blown his whistle and the game is on!

Then reality hits you. You're stuck on a tatty stage in a grotty pub, or—in our early days—a working men's club. In front of you, on a moth-eaten, swirly carpet, are a handful of blokes out for a pint, a bag of scratchings, and a chinwag. These blokes are moaning about their wives, or nattering about work or football or the weather. They're here for the beer, not music:

"Oh, there's a band on? Who am they?"
"Judas Priest, it sez."
"Judas Priest? Soft name, ay it?"

And there was our challenge. To get these disinterested blokes to take notice of us and win them over. To get the guy at the bar to pause his chat, put his pint of Double Diamond down, and have a look at us.

It wasn't easy. We'd play some club gigs to brutal indifference and, at the end of every song, resounding silence—or what the Zen-lovers call the sound of one hand clapping. Now and then, we'd get heckled, or even booed.

But it didn't often happen. Normally, through sheer willpower, brute force, and the majesty of heavy metal, we won them over.

I can't even remember the first gig I played with Priest. Weird, isn't it? You'd think it would be seared into my memory. I'm led to believe it was at a club called the Townhouse in Wellington in Shropshire in May 1973. That's probably true but I couldn't swear to it!

What I *do* know is that Priest played hundreds of gigs in our first three or four years. Getting to them was a palaver in itself. We'd all bundle into our van. A mate, Nick, would roadie for us. Nick was on the dole so we'd bung him a couple of quid (if we had it).

With five or six blokes who weren't big on showering all crammed into a little Transit around our amps and gear, it could get seriously toxic in that van. With all the smoking and farting, the air would get properly juicy. I swear sometimes you could hear it hum.

How did we cover up the stink? Patchouli oil was the big thing. Until Brut aftershave got invented, that is . . .

Like any band, we started off playing the same handful of venues in our local neck of the woods. We did the Midlands circuit. Walsall,

Dudley, Birmingham, Wolverhampton, Cannock, Coventry...if a rock club had a spare gig night going, we'd be there.

We'd always see posters for the handful of bands who were slogging away on the same circuit. The Steve Gibbons Band. The Trevor Burton Band. They were big in the West Midlands, but they never did too much anywhere else.

With all respect to them, we didn't want to be like that...and soon, we weren't. Thanks to our gift-of-the-gab manager, Corky, it wasn't long before we started getting gigs up and down the country.

I remember so many of the venues: The Top Deck in Redcar. The Top Hat in Spennymoor. The Drill Hall in Lincoln. Barry Memorial Hall. They all looked the same: long, noisy, smoke-filled rooms, with a bar down one side, and a gaggle of guys giving us the eye and thinking: *Go on, then! Impress us!*

Some of the names sounded great—Heavy Steam Machine in Stoke! Top of the World in Guildford!—but they were mostly working men's boozers that had adopted fancy names for their rock night. And they were full of working men, boozing.

Fifty years on, those early gigs can merge into a blur, but it's amazing to read old press cuttings. A 1974 review in a local paper in Sunderland said that "hardly anybody turned up" to the show, but at least praised our singer, "Bob Holford," for his "very powerful vocals."

Looking at an online list of our old gigs, I see that, apparently, on July 30, 1973, we played The Boobs of Tiffany in Merthyr Tydfil. *Really?* The Boobs of Tiffany?! I mean, obviously, I've never been into boobs, but you'd have thought I'd have remembered a name like that!

We got into the bad habit of nicking stuff from venues. Knives, forks, plates, pint glasses, ashtrays, chairs—anything that wasn't nailed down, and that we could use at home, was fair game. "*Quick, stick this bar stool under your coat!*" We got a bit of a reputation for that.

We began noticing we went down differently in different parts of the country. Up north, audiences were more generous in their reactions to us. South of Birmingham, people seemed more sophisticated, musically. Those gigs could be challenging.

A major exception was St. Albans. For some reason, Judas Priest could do no wrong there. They couldn't get enough of us. God knows how often we played St. Albans City Hall. It came to feel like a hometown show for us.

As we gigged and gigged and gigged, we started recognizing faces in the various crowds. People would see us and then come back for more. We began to establish a following, and it made us feel as if we were getting somewhere. That was a lovely feeling.

Every time we played in London a massive fan called Charlie would be down the front with his mob. He started our first fan club. Another guy who kept coming back was Richard Curwen, who is now a high-up at the BBC, running *Strictly Come Dancing*. We've become lifelong friends.

If we had a chance, we'd hang around the venue and have a pint after the gig and a chat with the punters. Normally, though, we had to pack our gear up straightaway, chuck it in the van, and drive home as quick as we could because we all had work in the morning.

Or, we would sleep in the van. *Oh, God! Sleeping in the van!*

If we thought the van was bad on the way to the gigs, think how rank it was afterward, with everyone sweating profusely and reeking of the night's alcohol and nicotine. Often, though, we had no choice but to kip in it.

If we were on tour, crashing in the van was cheaper than renting one room and everyone piling in there, assuming a B&B would even let us do that. So, we'd pull up in a lay-by and try to sleep with articulated trucks thundering past ten feet away all night long.

I always slept in the back. I'd stick a sleeping bag on top of the speaker cabinets and get three hours' sleep. If I was lucky. Then I had the genius idea of buying a foldable camp bed from the Army & Navy store in good old Stafford Street, Walsall.

That camp bed only stood six inches off the ground, but it was luxury! It was like lying on a feather mattress compared to those bloody speaker cabinets. Although, there again, the main reason I could sleep was that I was pissed out of my head every single night . . .

If we drove home after a gig, we'd leave our gear in the van overnight. There was no lift in Meynell House, and we couldn't face carting it all up to the flat at two in the morning. It was a rough area of Brum, but we were lucky and our stuff never got nicked.

It's a funny thing. It all sounds pretty grotty now and yet, looking back, those early days were some of the best times of our lives. Any band will tell you that. Those first years are fantastic, magical, because there is no pressure on you.

It's all a great adventure. Everything is new and exciting. You have no responsibilities, no distractions, no families. Your focus is totally on the band. You are on a mission. All you want to do is play the best you can, as often as you can.

It's a party you can't believe you are lucky enough to be at. When you play a dodgy club where nobody knows who you are, or cares about you, and you leave them cheering and shouting for more . . . well, you feel like conquering heroes.

Little things mean everything. A speaker might blow at a gig. We could never afford a new JBL speaker, but we could maybe get a refurbished one from a music shop in Dudley. We'd buy another patched-up one at the same time. We knew they wouldn't last long. We knew they'd blow again. But just for a bit, Glenn now had four speakers instead of three. And to us, in our little Priestworld, that felt *massive*.

Eventually, it all changes. Once you've got a record contract, loads of responsibilities kick in. You've got to make a record. You've got to tour it. You have obligations to fans. It starts to feel like a job: you become professional musicians. Don't get me wrong; it's still the best job going and you wouldn't want to be doing anything else. Even so, nothing equals those first, exciting days in a band when you are a gang, on a mission, taking on the world.

One caveat: I might have my rose-tinted specs on here. Because when I was in my forties, I quit Judas Priest by accident and I had to start out again from the bottom, playing tiny clubs with my new band, Fight. And it was a bloody nightmare!

So, the moral of the tale? Paying your dues can be fantastic—but do it when you're starting out, and full of hopes and dreams. Because it's a young man's game.

THE BOOK OF JOB(S)

I n the Bible, the Book of Job describes God unleashing torments on a wealthy man called Job to test the depths of his faith in Him. There is no shortage of tests and torments in metal, believe me, but the way to overcome them is to count your blessings and stay on the path of righteousness.

Never lose sight of the most profound scripture of them all: if you are lucky enough to be up on a stage, you are doing one of the greatest jobs in the world. And I'll start with the very best . . .

SINGERS

There is only one job that is of *Biblical* importance to me. A job that I love so much that it defines me, a job that is my very essence. It's being the singer in a heavy metal band.

Ever since I got clapped for "The Skye Boat Song," I've lived for singing. It is a soulful, spiritual experience for me. Always has been, always will be. The human voice is an amazing instrument. There's simply nothing else like it.

When you strip it right down, singing is such a brilliant feeling. Such a wonderful way to express yourself. That goes for whether you're onstage belting it out to thousands, like me, or some bloke singing out-of-tune down the pub on a Saturday night. I think both are equally valid.

What makes a great singer? First of all, and this may sound funny, *your heart has to be in the right place*. You have to mean it, and it has to be pure expression, or it just won't sound right. You must find the unique identity and character of your own voice.

When you've found those characteristics, you experiment like mad and come to understand how much you can do with your voice. How far you can take it. You're always learning as a singer, and the process, and the journey, are never over.

Having said all that, you generally start out copying other people. Trying to emulate them. I certainly did. When I was a kid, I listened to all sort of amazing vocalists—and I started at a very early age.

When I was about ten, my dad's sister, my Aunty Pat, gave me her old, red-and-cream Dansette record player as a present. I lifted the lid to find three singles inside it: "Rock Around the Clock" by Bill Haley, "Good Golly, Miss Molly" by Little Richard, and "Heartbreak Hotel" by Elvis.

Of the three, it was Little Richard that really got to me. I'd never heard such musical expressiveness before. He was belting it out, not holding anything back, and totally baring his soul. I still remember thinking, *Oh, my God! This guy's singing from the heart!*

As I got into my teens, and more into music, I grew heavily into people like Robert Plant, Janis Joplin, and Ian Gillan. I think it is fair to say that one common factor unites all of the vocalists that I love. It's a technical term: they like to *give it a bit of welly*.

I was attracted to Plant because of the extreme places that he goes to with his voice. The way he sings is so unleashed, and primitive, and primordial, and exciting. Hearing Robert Plant gave me the push to see just what my own voice could do.

Plant's female equivalent was Janis Joplin. I loved how she went onstage and just let it rip. There was so much angst, but it wasn't in the words she was singing, good as they were. No, it lay in her incredible wailing and screaming.

It was the same with Ian Gillan. I loved his high-registered stuff, but it was all about the texture and the intensity of his performance. There is something about a singer going all out in the way Gillan does that shows you they love what they do. That makes *you* love it, too.

I loved all sorts of voices: Sinatra, Elvis, Shirley Bassey. I went through a teenage phase of listening to soul singers like Al Green, Marvin Gaye, Sam & Dave. But the ones that get me, every time, are the ones that get into the upper reaches and go for it. Singers that *give it a bit of welly.*

The thing about metal singers is that you're always competing with that big, unholy noise all around you. Put simply, you have to be as loud as the band or nobody will hear you. I had no idea if my voice could do that when I first started out. Well, I know now that I can!

I've never had a singing lesson in my life. Maybe I should, because I occasionally hear horror stories about people needing operations on their throat because they're singing with the wrong technique. They're constricting their vocal cords and it ends up giving them nodules.

I've been lucky. I've never had anything like that and, touch wood, I hope I never will. I'm totally self-taught as a vocalist and I think that the vast majority of metal singers are the same. Is that a good thing or a bad one? I haven't got a bloody clue!

Sometimes, I'm not even sure if I'm singing from my stomach or my throat or my mouth. It varies. "Painkiller" comes from my throat and my chest. The ballads seem to come from the stomach. I never analyze the physical process. It just seems to happen naturally.

When I look at our set list before Priest go onstage, I know that once one song is finished and I go into the next one, I will need to do an entirely different style of vocal performance. I am mentally prepared and I'm running on instinct. As the sportsmen say, I'm in the zone.

I never analyze my voice, but there are plenty of people who do. If you venture onto the internet and type in "Rob Halford vocal coach," you'll find a whole load of singing experts who've taken it upon themselves to dissect my technique.

They're mostly classically trained singers and they sit with a camera trained on them as they listen to, and react to, my voice. Some of them are hilarious. "How does he do that?" they'll ask, eyebrows raised, as I scream my way through "Painkiller." "That's not humanly possible!"

These experts will go into the specifics of my phrasing and timing and explain how I hit the notes: "How does he get from *here* to *there?*" I've never met them, but they dissect my voice with forensic precision. Thankfully, they're usually complimentary.

A typical example is a young lady called Rebecca Ray, who analyzes singers on her *Rebecca Vocal Athlete* YouTube channel. She gives my vocals on Priest's version of Joan Baez's "Diamonds and Rust" a good theoretical seeing to.

"I love the vibrato to his voice—very theatrical," she says. "His diction is absolutely fantastic and his tonality is so clear and crisp. He's so in control, like a puppeteer with the musicians and audience. They don't even know it.

"He has got impeccable breath technique! I love the way he works with dynamics and he has this great range to work with. He's not overdoing it. You're not sure where he's going to go with his voice—he's such a confident performer . . ."

It's a funny thing, though. These vocal coaches gush and praise me to the skies on YouTube . . . and I bloody hate it! I can't even watch them. It's too close to home. They make me too self-conscious.

As the saying goes: *It's not them, it's me.* I have been lucky enough to get many compliments for my voice over the years, and yet I never know how to receive them. They make me feel uncomfortable. I don't know how to react.

Just the other day, I read that James Hetfield from Metallica put me at number three in his all-time list of metal singers.* It means a lot to

---

*James put Ronnie James Dio at number one in his list. No complaints there—I couldn't agree more! Ronnie was the greatest. I'm a far bigger fan of other singers than I'll ever be of myself.

me, coming from James, and it's lovely to know—but, as well as making me proud, stuff like that also makes me feel awkward.

I've never been good at taking praise. That reticence is definitely rooted in my downbeat Black Country nature. If someone praises my singing, or anything else about me, my natural reaction is to reply, "OK, cheers, mate!" and quickly change the subject.

People sometimes come up to me, usually in America, and say, "Oh my God, I love your voice! You are the best singer ever!" Or, in extreme cases, "Rob, your voice saved my life!" And, well, what am I supposed to say to *that*? Where can the conversation go?

That kind of comment has always made me feel so uncomfortable . . . but I've got a little better at dealing with it. *A little.* For years, I used to just feel embarrassed. I wanted to give them a punch on the arm, blush, and say, "Oh, shurrup!"

Now, I've realized that a compliment is a beautiful thing. That person has reached out to me and, as a recovering alcoholic and drug addict myself, I understand the healing power of music. It can get you through so many difficulties and challenges in life.

Maybe they might have been suicidal then heard a Priest song that made them feel better? Maybe they were down in the dumps, went to one of our shows, and got enthused? So, now, I try to accept praise in the spirit that it is given. I'm older and wiser and it's become easier.

And yet, for me, the ultimate irony of people praising my singing to the skies is that—I have said this a million times, but I'm still not entirely sure whether anybody believes me—I *hate the sound of my own voice.*

I always have. When I hear my singing back, no matter what my performance has been like, I feel vulnerable. I have put so much into it that I feel as if I'm naked. There's always a question going around my head: *Should I really be doing this?*

When Priest make an album like *Firepower*, I work like crazy on my vocals in the studio. But then, when I play the album back, I don't listen to me. I focus on what Richie is doing on guitar, or how Ian is playing bass. *That* is what grabs my attention.

I'm not particularly unusual in that. I think a lot of people in the creative world are the same. I saw a fantastic interview with the actress Maggie Smith, who was brilliant in *Downton Abbey*. She got asked if she watches her films, and said, "Good God, no! Why would I want to do *that*?! Why would I want to watch myself work? It's finished!" And that is kind of how I feel. *Do it, and move on.*

In any case, I still sometimes wonder if, at heart, I am just a frustrated opera singer. I worshipped Pavarotti. I can sing along with him on "Nessun Dorma" and roll the notes around my head, but when he hits that top C—my God, it's monumental! It blows me away, every time.

I can't conceive that a human voice is able to do what Pavarotti did. It is just so glorious. And that's what I think every time I see vocal coaches lavishing praise on me on YouTube: *Yeah, yeah, but I'm shit compared to Pavarotti!*

I'm grateful for my voice, but I'm never going to wax lyrical about it. The other day, I got out of bed and checked my social media. Someone had posted "Lightning Strike" and "Spectre" from *Firepower*. I listened to my voice on them for about a minute and thought, *Oh, that's not too bad.*

Don't get me wrong—being a metal singer is the best job going. It has brought me success, fame, riches, and joy and I wouldn't change it for anything. But if you want my honest verdict on how well I do it, here it is:

I'm not bad. But I'm no Pavarotti.

GUITARISTS

On the day after my twentieth birthday, on August 26, 1970, I bought a ticket to Ryde and went to the Isle of Wight Festival. And there was one attraction that weekend that towered over all of the others. My God, talk about a religious experience!

As a guitarist, nobody else was doing what Jimi Hendrix was doing. He reinvented the very concept of how to play guitar. Nobody had even thought of using the whammy bar on the amplification and the wah-wah pedals. Hendrix was an absolute game changer.

He was the greatest . . . but there have been so many game-changing guitarists over the years. Randy Rhoads. Ritchie Blackmore. Jimmy Page. Eddie Van Halen. Tony Iommi. Tom Morello. Once I start naming my favorite guitarists, it's hard to stop.

These great guitarists are all unique and all have their own identities. They find themselves in the same way that we singers do. They emulate their heroes, be it Hendrix or Eric Clapton or Stevie Ray Vaughan, then they practice and practice to find their own sound, tone, and phrasing.

They work and work until they arrive at their own, definitive place and identity. Until *they know exactly who they are.*

The Priest guitarists have all done that. Over the years, I've watched them work tirelessly to develop their own styles and textures. I've seen them explore the differentials of the pickups, their strings, their amp settings and speakers. I've seen them *grow.*

It means they all have a uniqueness in their playing that distinguishes them from anybody else. I can tell them apart with my eyes closed. I only need to hear a few notes: "Oh, *that's* Glenn Tipton! *That's* Ken Downing! *That's* Richie Faulkner!" They are their own signature.

Glenn is an amazing player. I've always said he is the closest there is to what I'd call a "singing guitarist." He thinks about every single note in the same way that a singer thinks about phrasing a verse or a line of a song. Glenn's phrasing is just like that of a singer.

The sound of Glenn's guitar, and the way that he plays it, is an extension of his character. That is equally true of Richie. Glenn is methodical, but Richie is wild. He's a wild guitarist. Their personalities pass through their instruments into their performances.

I admire guitarists, but I never wanted to *be* one. It was just too much bloody hard work! I knew that I didn't have the patience. I was happy using my voice and leaving difficult-to-play instruments to others.*

I love watching great guitarists. It blows my mind to see Richie Faulkner at work. I don't know how he does what he does. It doesn't

---

*I never even played air guitar as a kid. I don't think that bizarre ritual was invented until the seventies. Yet, nowadays, you get people going off to compete in the World Air Guitar Championships in Finland . . .

make sense that he can wrench the amazing noises that he does from his guitar, and that he can do it perfectly, night after night.

Just compare him to a classical player in a symphony orchestra. They are brilliant, but some of them can't play a note without reading sheet music. Richie, and guitarists like him, play thousands of notes every night and just remember them. I need an autocue just to remember my lyrics these days!

Judas Priest really moved up a notch and found our voice and our soul in 1974 when we brought in a second guitarist. A major inspiration for us to do that was Wishbone Ash. They were the first band I'm aware of to harmonize on twin guitars. We played their *Argus* album to death.

Ken Downing was our sole guitarist before that, and he's said that when he played solos onstage they sounded "empty." I know what Ken means by that. When you introduce a second guitar, you get so many more textures. It becomes like a wall of sound.

When Glenn Tipton joined Priest, our sonic possibilities increased tenfold. It made something really special happen. It's funny—you'd never have two drummers in a band, or two bassists, or two singers, but . . . two guitarists? From the first second we tried it, it made perfect sense.

It's the difference between having one horse pulling the *Steptoe and Son* wagon and having two.* With two horses, you can pull a heavier weight and you can go farther. That's a perfect analogy, because two guitars give you more horsepower—and, in metal, horsepower matters. *A lot.*

It's easily explained. Just try to imagine "Living After Midnight" without the guitar harmonies. It would sound like a different song. Or take one of the guitars out of "Victim of Changes." It would be so much *lesser.*

---

* *Steptoe and Son* was a classic sixties BBC sitcom about a down-at-heel father and son who used a horse and cart to collect scrap metal for a struggling "rag-and-bone" business. They loved each other but bickered like mad. Any similarities to Glenn and Ken are entirely coincidental . . .

Guitarists wax lyrical about different guitars, like they were classic cars or something, but I'm not like that. As a musician, I know a Fender Strat sounds different from a Les Paul, say, but that's as far as I go. As long as a guitar sounds OK to my ears, that's all that matters.

The one time in my career that I've picked up a guitar in earnest was in 1992, when I took time out of Priest and formed Fight. It felt important to me then to play guitar because that project was all about proving my self-worth: that I could make an album on my own.

I wrote all the songs for *War of Words* on the guitar in my bedroom in Phoenix. But I stuck to the riffs and rhythms and the basic, rudimentary compositions. I was OK at them, but I didn't attempt any more complex guitar heroics because . . . well, because I was too shit.

It's funny. I quite enjoyed playing guitar on that record, but I was also well out of my comfort zone. I had one dominating thought going around my head all the time that I had a guitar strapped on, and that thought was:

Rob, don't fuck it up!

I thought of playing guitar onstage when I went out live with Fight, but I decided against it. It was for the same reason that I wouldn't dream of playing guitar with Priest, and it's really simple: *The guitarists are way better at it than me. I'm not a guitarist. I'm a singer.*

I have to admit, sometimes when I watch other bands play and I see the singer pick up a guitar, I think, *Why, mate? What is that adding to the performance or to the music, exactly? Or are you just trying to show us that you can play guitar?*

I guess that sounds very bitchy and I've got no right to think like that. If that singer wants to strap on a guitar, it's none of my business. But, ultimately, it's not for me. Being a guitarist is one of the best jobs in the Book of Job(s), but it's just not my line of work.

BASSISTS

The Bible and music both have their headline acts: big-ticket characters who grab all the attention (you know, Jesus, Robert Plant, that sort of geezer!). Then, under the radar and in the shadows, you find the lesser-celebrated figures whose roles and work are equally important. And in the world of metal and rock, it's possible that no job is more unfairly marginalized, and yet more crucial, than that of the bassist.

Anybody who knows music knows that bassists are utterly vital. Working with the drummer, they form the rhythm section that is the central dynamic of any metal band. Bassists connect, join the sonic dots, and hold *everything* together.

Just like singers and guitarists, bassists start off emulating their heroes then work hard to define and refine their own personal sound. Ian Hill, Priest's own Bass God (that's the name that flashes up on my mobile when he calls me), had some very eclectic icons.

Ian loved Jack Bruce from Cream, Jaco Pastorius from Weather Report, and legendary jazzman Charles Mingus. He was also a big fan of Niels-Henning Ørsted Pedersen, a Danish jazz double-bassist who played with Count Basie, Dizzy Gillespie, and Ella Fitzgerald, among loads of others.

Maybe because of his love for the jazzers, Ian started off playing bass with his fingers, like Geezer Butler. It's interesting—the sound you get from moving the wire of a bass string with your flesh is totally different from the one you generate using a plectrum (or a pick, as we musos call it).

Ian played with his fingers on the first couple of Priest albums, and then the rest of the band suggested he should switch to a pick. Ian was initially resistant. That was how he'd taught himself to play the bass, and how he'd always played it—why should he change?

Luckily, Ian is very smart as a musician, and when he picked up a pick (pun intended!) he rapidly appreciated the benefits of playing with it. He realized a pick would allow him to play faster, and with more clarity, and to marry the timbre of his bass closer with the guitars.

Ian is a thinker and that quality extends to his bass playing. Just like Glenn and Richie on guitar, his personality comes across in his bass. I could no more tell him, "Play your bass like *this*," than he could say to me, "Rob, sing like *this*." Ian *knows* what to do.

Ian has never been involved in the songwriting in Priest, but that doesn't mean he doesn't contribute to the songs. Once he hears the riff and the melody, he makes the bassline his own. In fifty years, no one else in the band has ever written a bassline for Ian Hill.

There's a theory that, mirroring their role in the band, bassists have to be very solid, grounded characters. Ian certainly *is* that sort of guy, and he is as regular and reliable as they come, but, even so, I personally think that particular theory is bollocks.

Just look at Ian, then at John Entwistle from The Who, or John Deacon from Queen, or even Nikki Sixx from Mötley Crüe. Is anyone *seriously* going to tell me that they're all the same sort of character?! Yet they all bring their own soul and personality to their bands.

The Aussies have a saying that sums up a certain type of unshowy, low-level but talented guy who gets a job done with no fuss. They call them *quiet achievers*. That's Ian Hill, and that's bassists as a whole—the quiet achievers of metal and rock.

DRUMMERS

There aren't many funnies in the Bible, but there is an old joke among bands. You've probably heard it, but just in case you're the one person in a million who hasn't, I'll tell it to you now:

"What do you call someone who hangs around with musicians?"

"A drummer."

And, you know what? I've just told you that joke, but I don't like it. It bemuses me. It disrespects drummers—one of the most important jobs in the Book of Job(s), in metal, and in music.

Right from when I started listening to music, drums have always excited me. I love the way they make me feel. I remember watching Buddy Rich and then Gene Krupa on *Sunday Night at the London Palladium* as a lad and being totally blown away.

Other drummers talk about those guys in the same way that guitarists talk about Hendrix, as godlike geniuses, and they're right to. Before Rich and Krupa, drummers just sat in the background and kept the beat. That pair took drumming to a whole other level.

Yet at the same time as loving drummers, part of me can't help but think . . . why would anybody want to *be* one? What makes people want to sit on a stool with two lumps of wood and hit things? It's a mystery to me. But thank God that people do.

Drummers can get unfairly relegated to the background and yet on *Top of the Pops* in the sixties, for some reason, they always sat right at the front of the stage. I still remember intently watching Dave Clark in the Dave Clark Five. He is a brilliant drummer.

A drummer is the heartbeat of a song, but there are so many different types and approaches. In terms of technique and style, there is a world of difference between Ginger Baker and Ringo Starr. Between Charlie Watts and Carmine Appice. Between Ian Paice and Scott Travis.

Some drummers just have a bass drum, a snare, a couple of toms, and a couple of cymbals. Charlie was like that, and so is Ringo. Others want a hundred drums. It all depends on the individual and the music they are playing.

In Priest today, Scott Travis needs two bass drums because he uses the double-kick pedal, as we call it. He has side toms, rack toms, and half a dozen cymbals because we need that variety of sounds and textures. For some songs, he might only play one drum and one cymbal.

Of course, Scott is a long way from being the only drummer we've ever had in Judas Priest. I must admit that the only other band to have gone through so many different stickmen, for so many different reasons, is Spinal Tap.

I don't think that's a bad thing. It's not unusual for bands to change musicians as their sound develops, and I think the variety has given us something. Listen back to our albums and it is possible to detect who was on the drum stool at the time by their style of playing.

I brought our first drummer, John Hinch, with me when I joined Priest from Hiroshima in 1973. John was a very basic, no-frills drummer, which I don't mean in a derogatory sense because that was exactly what we needed at the time. He got the job done.

When we moved on to music that required a little more technique and style, we had to let John go because he wasn't really keeping pace with us. The same was true of Alan "Skip" Moore, even though he did a good, solid job on *Sad Wings of Destiny*.

When Roger Glover from Deep Purple produced *Sin After Sin* in 1977, he hooked us up with a session drummer, Simon Phillips. Simon was young but an old head on young shoulders and incredibly talented. It's no surprise to me that he went on to play with Michael Schenker, The Who,* and Toto.

After *Sin After Sin*, we auditioned a lot of drummers and we chose Les Binks. Les was a lovely guy, but what took some getting used to was that he was our first full-time member who wasn't a Midlander. Suddenly there was a Belfast accent floating around among all the yam-yams:

"*Ey Rahb, 'll you pass me dahse droehmstecks, please?*"

Despite his dodgy voice, Les fitted in and he made two albums with us, *Stained Class* and *Killing Machine*. He was quite a fancy, complex, technical drummer and after a while we decided we needed someone to give us more traditional, straightforward heavy metal *power*.

Which was where Dave Holland came in. We poached Dave—well, I suppose we nicked him—from Trapeze, a Cannock band we all liked. Dave settled down onto the Priest drum stool for the next ten years and became part of one of the classic line-ups of the band.

Dave was there right through our major breakthrough years of *British Steel*, *Screaming for Vengeance*, and *Turbo* and was a laid-back guy and a proper methodical, keep-it-simple drummer. With Dave, we always knew we had a solid musical foundation to build on.

It took a lot to rile him, but we managed it. When we came to record *Ram It Down* in Puk Studios in Denmark in 1988, Dave was not in a

---

*Priest have never had a wild, extrovert drummer like Keith Moon, and thank God for that! For us, the drummer has to be the anchor of the band: tight and *disciplined*. Moon was a brilliant drummer but he was also pure chaos. There's never been anybody like him since.

good place. He had a right strop on in the studio, for whatever reason, and totally lost his normal open-mindedness to our ideas.

"Dave?" Glenn might ask him. "Do you want to try a bit of a looser beat on this one . . . ?"

"Dow tell me what to do!" Dave would snap back. "*I'm* the bloody drummer!"

It was making things awkward and we tried a work-around. At that time in the eighties, drum machines were all the rage. We sampled a lot of Dave's beats and, rather than his live drumming, we programmed the machine to get the rhythms we wanted.

Dave got the right hump about this and was mardy all through the tour that followed the album coming out. He'd sit in silence on the tour bus, he barely talked to us, and he quit the band at the end of the tour.

It was a shame that it ended like that because, if I am honest, I think that Dave had a point. Drum machines *aren't* as good as using a real, live human. Listening to *Ram It Down* now, the drums are a real weak point. I think using the drum machine was a mistake, and we'd certainly never do it again.

We lost touch with Dave when he quit the band, and so we were all shocked and devastated when, nearly twenty years later, he got sent to jail for sex offences. His trial was as much of a bombshell for us as it was for everybody else.

This book about music is not the place to go into whether or not Dave did what he was found guilty of. I haven't got any more idea about that than the next bloke. He never reached out to us when he came out of prison, but, then again, I suppose we never reached out to him, either.

Sadly, Dave died of lung cancer in 2018, when he was apparently living in Spain. I didn't even know he'd moved there. Ultimately, I prefer not to think about the tragic events later in his life and remember him for what he was when I knew him: a great, great Judas Priest drummer.

Which is also the perfect description of Scott Travis. Dave's successor slid behind our drum kit more than thirty years ago and he is still there. Even though he does sometimes complain that, "You still treat me like the new guy!"

The story of how Scott came to join us is well known. He was such a colossal Priest fan that he planned to set up his drum kit in the car park of one of our arena gigs in his home state, Virginia, in 1986. He hoped that we'd get off the tour bus, hear his paradiddles, and offer him a job!

It sounds borderline creepy, like when a stalker fan camped in the front garden of Agnetha from Abba and she ended up having a relationship with him. But Scott eventually found his way to us by a more conventional route. I met him via his LA band, Racer X, and saw he was a phenomenal drummer. So, when Dave quit Judas Priest, it was a no-brainer to offer Scott the job . . .

Well, not quite. It feels silly now, but my sole reservation was that Scott is a Yank. I wondered if it might dilute Priest's identity as a British heavy metal band. Luckily, I quickly got past such daft notions, and the rest is history.

When Scott joined, he was a perfect fit from day one. We realized at once how important to Priest he would be, which was why we featured him playing that amazing drum phrase right at the opening of the title track on his first album with us: *Painkiller.* That was a deliberate decision and his showcase moment. It was Priest telling the world:

This is Scott Travis, and THIS is what he can do!

Scott is an amazing combination of a powerhouse and a great technical drummer. His brilliant talent is that he can play every song from our fifty-year repertoire and reproduce the style of the drummer that we had at the time. He's like the Mike Yarwood* of the drum world.

As well as dodgy jokes about drummers, the idea also exists that at any metal or rock gig, the most boring interlude is a drum solo. In fact, a lot of people maintain that it's a handy moment for audience members to pop off for a pint and a piss.

---

*Mike Yarwood was a famous impressionist on British telly, back in the day. He'd always finish his shows by saying "And this is me!" and singing a schmaltzy little number. Thankfully, Scott doesn't do that.

I don't really buy into this notion—like I say, I love the way that drums make me *feel*—but a cool thing about Scott is that he half-agrees with it! Sometimes, if we're putting a set list together and we tell him he will be doing a big drum solo, he will wince.

"Aw, hell, guys! Have I *got* to?"

"Yes!"

Luckily, Scott always does it and he always makes a thrilling, fantastic, thunderous racket. Our fans love his solos and lap them up . . . and I guess any who aren't in the mood can always pop off for a pint and a piss.

BAND MANAGERS

In metal and rock—and any music, really—the glamour ticket is being up onstage, spilling out your heart, taking the applause of the fans. But there is one behind-the-scenes job that is so crucial that, if it's done wrong, the whole house of cards can come crashing down.

Every band needs a great manager. You're nothing without one. A great manager maximizes your potential, from getting you gigs and festivals in the early days to protecting your image and negotiating the best record deal possible. He* looks after you as artists and as people. A good manager lets you focus on making the best music you can, and playing the best shows you can, by taking all other forms of pressure off you. He lets you think, *I don't have to worry about any of that—it's all in hand!* He stresses about shit so you don't have to.

Artist managers are so important that the best go down in music history. Colonel Tom Parker with Elvis. Brian Epstein with the Beatles. Peter Grant with Led Zeppelin. Malcolm McLaren with the Sex Pistols. Even Simon Fuller and the Spice Girls, I suppose.

The best managers are both visionaries who can plot the future of their acts, and ace administrators and delegators who keep everything

---

* Many of them are "he," but not all of them, as you'll soon read in these scriptures . . .

ticking over immaculately day by day. And, in an industry populated by chancers and cowboys, they're gold dust.

All artists long for all-seeing managers like that to help them plot their course. But they don't come cheap, and many bands starting out have no choice but to rely on a mate to give them a hand. And Judas Priest were no exception.

Our first manager, back in the early seventies, was Dave "Corky" Corke. As I recounted in *Confess*, Corky was a legend in his own lunchtime and in the Priest story. He was a proper character, a one-off.

He was a little bloke with corkscrew hair, glasses as thick as the bottom of a beer bottle, and the gift of the gab. He hung around with the band, then sort of appointed himself as manager. That was OK. There wasn't exactly a long queue of people wanting to do it.

Corky was a wide boy with a heart of gold. He could sell ice to Eskimos. The best way to describe him is that he was a Brummie take on Del Boy from *Only Fools and Horses*.* Yet I'll say this: in our earliest, struggling days, he was a godsend for us.

Corky got on the phone and got us gigs despite not even having an office. He started off sitting outside a call box in his car, waiting for the phone to ring (he'd told people that was his office number). Then he hot-wired a phone in a lift and commandeered it for his purposes.

When Corky finally got himself an office, I went to see it. It was a bare room with a telephone on the floor. It didn't have a chair, a printer, a fax machine, a desk, or even any pens or paper.

"It's a bit . . . empty, ay it, Corky?" I enquired.

"It's got a phone, Rob!" he grinned at me through his massive specs. "It's all I need, mate!"

And it was. When his phone wasn't disconnected for nonpayment of bills, Corky was never off it. He played it like a maestro. I overheard

---

* *Only Fools and Horses* was a BBC TV sitcom about a lovable rogue London market trader, Del Boy Trotter, his goofy brother, Rodney, and their company, Trotters Independent Traders (or TIT for short). Honestly, I can't recommend it highly enough.

one or two of his calls to venue managers, hyping us up, and they made me boggle.

"I manage Judas Priest, who are about to be massive!" he'd say. "And you can have them for £15!"

"I'm not paying £15!" the suspicious promoter who'd never heard of us (nobody had!) would reply.

"Go on then, £10! They've got a massive following—you're getting a bargain here!" And he'd bang on until they'd agree just to get him off the blower.

Corky's scruffy first-floor flat in Meynell House in Birmingham became Priest's unofficial crash pad. We'd hang out there for days drinking, getting stoned, and jamming. Ian spent so much time there that he ended up moving in.

There were always people after Corky, normally for money. One time, he came away with us for a few nights to play dates in the depths of winter. Ken's girlfriend, Carol, and my sister (and Ian's future wife) Sue, stayed in Meynell House while we were gone.

Corky forgot to give them the flat keys before we left, so they couldn't get in. A bloke downstairs loaned them his ladder and they climbed up to the balcony, got in by wrestling the slats off a window, and left the ladder there for the morning.

The next morning, Sue went to climb down the ladder to get in her car to drive to work. She glanced down and saw, standing at the bottom, in deep snow, a man straight out of *Monty Python's Flying Circus*, in a bowler hat and overcoat, clutching a briefcase. He was a debt collector.

"I have some papers for a Mr. David Corke," he shouted up.

"We can't open the door!" my sis said. "But if you want to come up here, you can give them to us."

As if it was the most natural thing in the world, the official shook the snow from his shoes, climbed up the ladder, served the papers, tipped his bowler hat, and climbed down again. Which Corky was obviously *delighted* about when we got home.

Yet, for all of his foibles, Corky was very serious about Priest. He knew we had something and could see our potential. He'd come with us to all of our UK gigs and give us his appraisal and suggestions at the end. We always listened because he always made sense.

He worked hard, but, *my God*, he played hard as well. Corky was a nonstop practical joker with a wicked, almost surrealist sense of humor. We always had to be on our toes around him because we never had a bloody clue what he'd do next.

He bought a weird pixie hat, with pointed ears attached, from a joke shop. For weeks, Corky and that hat were inseparable. I'd get up from the sofa in Meynell House, wander to the bathroom for a piss, and a manic bespectacled pixie would leap out in front of me: "Booooooo!!"

"*Aaargh! Fucking hell, Corky!*"

That sodding pixie hat came to a few gigs with us. Going to towns with no motorways, slogging down B-roads in our Transit for hours on end, could be bloody boring. Corky decided that his comedy hat was just the thing to liven up journeys.

I remember tootling down a country lane on the way to Bath. Glenn was driving. Corky saw a cyclist in front of us, put his pixie hat on, and told Glenn to slow down. As we passed the cyclist, Corky rammed his head out of the window and screamed at the top of his voice.

"*Huuuuuuuuuuuuuuuurgh!*"

The shocked guy jumped out of his skin and toppled off his bike into a ditch. Corky told Glenn to pull into a little siding farther down the road. Five minutes later, when the poor cyclist caught up with us, Corky did it again. And the bloke fell off again.

It was ridiculous, arsehole behavior and we should have told Corky off. The problem was, we were all laughing so much we couldn't speak.

I'll give him this: Corky varied his pranks. One time, he picked out some bloke at random from the phone book—a blameless middle-aged guy named Arthur Tedstone—and he made his life an utter misery.

Corky would get on the phone and order things to be delivered to Mr. Tedstone's house: pizzas, cement, lawn turf, *anything*. Then he'd sit opposite his house in his car, watch poor Arthur explain to the pissed-off delivery guy that he hadn't ordered the stuff, and laugh his head off.

On Priest's first international dates, in 1974—and, again, credit to Corky for fixing those—we were totally flying by the seat of our pants.

As we left for Germany, Corky was still fixing up the itinerary. He instructed us to ring his phone box at a certain time every day.

"Alright, lads, quick, write this down!" he'd gabble as soon as he picked up. "You're doing three nights at the Zoom Club in Frankfurt, starting tomorrow. Ask for Hans . . ."

It was laugh-a-minute with Corky and, as the people he spent the most time with, Priest were always in the firing line for his infamous stunts. Then, one day, we managed to get our revenge. It was fucking brilliant.

We were playing a festival in Finland in 1976 with Caravan and the Climax Blues Band. The Finnish promoter hired an old Second World War piston-engine cargo plane and flew us three British bands and all of our gear out together. Corky was quite a nervous flyer.

It was the height of summer in Finland, when they have twenty-four-hour daylight, so when we went onstage at ten o'clock at night, it was as bright as midday. It was an amazing experience, so we were all in high spirits on the flight back the next day. And then Glenn had an idea.

Glenn explained his brainwave to the rest of Priest and to the other two bands. We all thought it was hysterical. In fact, Glenn told everybody on the plane except for Corky. Then he had a word with the lady who had been dishing out the drinks and sandwiches.

"We've got this manager, Dave Corke," he said. "He's always playing pranks on us and we'd like to pay him back. Do you think we could have a word with the captain?"

We were clearly on a very rock-and-roll plane, because the attendant grinned and took Glenn to the cockpit to talk to the pilot, who agreed to his ruse. I was sitting by Corky. Glenn returned and took his seat on the other side of him—and the attendant got on the plane's Tannoy.

"Ladies and gentlemen, I have to inform you that the captain has told me we may have an issue with the plane's fuel levels," she said. "But please don't panic. I'll keep you updated."

"Eh? What did she say?" Corky asked me and Glenn.

"What? We weren't listening."

"She just said something about a problem with the plane's fuel!"

"Did she? I'm sure it's nothing. Don't worry about it."

I glanced behind me to see Caravan and the Climax Blues Band grinning their heads off. Ten minutes later, the attendant, who was clearly a very talented amateur actress, got back on the mic.

"I have to warn you, I'm afraid we're unable to guarantee our fuel level is sufficient to land," she said. "I will let you know all developments."

"Oh, shit!" said Corky. "Fucking hell!"

Glenn and I glanced over at each other and just about managed to keep a straight face. Between us, Corky was seriously losing it. He was sweating like a pig and gripping the sides of his seat. At which point, the attendant *sprinted* past us and got on the Tannoy again.

"Ladies and gentlemen, we need to make an emergency landing in the sea!" she gasped. "Please assume the brace position! Remove all sharp objects from your persons and take off all shoes or high heels!"

Corky was wearing long Chukka boots laced right up over his ankles and somehow, in one panicked movement, he pulled them right off. It was like a David Copperfield trick (or, more likely, Tommy Cooper*). While he was doing it, Glenn and I were howling.

"Oh, my God! Oh my God!" Corky gibbered. "Oh, fuck! We're doomed! I don't want to die! I've got so much to live for . . . oh, God! Help me, God!"

We'd never known Corky was so devout! Glenn and I were cracking up either side of him, but, in his desperate state, he assumed we were both as hysterical with fear as he was: "*Oh, shit! I don't want to go like this!*"

He was out of his mind. It was time to calm him down, so Glenn and I started saying, "Corky, mate, it's fine! It's just a joke!" He didn't believe

---

* Tommy Cooper was a fez-wearing British TV magician and comedian whose tricks always accidentally-on-purpose went wrong. He was the king of the genius one-liner: "I went to buy camouflage trousers—I couldn't find any!" Or: "I'm on a whisky diet. I've lost three days already . . ."

a word of it. "Are you stupid?" he yelled at us. "It's not fine! We're all going to die!"

It wasn't until the attendant came over, knelt in front of him, and told him that it had all been a wind-up that the penny dropped for Corky. He looked around, realized that everybody else on the plane was laughing their heads off—and he lost it again, in a *very* different way.

"You fucking arseholes!" he bawled. "Why did you *do* that? That was really fucking shitty!" We had landed and were halfway back to Birmingham in the van before he finally cracked a reluctant smile. "OK, you bastards, you got me. I'll get you back . . ."

And we knew that he would.

Corky was a great bloke and is a major part of the early Priest story. We'll never forget him and we will always be grateful to him, because he gave us a big push when we really needed it. But, at the same time, we knew we couldn't go on with him forever.

After *Sad Wings of Destiny*, we realized that if we wanted to take the next big step forward, Corky and his *Only Fools and Horses* school of management had to go. We had a painful conversation in which we told him we'd decided it was best if we went separate ways.

Corky was hurt and upset, and I don't blame him. Yet I think he tacitly accepted that we were moving into a different world where he might be out of his depth. Was he bitter? Maybe. But he took it on the chin and wished us luck. He was a class act.

And our decision proved to be the right one. Instead, we signed to a more conventional music-management company called Arnakata, who looked after Be-Bop Deluxe and the Tourists. The latter had a talented female singer named Annie Lennox.

Two brothers ran Arnakata. I was never quite convinced that they *got* metal, or Priest, and our relationship was very formal. But they had the professional standing and contacts that Corky lacked and they got us a major label deal, with CBS.

Arnakata were solid while never being great. We did five years with them, and then it came to a very strange end. On the day of Priest's first ever show (well, out of two) at Madison Square Garden, one of the brothers said they had to quit managing us because he had personal problems.

Huh? Yet, if I am honest, I wasn't sorry to see them go. By now, Priest were a much bigger band than when we signed to Arnakata. When we started casting around for replacement management, there was no shortage of applicants.

Herbie Herbert, who did a great job managing Journey, gave us a full-on sales pitch on why he was the man for the job. He was impressive, but he was very rooted in America. I thought we needed a British manager: What if we were sitting with a problem in Birmingham, and Herbie was on the other side of the world, in San Francisco?

And then we met Bill Curbishley.

"Wild" Bill, as he sometimes went, was a tasty character. An East Ender, he was rumored to have gangster connections and had been to prison for armed robbery (he says he was innocent). But we were attracted to him by the fact he is a brilliant artist manager.

Bill had done fantastic work guiding the career of The Who, an amazing British band. He had overseen their groundbreaking concept albums, *Tommy* and *Quadrophenia*, and helped to turn them into movies: he'd even coproduced the latter. He was an ideas man and a bit of a genius.

Bill didn't pretend to be a heavy metal maniac. He simply did his research and told us where he thought Priest stood—in America, the UK, Germany, the world—and what we could achieve.

As I said, the greatest managers are visionaries. At our first meeting, Bill explained precisely what Priest could expect to do, and earn, over the next decade. He was bang on. It all came true. Then, years later, he had the bright idea for our own concept album: *Nostradamus*.

Bill Curbishley is a strong man and I like that. Sometimes, managers just have to be confrontational. I've hated confrontation since I was a kid, but managers need to shout and bang the table—with record labels, agents, promoters, whoever. It goes with the job.

Bands can get miffed when their manager looks after multiple acts. They begin to feel neglected: *He's spending more time with them than he is with us!* Yet even when Bill added Robert Plant and Jimmy Page to his roster, we never felt like that. He is a king among managers.

When Bill started taking more of a back seat in recent years, he handed the reins of Priest's day-to-day management to one of his colleagues, Jayne Andrews. That was a great decision. Jayne grabbed those reins with both hands and has been steering us ever since.

Jayne loves Priest to death and is fiercely protective of the band. She has a ferocious reputation in the music industry as a fighter, and I love that. It's no good for any band to have a manager who is a pushover. I know she always has our back, 100 percent.

Jayne has had to fight all the harder, of course, because she's a woman. The music industry has always been a sexist cesspit, and when she took over, she met with some initial disrespect: "Ah, she's just a chick! What does *she* know about rock and roll?"

Attitudes are healthier nowadays but that was what Jayne initially had to fight against. Sharon Osbourne had to deal with the same shit when she started managing Ozzy, as did Wendy Dio with Ronnie. I don't think anybody would dare to disrespect any of those three women now!

I can't overstate how important it is to have a good manager. Priest are so lucky to have had three great ones in Corky, Bill Curbishley, and Jayne Andrews. To date, *as far as I know*, Jayne hasn't run our business from a phone box or donned a pixie hat to scare cyclists off their bikes.

But you know what? That's probably for the best. I'd like to think we've moved on . . .

LAWYERS

Some occupations in this Book of Job(s) aren't as glamorous as the others, but they are still deeply essential. If any young band is crazy enough to approach me for advice, I always tell them two things: get yourselves a good manager and a good lawyer.

Where there's a hit, there's a writ. The metal and rock world is littered with litigation and contractual conflict. People say that lawyers are like piranhas, and there may be a lot of truth in that, but a good lawyer will save a band's arse on countless occasions.

Artists require lawyers on a day-to-day basis to check and double-check every contract they sign, with record labels, promoters, merchandisers, whatever. Because, let's be bloody honest here, most bands are as good at scrutinizing legal contracts as solicitors are at singing!

Yet in addition to that routine business, sometimes a one-off, special, or disastrous circumstance will come along in which a lawyer will not just make you a bit of money but can save your whole career. *Save your life.*

Priest's most high-profile, car-crash lawsuit, of course, came in Reno in 1990. Flying in the face of common sense and basic human nature, we were accused of hiding backmasked messages in our music urging our fans to kill themselves.

Even more than thirty years on, I shake my head while typing that sentence at how bloody daft the whole thing was. Yet in the wake of the tragic suicides of two of our young fans in Nevada, we were sued by the boys' parents and summoned to the state for a high-profile trial.

I was accused of spitting the words "Do it!" during our cover of Spooky Tooth's "Better by You, Better than Me," allegedly urging fans to top themselves. We had also supposedly backmasked messages such as "Fuck the Lord, fuck all of you!" on our *Stained Class* album.

It was palpable nonsense, but it was nonsense that we had to take hugely seriously, given the human tragedy that had unfolded and the weight of the accusations against us. Our management hired a team of top US lawyers and we began intensive pre-trial meetings.

These lawyers didn't know a thing about Judas Priest or about heavy metal. They didn't need to. They were purely concerned with the facts and with the essence of the case: Had we really done this evil, hideous thing we stood accused of?

We answered every question our lawyers asked us, they assessed us as people, and they quickly realized: *These musicians seem like OK guys! They're not angry, bitter, malicious monsters! Why would they try to take someone's life—to kill their fans? They obviously didn't do it!*

Our lawyers sussed that the accusations against us were absurd. They realized from the outset that the whole case was ridiculous and none of the charges made sense. It really helped our morale that they felt so strongly and were so supportive of us.

Pre-trial, they grilled and grilled us, and prepared themselves to within an inch of their lives. They went into court with a trolley piled high with, literally, thousands of pieces of paper. They knew that if the judge asked them a question, they needed the answer right there, at their fingertips.

When the case started, the prosecuting lawyers were very showy and dramatic, and we initially wanted ours to be more like them. Our lot were being low-key and methodical, and we felt they should be more shouty and aggressive and start thumping the table.

Priest were furious at the awful thing we were being accused of, and we wanted our lawyers to sound just as angry—*but we were wrong.* We soon realized that their cool, calm, and collected approach in the courthouse was the correct one. We came to trust them.

When I took the witness stand and played the judge other Priest songs backward, uncovering nonsense, apparently backmasked lyrics such as "Hey, Ma, my chair's broken," it helped clinch our case. Even though we were innocent, it was still a huge relief to be cleared of the charges. I always had a fear that, against all reason and logic, we might get found guilty.

That crazy trial dates from an era when major bands, and artists such as Ozzy, were getting sued left, right, and center over their songs. You don't get those cases now because the courts came to their senses and realized they were a waste of time and money—and utter bollocks.

Lawyers aren't magicians. They can't always get what you want, as the Stones nearly said. I'll give you an example: for many years now, we've had a legal firm offering increasing sums of money to our old record label, Gull Records, for rights to our first two albums. We want to own them, because *Rocka Rolla* and *Sad Wings of Destiny* are important chapters in the Judas Priest story. We'd love to give them proper high-quality reissues—but our lawyers keep getting knocked back. Ah, well. We'll keep trying. Maybe one day . . .

The other occasion that a lawyer saved my ass from disaster happened outside of Priest. It came in 2013, when I fired the former manager of my solo career, John Baxter, and he sued me for $50 million for fraud, breach of contract, and "intentional interference with contractual negotiations."

Getting sued for $50 million is enough to put the shits up anyone, but my high-flying lawyer, David Steinberg, guided me through the proceedings and got me a great result. David had amazing gravitas in court, despite sporting an Art Garfunkel–style white Afro haircut. Which was an achievement.

If you're in a successful metal or rock band, the next lawsuit can arrive at any time. Are lawyers a necessary evil? Yep! Are they piranhas? Maybe—but you'd much rather they're ripping the other guy's flesh off rather than yours . . .

THE BOOK OF
PSALMS AND TESTAMENTS

The Bible is subdivided into many books, and metal bands' scriptures are no different. I suppose that our songs are our psalms and our albums are our testaments. They're our sacred texts but, believe you me, bringing them to life requires plenty of blood, sweat, and tears.

How do Priest set about writing our heavy metal hymns? Where do our inspirations come from for riffs and for lyrics? How do we select our producers and studios? And how do album titles and artwork emerge from the creative mayhem?

And the biggest question of all: How do we summon the divine patience and the infinite wisdom to deal with the bane of every musician's life—record companies? Read on, metal maniacs, and all will be revealed . . .

SONGWRITING

Songwriting is the most sacred element of the whole business of being in a band. For all of your energy, and your hopes and dreams, and your talent as a musician, without songs you are nothing. But where do these magical psalms come from?

It makes sense to describe writing songs as sacred because there is a mystical element to it. I love the process of starting a day with zilch and ending it with a song that will last forever. It's an amazing, exhilarating feeling, but how does it happen?

How do you come up with a melody? Where does the inspiration come from for lyrics? I'm asking a lot of questions here because, ultimately, songwriting is so hard to analyze. It's all about feelings, and emotions. It's an abstract, nebulous process, but somehow it all comes together. *It works out.*

You're never taught how to write a song. You don't get lessons. When you first start out, all you have is the knowledge of all the great songs you've heard (which you start off copying: everybody does!) and the wish to somehow cast a spell and create something new.

When you're starting a band and trying to write your first songs, you're totally naive. You're going through a birthing process; making it up as you go along. So, it's a source of real pride to me that, nearly fifty years on, I think the songs on our debut album, *Rocka Rolla*, still stand up.

It's a flawed record—the production still makes us cringe—but I'm so pleased the songs aren't shit. People still reference that album. Some fans say it's one of the best we've ever made! I haven't listened to it in forever, yet I can still hear every single song in my head.

Priest songs are nearly always born on the guitar. It's the riffs and rhythms that inspire me. It's always been the way. I would hear Ken or Glenn jamming or playing around on their guitars, and a fragment of sound would trigger an idea in me. It's the same now with Richie.

Virtually everything starts with the guitar. Once in a blue moon, I might think of a vocal melody first. It appears in my head out of thin air and I sing it and send it to the guys on voicemail. That's a real rarity, though. Usually, I need the substance of the skeleton of a song to inspire me.

Sometimes, you can be lucky and a song falls into your lap. It's a well-known tale how, making *British Steel*, Glenn woke me up, jamming in the middle of the night, and I went down and asked him to stop "living after midnight." *Voila!* One of our biggest songs! But that kind of happy accident doesn't come along very often.

In fact, when it does, we don't always trust it! It seems too easy. I think we have an unspoken attitude in Priest that songwriting has to be hard graft and elbow grease: blood, sweat, and tears. We almost feel guilty if a song emerges fully formed: *"It cor be any good, can it?"*

More normally, writing songs is like being in a battle for us. I think this is true for all musicians. It can be a challenge and a frustration, but it's one that we enjoy. It can feel exactly like doing a jigsaw puzzle: *"My God, this is going to be a great song, but we're missing something! What is it?"*

Writing songs is a head game. You have good days and bad. It can be so rewarding and yet give you so much angst. And on the days when it's a struggle, you start to wonder: *What is going on? Have we lost the plot? After all these years, has the well finally run dry?*

What we have learned, when it's just not happening, is not to force it. Stop for a while. Breathe out. Head down to the pub (in the old days!). Have a nice cup of tea (nowadays!). If we give ourselves a bit of space, one of us will come up with a bright idea. A spark that lights the fire again.

Songs can take forever to germinate. Back in the mid-seventies, Priest did a British tour that included a few Scottish dates. After one of the gigs, we slept in the van by Loch Ness. I gazed at the loch, which was like a black mirror, wondering if there was really a monster in there.

Hmm—there might be a good song in this! Well, there was, but it took a while to come out! The idea rattled around the back of my brain for the next thirty years before the song finally saw the light of day as "Lochness" on *Angel of Retribution* in, ahem, 2005:

> *Grey mist drifts upon the water,*
> *The mirrored surface moves . . .*

Well, as I always say, you can't rush these things!

Songwriting is teamwork. It's joint creative endeavor. When we go in to make a Priest album, we never say, "Right, we need a bunch of fast songs and a bunch of slow songs." It's never like that. We just know, *feel* instinctively what we need to make up an album.

Making an album is like being at the birth of a child: a metal baby! You go in with nothing, you work together, and then, at the end, *there it is!* Your child for 1978, or 1990, or 2018! You hold it and it's a beautiful thing. You've worked so hard and you can't quite believe it's there.

We've written the last four albums in Glenn's studio in Worcestershire, and I have a routine to ease myself into the songwriting day. Before I do the one-hour drive to Glenn's gaff, I go down to the kitchen in my place in Walsall and I make what I call my schoolboy lunch.

It's almost a religious ritual. It never varies: I'm very much a creature of habit. I make myself a cheese-and-tomato toastie and wrap it in tin foil, put it in a Morrisons sandwich bag, pick up a KitKat and a bag of crisps, and head over to Glenn's place.

I always drive on my own to the writing session, and while I'm driving, I can hear the music of all the songs we are working on in my head. That can actually be a bit scary—I'm not sure if that ability is a blessing or a fucking curse!

It's dangerous and probably a bit stupid, but sometimes I try to record while I'm driving. Inspiration will suddenly strike me—*Oh my God! I've got a vocal melody for this one!*—and I grab my iPhone and start yelling into it, trying to avoid the trucks around me as I do it.*

I'll get to Glenn's studio at midday, eat my schoolboy lunch, and we'll crack on. We'll write until around six o'clock and then we'll knock off. We never do any longer, even if we're having a great creative day. That's just the time span that works for us nowadays.

I sometimes get asked if I think Priest's songwriting has undergone any quantum leaps over the years. I'm not sure. A lot of people say we made a great leap forward when we wrote *British Steel*. I can see that, but mostly I think we've always been steady and consistent.

---

* So, if you ever read that Rob Halford came to a sorry end by driving into the back of a lorry, in the middle lane of the M5, on the way to a Judas Priest songwriting session . . . you'll know *exactly* what happened.

One thing has never changed. Some bands like to go into the studio to make an album with a lot of material already written, but we've never done that. In the seventies and eighties, we never had bloody time— we made an album a year and spent the rest of the year touring it!

I suppose some bands might panic at going into the studio empty-handed, on a tight recording deadline, but we never have. Call it living on a wing and a prayer, or call it self-confidence, but we've always known we'll do what we have to do—that we'll, well, *deliver the goods.*

Some albums come together quicker than others, of course. I look back on the sessions for *Turbo* and I shake my head. What with all the booze and drugs and partying going on, we were spinning ourselves some pretty tall tales:

"Let's do it in the Bahamas! No, it's not working here, let's go to Miami! Fuck it, it's still not happening; let's go to Los Angeles! Yeah! Why not? We're BOUND to be more focused there . . ."

Your psalms and testaments are sacred to you, but sometimes you hear other songwriters' musical hymns and just bow down in worship. Even today, musicians still wonder in awe how Queen managed to write "Bohemian Rhapsody." Where did *that* come from?!

It's one of those special songs that's touched by the hand of God. If you dissect it, it's so complex but everything works. And, for any fan, that is the joy of music: hearing a song that is so great that you end up laughing in amazement and delight.

When you hear genius songwriting like that, or by people like Lennon and McCartney, or Jagger and Richards, or Page and Plant, it's like a beacon. It drives you on to try to reach those lofty heights yourself. Will you ever make it? Maybe not, but you can try!

I've been in Judas Priest for nearly fifty years now and there are two elements of life in the band that give me more pleasure than anything else. One is going out on tour, on a pilgrimage, and performing live— and the other is writing songs. Making magic from nothing.

Finessing them in the studio is fine, but the most important moment is hitting on that first germ of an idea, that first nugget of a song. Today, I'm never happier than when I've just eaten my school-boy lunch and I'm sitting down, with Glenn and Richie, to fit the fragments together.

Yeah. To get that jigsaw finished.

RIFFS

In the beginning was the riff. And it was *loud*.

This is so obvious that it should hardly need saying, yet at the same time you can't say it too many times. Great riffs are the engine that power metal and rock. Riffs aren't the be-all and end-all of a song, but they are its anchor. Think of the classic metal riffs: Black Sabbath's "Iron Man" or AC/DC's "Highway to Hell." They embed themselves in your brain and never leave.

Nor do you want them to. If you think of a song like Deep Purple's "Smoke on the Water," you can't help but sing the riff in your brain: "Duh duh *duh*, duh duh duh duh! Duh duh *duh*, duh duh!" Zeppelin have so many like that. The riff says everything about the song.

How do you find a great riff? You don't. You have to wait for it to find *you*. You can't wake up one morning and say, "Right, today I'm going to write the greatest riff in heavy metal!" All you can do is pick up your guitar, jam, and hope that inspiration strikes.

When it does, you *know*. The second I heard Glenn play the riff to "Hell Bent for Leather," I knew he had made heavy metal magic. It felt like he was bottling lightning. Riffs like that come out of thin air—how the fuck did *THAT* happen?! They're pure creativity.

When Priest are writing a song, the riff is always our starting point. It's the key to the lock, the template for everything else that happens in the song. We never write a song and then say, "Let's put a riff in there as well." It doesn't work like that.

Richie will come up with killer riffs from nowhere. He will be noodling in the studio, and I may only be half-listening, but then a riff or a chord sequence will just leap out at me. This used to occasionally lead to some frustrating conversations:

"Wow! Richie, stop! What did you just play?"

"Huh? What?"

"What did you just do? Ten seconds ago?"

"Er, I can't remember!"

So now we always tape everything Richie does, even if he's just chilling out and jamming away, in his own little world, in a corner. We don't want to miss the magic. We don't want to miss the golden riff.

As a lyricist, having a fantastic riff to work off is manna from heaven. It pushes me and it inspires me. Every riff contains an emotion and its own message, and the best ones make it really obvious to me where my words need to go to convey that message.

Look at "Breaking the Law." The second I heard that song, I was singing with the riff: "There I was completely wasting, out of work and down." *Where did those lyrics come from?* No bloody idea! I just instinctively sensed that the riff demanded harsh words of rage and frustration.

You can't dissect or analyze a classic riff. You can only be grateful for it. It's a gift from the rock gods. The moral? Not every rock or metal song has a fantastic riff—but there are simply no *great* rock or metal songs that don't.

LYRICS

I have a book that is very dear to my heart. It's forty-five years old, but it's in extremely good nick for its age.* Published in 1977, it's my well-thumbed copy of *Roget's Thesaurus*, and it has helped me to write the lyrics for every single Judas Priest album from *Sin After Sin* onward.

As soon as I joined Priest, I took on the role of being our lyricist. I was very happy to. I've always loved words. English literature was one of my favorite lessons at school, though I always found classic authors such as Chaucer and Shakespeare a bit foreboding and impenetrable.

---

* That's because I look after things, the same as my dad did.

Instead, as I grew into my teens, I got well into science fiction and fantasy. I loved the escapism of it. Tolkien and Isaac Asimov were big favorites, as was Mervyn Peake and his *Gormenghast* trilogy of novels. His imagination, and his precise use of language, really excited me.

It's a funny thing. I've freely admitted that, when I started out singing, I took my lead from Plant, Joplin, and Gillan. I tried to belt it out just like they did. In terms of lyrics, though, I've never taken inspiration from, or tried to copy, anybody.

I don't know why that is, but I've never once read another band's lyrics, or heard the words of a song on the radio, and thought, *God, I wish I could write something like that!* It's never happened. I think I've always ploughed my own particular furrow.

If there's a theme to my lyrics—and I think there *is*—it's the battle between good and evil. That has undercut everything in human history forever, whether it's culture, politics, fashion, art, music, or whatever. It's the eternal yin and yang.

The important point is that good always triumphs over evil in Priest songs. *Always.* Look at "The Sentinel" or "Sinner." It's important to me that, even if a song deals with a bleak subject, its central message and lyrical conclusion is uplifting.

I remember taking a deep breath before I started writing the lyrics for our first album, *Rocka Rolla*. Because it was our professional debut, I knew that, potentially, more people would be listening to us than ever before (although it didn't really work out that way!). I couldn't help but worry: *Am I doing this right?*

But I long ago left that kind of doubt about my lyrics behind. Now, I try to match the volume and sound and aggression of the music. You can't wimp around when you're dealing with something as strong and as powerful as "Painkiller." You've got to give it some big, hairy, metal balls:

Faster than a bullet, terrifying scream
*Enraged and full of anger, he is half man and half machine . . . ***

*****I hate to blow my own trumpet, but I love that lyric. I think it's fucking great! I'm definitely prouder of my lyrics than I am of my singing.

The other crucial point is that, although I write all the lyrics in Priest, I'm speaking for the band. We all have to agree on the message we want to send out. They leave the words to me, but they have to like them and what they represent.

For that reason, I've never strayed too far into cathartic songwriting and baring my soul, in our lyrics—but there are exceptions. During my many years in the closet, living a lie about my sexuality, I couldn't help but sometimes pour my angst and pain into our words.

The famous one is "Raw Deal" from *Sin After Sin*, of course. I'd never even been to America at the time, but the song was a lustful account of ogling guys in a famous New York gay hangout, Fire Island:

> *Them steely leather guys were fooling with the denim dudes*
> *A coupla colts played rough stuff . . .*

On the same album, "Here Come the Tears" was very maudlin and a definite wallowing in self-pity.* It was me, at twenty-six, sighing that I was all alone and probably always would be, seeing that homosexuality was, in those days, still the love that dare not speak its name:

> *Looks like it'll always be the same*
> *No one here to comfort me*
> *Here come the tears*
>
> *All alone, no one cares*
> *So much love to give to you all out there . . .*

In truth, I'm in two minds about that song now. Gay fans have written to me saying it really helped them in their lives, because they felt the same, and that's great. At the same time, I glance at those words and I occasionally think: *For fuck's sake, Rob! Give it a rest!*

Again, because I'm speaking for all the band, and not just for me, I rarely write social commentary lyrics in Priest songs. I don't think all

---

*Just in case Coldplay think they invented moping in rock—I was doing it twenty-five years before they did!

of the band share the same politics and worldview, so I don't climb on a soapbox. It would be presumptuous.

Despite that, "Breaking the Law" was a direct reference to Britain under Thatcherism at the start of the eighties, and the frustrations that a lot of working-class people felt. An even more interesting case is "Jawbreaker" from *Defenders of the Faith.*

Because I've admitted its central lyrical motif is a big fat cock, some people treat it like a joke, a cartoon. It's actually a serious song, about war and anarchy and revolution in places like Cuba or Ethiopia. But I guess that gets obscured behind the, er, big fat cock.

Yet although I've rarely allowed myself to bare my soul or get political in Priest lyrics, I had a lot more freedom when I had my solo band, Fight. Because I wanted to differentiate the project from Priest, I let myself go off in some interesting lyrical directions.

The title track of the *War of Words* album was all about censorship in America. "Contortion" dealt with Man's inhumanity to Man: "Money sucking greed / Watch the human gluttony." On Fight's second album, *A Small Deadly Space,* "Gretna Green" was about domestic violence.

One of the (very few!) benefits to getting older is that I think I've got better as a writer. My lyrics have become deeper and more interesting. I know how to use one word rather than five. I'm particularly proud of the *Nostradamus* lyrics. I think I did a decent job on that album.

Riffs come first when we write our songs and lyrics come last. They're hugely important to me and I take them incredibly seriously. Once we have chosen the ten pieces of music for an album, I lay ten blank pieces of paper on Glenn's kitchen table.

I generally start with a title—let's take the example of "Firepower." I will write that down, then underneath I write bullet points of words that relate to that idea: smoke, lightning, thunder, storm, danger, heaven, hell. I look at them for inspiration, and then I'm off. *At work.*

I'll circle and prowl around the table, adding verses and tweaking lines as I think of them. *That shouldn't say "if"; it should say "why"! That shouldn't be "red"; it should be "scarlet"!* I'll walk from place to place, from sheet to sheet, lost in my own little creative world.

Like all writers, it's a mix of inspiration and perspiration. The lyrics all influence and seep into each other, and sometimes the inspiration—the first flash of idea—can leapfrog from song to song. The perspiration is the hard graft of fitting it all together.

Sometimes, I will listen to the Priest music that needs lyrics and think, *What the fuck am I going to do with this?* I've got an empty head and a sense of terror: the horror of the blank page that every writer knows. I stare at the sheet of paper and it's just not happening.

Some people call that writer's block, but I hate that negative phrase and I never use it. If I'm getting nowhere with a lyric, I just walk away for a while and come back to it later. I know that, eventually, the idea will emerge. It's in my head, waiting to be released.

When it comes to other lyricists, most of the ones I love are in my own domain of music. Zeppelin have had some fantastic lines, and so have Sabbath. Tool have really smart, intellectual lyrics. Outside of metal, I love David Bowie's words. He was the absolute lyrical master.

Some lyricists, like Bob Dylan, Lou Reed, and Patti Smith, have had their lyrics published in little books, like they're poetry or something. I'm not sure I'd want to do that, exactly, but I do have an idea for a similar project that I think could be quite exciting.

I'd like to give my lyrics to some well-known graphic artists, and invite them to draw their artistic interpretations of the songs. The finished book could have the lyrics on the left-hand pages, and the illustrations bringing them to life bang opposite them.

Yeah! *The Illustrated Lyrics of Judas Priest.* We will do that, one day.

STUDIOS

If making an album is like giving birth to a heavy metal baby, the studio is the delivery room. It's the precious space where you coax your beloved offspring into life, and so you need to feel relaxed, safe, happy, and comfortable there. It's hard to be inspired if you're not.

Exactly like childbirth, you need somewhere that is clean, professional, and nurturing, where everything you need is on hand. You don't want to be crafting a record—or popping out a bab*—in a grotty old shithole with signature notes of mold and mouse droppings.

There's a strange paradox with studios. Once you're in a control room or in front of a microphone with the doors firmly closed, you could be anywhere in the world. Yet the facilities and the environment shape your mindset and, by extension, the music you make.

In our very earliest years, Priest pissed about in a couple of tatty little Midlands studios making demo tapes. Corky fixed the sessions up. We had bugger-all money, so we paid rock-bottom, cheapskate rates, and we got exactly what we paid for. They were a bit grim.

Our first proper studio came when we made *Rocka Rolla* in 1974, and it was a real premier-league introduction. We went down to London to Basing Street Studios, the top-of-the-range studio established by Island Records founder Chris Blackwell, which is now known as Sarm West.

Our gobs were hanging open at the gleaming facilities and technology of Basing Street: we felt like we had wandered onto the starship *Enterprise* from *Star Trek*. I half-expected to see Glenn beaming some bugger up, and Ken trying to chat up Lieutenant Uhura.

It was a flawed experience, though. Our first label, Gull Records, said they could only afford for us to record at night. We had no money for a B&B, so we had to spend daytimes trying to sleep in our stiflingly hot van in the middle of the busy tourist area of Notting Hill. No bloody chance!

It was shit, so Gull stuck us in Rockfield Studios in Monmouth, Wales, to record the follow-up, 1975's *Sad Wings of Destiny*. At least we each got a bed for the night there—and it began a long sequence of Priest hunkering down to make records in residential studios.

That's a funny process. Bands staying for weeks together in a studio complex is born of necessity, but when you first start doing it, it feels

---

* Just in case you don't know—"bab" is Black Country slang for a baby. As in: "'Er's a lovely bab, ay er?"

like an adventure. You're there to work, but it can also feel a bit like a school trip, or a lads' holiday. It can be a real bonding experience.

Rockfield was right out in the countryside and very hippie-esque at that time. I seem to recall patchouli and flared loon pants in abundance. So, Priest settled in to do what any self-respecting band would have done—work hard, and play even harder.

We'd record in the daytime with the producers, Max West and Jeffrey Calvert,* then get totally pissed every evening. We were all skint, so we hardly left the complex. Being broke was OK, because we didn't need to venture out: there was plenty of booze there.

Oddly enough, the other day, out of the blue, somebody sent me a photo of Priest at Rockfield, eating dinner and getting bevvied. And I could only think: *My God, we look fucking young!*

We went wild in the country again when we did *Sin After Sin* in 1976 at Chipping Norton Studios in the Cotswolds. That is in a lovely part of the world, all very nice and refined and English, and we even had a bit of dosh by then to go to the occasional country pub.

I like remote studios like that, that are so comfy that you feel like you're at home. I've never liked working in city studios: they tend to be too businesslike and sterile. The sole exception is that I'd like to record in New York one day. But New York is its own category of place.

When you're recording in an environment where you're relaxed and happy, it puts you in the right frame of mind to work. And Priest have never been more chilled yet focused in a studio than we were in John and Yoko's old gaff, Tittenhurst Park, making *British Steel* in 1980.

We loved bombing around the place gawping at John and Yoko's old decor touches (those side-by-side, his-and-her toilets!), but the idiosyncratic nature of the house also helped to shape the album. You think that studios are all identikit, interchangeable units? Think on!

---

*Max and Jeffrey were better known as Typically Tropical, who were one-hit-wonders earlier in 1975 when their faux-Caribbean kids' pop song, "Barbados," went to number one in Britain. Ask your gran about it. Actually, best not to. You might give her nasty flashbacks.

Our producer, Tom Allom, had us jamming together on *British Steel*, rather than all doing our bits separately, as we had before. That didn't mean we were all in the same room. We were linked by headphones, but most of the time we couldn't even see each other.

It was all about acoustics. Glenn and Ken were in the studio room, Dave Holland set his drums up in the stately home's lobby, and Tom sat me in a storage cupboard to do my vocals. I wasn't so sure about that, until he played them back to me, and I realized: *Yeah! That's the place!*

Romping around a mansion that a Beatle had lived in, pulling fantastic songs out of the air, and making a killer album, we were as happy as pigs in shit at Tittenhurst Park. In fact, we should probably have made more records there. Instead, we did something completely different.

Priest made our next three albums—*Point of Entry* (1981), *Screaming for Vengeance* (1982), and *Defenders of the Faith* (1984) at Ibiza Sound Studios in the sunny Balearic Islands. Why did we go there? Well, initially at least, let's put it down to the Chancellor of the Exchequer.

Back in the early eighties, there were some mad tax laws flying about in the UK, hitting higher earners, which we had just become after *British Steel*. If you didn't spend a few months a year out of the country, you had to hand the government a serious pile of wedge.

We were never one of those bands who emigrated to avoid paying UK tax—we're too British for that. We love this country. At the same time, if we could make a record in the sun and save a bit of dosh at the same time, what was not to like? So, it was *Ibiza, here we come!*

In the same way that the right studio can help to make a record, the wrong one can ruin it. There was nothing wrong with the actual studio in Ibiza, but the problem was its location. *Sun! Sea! Sex!* Priest went into making *Point of Entry* as if we were lads on the piss in Magaluf.

It's no surprise that I can hardly remember making that album. There were *so* many distractions, and we gave in to every one of them. We were in Ibiza for weeks, but I blush to think how few hours we actually spent in the studio. It was a criminally low proportion.

On a typical day, we'd meet up in the studio in the early afternoon, still pissed or hungover from the night before. We'd work until tea time, maybe do a couple of hours after we'd eaten, and then it would start:

> "Anybody fancy a pint?"
> "Yeah! I wonder what's happening at Pacha?"
> "Let go down to the Old Town and find out . . ."

And off we'd go. We'd stumble back to our rooms at dawn, then do it all again the next day. I think I spent more time ogling the talent on the local nudist beach than I actually did in the studio.

That pissing about took its toll on our songwriting and concentration levels. We knew *Point of Entry* had fallen short and when we went back the next year, to make *Screaming for Vengeance*, we made sure we put in a good shift every day before we went out and got bladdered.

Our last trip to Ibiza, to make *Defenders of the Faith*, famously started off in pretty bonkers fashion. We got to the studio to find the owner, Fritz, had got a bit lax with his payments, and bailiffs had moved in and stripped the whole complex bare!

There was no mixing desk, no mics, no furniture even—the place was a shell! We were on a record-label deadline, so had no choice but to bail Fritz's gear out and help him to cart it back into the studio. It's a funny story now, but, believe me, we were seriously pissed off at the time.

That was our last recording trip to Ibiza, but we all fell in love with the island. Most of the rest of the band ended up getting their own places there. Ian bought a villa; Glenn bought a place that he still owns; and then there was The Strange Case of the Dave Holland Hotel.

Our drummer bought quite a big house on the island and decided he wanted to rent out the rooms when he wasn't there. Like Airbnb thirty years ahead of its time! The only problem was that Dave was far too cheapskate to kit out the place with the stuff his guests would need.

So, at the start of our *World Vengeance* tour, Dave asked all of the tour party—band members, management, road crew, everybody— the same burning question:

"If yow dow use the soap or shampoo in your hotel room, can you save them for me?"

"Huh? What for?"

"It's for me hotel!"

Our long-suffering tour manager, Jim Silvia, got lumbered with carrying boxes and boxes of miniature hotel toiletries from city to city and then, at the tour's end, shipping them to Ibiza in a crate. He needn't have bothered. The Dave Holland Hotel never opened its doors.

Do you know the phrase "Out of the frying pan, into the fire"? Well, it applied to us big-time when we made the leap to our next residential studio. After surviving the years of madness and distractions of Ibiza, we decided to make the *Turbo* album in 1985 in . . . the Bahamas.

Through the mists of time, I'm not even totally sure now whose bright idea it was to record at Compass Point Studios in Nassau. I think it might have been Tom Allom, as our producer was by now living in Miami, so it was nice and handy for him. In any case, things soon went tits up there.

Very tits up.

I've got to take a lot of the blame for this one. I was going through a major personal meltdown. Drinking like fuck, doing loads of drugs, and locked in a dysfunctional relationship; I was in no shape to make a record. I was in no shape to do *anything*.

We could have been in Abbey Road Studio Two with Sir George Martin and I'd still have struggled to get the job done. Having said that, I wasn't the only bloke taking my eye off the ball. Dope, Red Stripe, rum, sensational women . . . there was a lot to distract a heavy metal band in Nassau!

I'd stagger into Compass Point the worse for wear, scribble down some ropey lyrics, and bang out a vocal with one eye on the clock, and then run off to carry on partying. And why would a band want to be in the studio when the world's most gorgeous beaches are right next door?

In fact, what impressed me the most about Compass Point, through my alcoholic and druggy haze, wasn't the setting or the facilities, but the fact that in the studio next to us was a giant of romantic Mom-pop: Julio Iglesias.

Julio was there to film a video. I'm a sucker for his music and I couldn't let the occasion pass without meeting him. His people said it would be OK to say hello while he was being made up for the vid. I nervously entered his sanctuary to find him . . . setting fire to his hair.

Well, not exactly. Julio was holding a cork over a candle and, when it was smoldering, applying it to his hair and eyebrows. Apparently, Pavarotti used to do the same (it must be a Latin thing). It covers up any streaks of gray creeping into their immaculate coiffures.

I introduced myself and told him I was a huge fan and the singer in a heavy metal band. He was charming and gracious and we chatted for a few minutes. I left chuffed at having met a true musical maestro and, of course, sank a lake of Red Stripe to celebrate.

I'd never have expected Julio to remember me, but years later I went to see him perform in Phoenix. When I went backstage after the show, he recognized me straightaway: "Ah, Rob, the Minister of Metal!" I felt honored. I've certainly been called far worse than *that* before.

We were getting nowhere with *Turbo* in Nassau and decided to bail out. It took sessions in Miami and Los Angeles, and me surviving a suicide attempt and getting sober in rehab, before we could finish the album. In retrospect, it's fucking amazing how well it turned out!

Priest made a couple more trips to exotic studios. In 1988, a Danish guy named Jon "Puk" Quist came to us and said, "Hey, guys, I've got the best studio in the world!" It was a persuasive line, and so we recorded *Ram It Down* at his Puk Recording Studios in Denmark.

Puk was the most remote place I have ever been to in my life. There was nothing for miles and miles—no bars, restaurants, shops, houses, nothing. I remember we had to walk across a pig farm to get from our rooms to the studio. That was a bit bloody whiffy.

As a studio complex, Puk had everything: state-of-the-art equipment, great recreation rooms, an Olympic-size swimming pool, a sauna, solar sunbeds. Who knows? Maybe it *was* the best studio in the world—*but it was so bloody boring!* We never went back.*

Painkiller in 1991 is one of the most extreme and focused albums that Priest have ever made and maybe that owed a little to the studio. We made it at Miraval, a beautiful but very sparse residential complex deep in the South of France.

Miraval was about ten kilometers from the nearest town, Cannes, and surrounded by lush vineyards. When we were there, it didn't even have a television or telephones. There was nothing to do except focus on the music, and the result was an album that we are incredibly proud of.

So, Judas Priest have certainly done our share of gallivanting to exotic residential studios all around the world—yet I know for a fact that we will never do it again. Because we've *been there, seen that, done that.* It's a young man's game, and we are not young men any more.

Over the last twenty years we have recorded five studio albums, and we've made them all either at Old Smithy Recording Studios or, more recently, at Glenn's home studio. Both are in Worcestershire and within an hour's drive of my home in Walsall, and that suits me down to the ground.

I'm in my seventies now. I don't want to be out of my head clubbing in Ibiza, or pissed as a twat in the Bahamas. In fact, I find the very notion horrific! However, the great thing is that *I* may have mellowed in that way, but Priest's music certainly hasn't.

The first time we recorded at Glenn's studio, for *Redeemer of Souls* in 2014, I knew it was perfect. It puts me—puts all of us—in exactly the headspace we need to be in. And, of course, it gave us *Firepower*, one of the most powerful, ferocious albums Judas Priest have ever made.

I can scream my tits off at Glenn's place on a track like "Lightning Strike," then I can go and sit in his kitchen, have a cup of tea and a Hobnob biscuit, and watch a bit of TV. And when we finish at six

---

*Puk burned down in 2020. Which is a shame because, boredom factor aside, it was a lovely place.

o'clock, I can hop in my motor and drive home to Walsall. Job's a good 'un!

I talked a lot in *Confess* about the workers in factories like G. R. Thomas Ltd., a metalworks company by my childhood home in Walsall, and how our band shares their mentality. Well, when those workers clocked off each evening, they didn't all go and get pissed in a shared house.

No. They went home to their families: their loved ones. Nowadays, that is exactly what I want to do, too. Because—and this might just be the truest, most meaningful statement in the whole of *Biblical*—the longer you are in this metal and rock game, the more you need your slippers.

PRODUCERS

The Bible reckons that God handed Moses the Ten Commandments and ordered him to spread His word among the people. The prophets most responsible for conveying metal and rock bands' holy testaments to the masses are their record producers. They are The Chosen Ones.

Outsiders may lazily imagine that producers are mere technicians who do little more than push "Record" and twiddle a few knobs. This could not be further from the truth. Great producers are creative figures who can spot potential in a song that even the band doesn't know is there.

When you are making an album, the producer basically becomes an additional member of the band. They listen to every song with the detachment the band simply can't have, and decide how to get the maximum out of all of that song's components.

There has to be a huge amount of trust between a band and their producer. Musicians, especially songwriters, are incredibly possessive about their songs. They're their little babies, and now they have to hand them over to a producer to help them to grow.

That's where a producer proves their worth. They have to come in with ideas—"What if the guitar line did *this*?" "Could we give the drums more weight *here?*"—to improve the songs, and they have to do so while not upsetting band members who might, just possibly, have fragile egos.

Producers have to be peacemakers in the studio to the extent that they may sometimes feel like therapists. They have to gently coax musicians out of their most outlandish desires:

> **Producer:** "I think we have too many lead breaks on this song."
> **Guitarist:** "No, man! The song needs them! They have to be there!"
> **Producer:** "Yes, but maybe not forty-eight bars? Maybe we could try it with just twelve?"

Or it might go like this:

> **Singer:** "I've written ten verses for the next track."
> **Producer:** "We can't have ten verses. We can only have four."
> **Singer:** "But I was up all night writing them! We need all ten because they tell a story! They have a message!"
> **Producer:** "But maybe you can tell that story so much *better* in four . . ."

Great producers, such as George Martin, Quincy Jones, or Jim Steinman, become as famous as the artists they produce, and deservedly so. In some instances, record companies will even communicate with the producer as an album is made, rather than directly with the band.

That was certainly the case in 1974 when Priest made *Rocka Rolla.* We were totally wet behind the ears in those days, whereas the producer that Gull Records had fixed us up with, Rodger Bain, was already a veteran of making albums with Black Sabbath and a band we had toured with, Budgie.

Rodger was very easy-going, to the extent that he was fast asleep and snoring on the studio couch as we wrapped up the album, but we had faith in him. With his pedigree, we thought he'd be able to capture the Sabbath-like power and volume we wanted on the record.

That was why it was such a shock to hear his final mix on the album and realize it was so quiet and muted. It was a proper letdown. Ken had a theory that Gull had told Rodger to dial down our metal side and make us more radio friendly, and there might just be something in that.*

Priest were so bitterly disappointed with the sound on that album that we were determined to take care of the production on the next record ourselves. We stamped our mark on it, even though we were, again, working with producers who were bigger names than we were.

Max West and Jeffrey Calvert had just got famous for fifteen seconds for flying to Barbados on, ahem, Coconut Airways, but they weren't really pop stars. They were two studio engineers who had got talked into making their novelty number one by a record label.

Two lovely guys, Max and Jeffrey knew their way around the studio, but they freely confessed they didn't know the first thing about heavy metal. That was OK: *we did*. Glenn parked himself behind the console and we definitely earned our coproduction credit on *Sad Wings of Destiny*.

Max and Jeffrey were expert technicians who knew exactly where the mics had to go—right against the cabinets? Above them? Below?—and Priest focused on getting the right sound, power, and texture. And we succeeded. When we heard it back, it sounded bloody great.

I must confess that studio success maybe went to our heads a bit. We had signed to Columbia Records, by 1977's *Sin After Sin*, and our new label gave us a proper big-name producer: Roger Glover, the former bassist with Deep Purple, a band we all worshipped. Fantastic!

Within a week, we'd told Roger to sling his hook.

It's hard to say why. I think it was a communication breakdown. Roger was coming in with the experience of selling millions of albums

---

* Not that the plan worked—you certainly never heard anything from *Rocka Rolla* on the bloody radio! Or anywhere else, come to that . . .

behind him and was very opinionated. We knew the sound we wanted and we had a successful production under our belt. So, we butted heads.

Firing Roger was probably a mistake. We were on a tight deadline, we had enough on our plate trying to write the songs, and the slick studio—Ramport in south London, owned by The Who—took some getting used to. *Uh-oh*. Maybe we weren't such top producers yet, after all!

After struggling for a couple of weeks, we ate some humble pie and put a call in to our management: *"Er, will you ask Roger if he will come back, please?"*

He did, and to his credit he didn't do it with an "I-told-you-so!" attitude. Roger knew where we were coming from and, being in a band himself, he admired that we were prepared to fight for our musical vision and not just roll over for him. We worked great together after that.

Following that album, we had a couple of producers who were fairly low-key and studious. Dennis MacKay on *Stained Class* and James Guthrie on *Killing Machine* were both very methodical and professional. They both did a good job and I have nothing negative to say about either of them.

We didn't laugh and drink and party with them, though, or form a lifelong, blood-brother friendship and creative partnership that survives to this day. That didn't happen until we met Tom Allom.

They say that opposites attract. That must be true, because when Priest first met Tom, it was clear we could not have been from more different backgrounds. In fact, scratch that: we seemed to come from different bloody planets!

Tom was a little bit older than us and he sounded as if he belonged in the House of Lords or an officers' mess rather than a recording studio (hence our nickname for him: the Colonel). His clipped, immaculately enunciated tones made a comic contrast with our yam-yam mumbles:

> "Robbo! Could you give me a bit more *oomph* on the vocals, dear boy?"
> "Ar, if yow like, Tom!"

Yet despite our different class and backgrounds, we hit it off with Tom from the off. He was just a great bloke and a larger-than-life personality, and in no time at all he was part of the band in the studio. *Part of our gang.*

Musically, Tom was classically trained. He knew everything about crotchets, quavers, and time signatures, and could play the piano. But he was also up with metal. He'd engineered the first three Sabbath albums, and he did his research on Priest before we met, which impressed us.

We first worked with Tom on the *Unleashed in the East* live album and he did a great job on it. So, when we came to record *British Steel* with him in 1980, we already had respect for him. That soon grew massively.

As a producer, and as a human being, Tom is a joy to work with. He brings out the best in us. He always knows what microphone to use, when to bring the music up and when to fade it down, how to nail vocal harmonies. You just feel safe: *This bloke knows what he is doing.*

The relaxed yet intensive atmosphere Tom created on the *British Steel* sessions was perfect for us. He deserves as much credit for that album as we do. Because we felt so at home with him, it gave us the confidence to be creative.

An example: When we were recording "Metal Gods," fuck knows why I suddenly thought, *This song needs some added cutlery!* But I did.

"Er, Tom, shall I shake some knives and forks so it sounds like robots marching?" I asked him.

"Terrific idea, Robbo, old boy! Trot off to the kitchen!"

So, I gave a Tittenhurst Park cutlery drawer a good rattle as Glenn and Ken were riffing away. And the rest is history.

Tom worked us hard for the month that it took to write and record the album from scratch, but he also joined in big-time after we finished for the day. Some producers try to stop their bands from partying too hard. Not Tom. In fact, he'd usually be leading the charge.

"Six o'clock, chaps!" he would proclaim. "Sun is over the yardarm! Anyone for a gin and tonic?" An uproarious evening would invariably follow.

In the studio, Tom was the sixth member of Priest for the next decade. He was with us through our adventures and misadventures, right from the three albums we made in Ibiza through the madness of *Turbo* in the Caribbean then the more sober *Ram It Down* in Denmark.

When Priest were finishing *Ram It Down*, we had what a few fans still regard as our *infamous* encounter with some very different producers. We went off to Paris to make three tracks with Stock Aitken Waterman (aka SAW).

We were—how can I put this?—not an obvious match. That production trio was ruling the pop roost and the UK Top 40 with upbeat chirpy hits by Kylie, Rick Astley, Big Fun, and Samantha Fox . . . and we were Judas Priest, heavy metal maniacs. *What the fuck were we doing?*

Some sniggered that working with SAW was going from the sublime to the ridiculous, but I don't agree with that. I think it's narrow-minded and rude. I've always had a lot of respect for great pop music well done. It was totally my idea, and you know what? I stand by it!

When I first suggested working with SAW, one or two of Priest were a bit iffy about the idea, to say the least. But I Made One of My Speeches (I'm quite notorious for those), they heard me out, and we reached a decision: *OK, let's give it a go! What harm can it do?*

We flew to Paris and spent two days with Mike Scott, Matt Aitken, and Pete Waterman. In that brief time, we recorded three songs with them. It was unbelievably fast, and it provided a fascinating insight into the world of pop production and the way those guys worked.

We got on with all of them, but we bonded the most naturally with Pete Waterman, a West Midlander like us. I must say, Pete can natter for England. You know how women can get called "bubbly"? For some reason, it's not said about blokes—but Pete Waterman is *bubbly*.*

We did a version of The Stylistics' "You Are Everything," and SAW wrote two songs for us on the spot—*Bish! Bash! Bosh!* I thought the results were brilliant, a great meeting of pop and metal, but then we had the big dilemma: *What do we bloody do with these, then?*

In the end, we didn't release them. It could have been the kiss of death for our career if our most hardcore metal fans had been so

---

*Pete "Bubbly" Waterman! I hope that catches on!

disgusted by us making "pop crap" that they just stopped coming to see us. I guess we chickened out. But I'm still so glad we had that adventure.

It certainly showed us a whole other world of producing! And I like to think that if we were ever to release those songs now, nearly thirty-five years on, even our most hardcore metal fans might say, "You know what? Those SAW songs are absolute belters!" *There again, I've always been an optimist . . .*

Back in the metal world, we had by now made eight albums (including live records) with Tom Allom. He'd always been on our wavelength. He'd helped us to adopt synth guitars on *Turbo*, because he agreed we had to try new things. Creatively, nothing is worse than being in a rut.

Yet this was the irony: we also didn't want to fall into a rut with Tom. When it came time to record *Painkiller*, we felt we needed a change. We wanted to reinvent ourselves with that album, and maybe it felt as if everything had got a bit too *cozy*.

Tom was a little upset when we told him we wanted to go separate ways, but he took the news with the stiff-upper-lip class that you would expect and wished us luck. And we turned to Chris Tsangarides, who had engineered with us on *Sad Wings of Destiny*.

Well, we turned to Chris—but, mainly, *we turned to ourselves*. We sensed that *Painkiller* was a crucial record for Priest and we knew *exactly* how we wanted it to sound. We were fully in control of its production. Glenn spent as much time behind the desk as Chris did.

It worked. We got the sound we wanted. As well as some production input, Chris did a brilliant job on the engineering, mixing, and mastering, and *Painkiller* did what we needed it to. It reestablished Judas Priest as a hard-edged, uncompromising heavy metal band.

At this point, of course, with the skill and timing that I'd like to think are my calling card, I reacted to Priest making a killer album by accidentally quitting the band. If nothing else, my unintended exit at least gave me some cool new producer experiences.

I've never gone for the idea of the genius auteur producer who terrorizes his artists and rules the studio by fear. It just sounds to me like too much bloody hard work! So, for my Fight solo project, I turned to a studio wizard whom I knew and liked.

Attie Bauw was a cool, level-headed Dutchman who had engineered on *Painkiller*, and he and I had a very easy-going relationship on both *War of Words* and *A Small Deadly Space*. I sat behind the console with him in Amsterdam and Phoenix and earned myself my coproducing credit.

That experience was certainly nothing like the one that followed it, as I got catapulted a million miles out of my comfort zone. And I loved it.

I went into my middle-aged electro-goth phase in the nineties, and did the 2wo electronic project with John Lowery (aka John 5). It was a total revelation to me. At the time, I loved techno-industrial music, but I soon realized I didn't have a fucking clue how it got made.

John 5 and I vanished to a studio in Bryan Adams's house in Vancouver with a producer, Dave Ogilvie, from the Canadian electro band Skinny Puppy. Dave worked with Nine Inch Nails' Trent Reznor, and Trent had said that he would release my album on his Nothing Records label.

It was all exciting—but the process was nothing like sitting in a studio jamming with Priest and Tom Allom. Instead, Dave Ogilvie and a crack team of engineers were perched at their keyboards and on their laptops, magicking up weird and wonderful electronic sounds out of the ether.

I chose the ones that I liked and laid lyrics over the top of the beats. By then, email had just been invented, so Dave was whizzing sound files over to Trent in New Orleans for his ideas and input. I felt both inspired by the process and completely out of my depth.

2wo gave me a whole new angle on what a record producer could do, and be. It was a fascinating world—but it wasn't my world. The album, *Voyeurs*, died on its arse and I knew it was time for me to get back to heavy metal. Now, who could help me?

When I started recording as Halford, I knew I needed a full-on, balls-to-the-wall metal producer. I got one in Roy Z, who had made two solo albums with Bruce Dickinson. And this pairing exemplified a funny irony that occurs if you stick around the music business for long enough.

Priest had started out in awe of our big-name producers, Rodger Bain and Roger Glover. Yet if a band enjoys a long, high-profile career, they get to the point where the boot is on the other foot and producers are overawed to be working with *them*.

Roy Z was a major, major Judas Priest buff. He did a cracking job on my two Halford albums, *Resurrection* and *Crucible*, but what really did his head in was being invited to produce a Priest record when I rejoined the band in 2003. Roy just couldn't believe his luck.

He transferred from Sound City Studios in LA to Old Smithy in Worcester and gave us exactly what we needed when I got back behind the Priest mic for *Angel of Retribution* in 2005. We thanked Roy kindly for his efforts as a producer—and then we went self-sufficient.

By now, Judas Priest had been making albums, and hanging around recording studios, for forty years. We were not the wide-eyed, dopey ingenues who had made *Rocka Rolla*, and we were pretty sure we knew enough about producing to do a decent job ourselves.

So, we did exactly that for *Nostradamus*—or, rather, *some of us* did. I contemplated rolling up my sleeves and getting heavily involved behind the mixing desk, but then I decided to leave the job to Glenn and Ken.

If I am honest, my main reason was self-preservation. I love both Glenn and Ken to death, and I always will, but it's been well-documented over the years that our original twin guitar titans, fantastic dual riff-machine that they were, didn't always see eye to eye.

A band is a family, and I shall talk more later in *Biblical*, in the Book of Lamentations, about how it feels when family feuds end up tearing that band apart. For now, I'll just say that I'd spent years being a mediator between Glenn and Ken, and I just couldn't face it this time around.

I didn't want to be stuck on the mixing desk between the push-me, pull-me of Glenn shoving the faders in one direction and Ken yanking them in the other. They might have been on their best behavior—but they might not. That was the thing with those two. You just never knew.

Attie Bauw was also on the production team and I trusted him to manage the situation. So, I left them to it, and the three of them did a fantastic job. I didn't hear the final mix of *Nostradamus* until we held an album playback for the label, in New York—and it sounded fucking brilliant.

After Ken did his abrupt exit stage left from Priest in 2011, Glenn produced our next album, *Redeemer of Souls*, with metal producer Mike Exeter. As Glenn steps back from live performances, due to his Parkinson's, I can see him doing more of our productions in the future.

Yet, you know a funny thing about producers? So often in metal and rock, like in life in general, you end up going full circle. As Priest geared up to make *Firepower* in 2018, we found ourselves going back to the future.

Just like *Painkiller*, nearly thirty years earlier, we knew *Firepower* was a crucial album. We realized that we had to redefine, and reestablish, ourselves in the metal world again, and that quest took us back to the man who'd helped power our initial breakthrough: Tom Allom.

Tom was in semi-retirement when we contacted him, but, like an old cop who can't resist the call of one last job (oh, and another one, and another one), he leapt at the chance to work with us again. Yet we sensed we needed one extra piece for our sonic jigsaw.

As well as the classic Priest magic Tom has always given us, we knew we also needed a sharp, current edge from somebody who was steeped in more contemporary metal production. Which was when the metal gods kindly delivered Andy Sneap to us.

Andy is a shit-hot producer who's worked with Megadeth, Exodus, and Trivium, among many others. He wrote to Glenn out of the blue, saying he'd love to be involved with Priest in any way possible. We met him, liked him, and then we had a crazy idea:

Why don't we try using Andy and Tom together?

It was a bonkers plan, in some ways. Tom and Andy had never met, and there was obviously a big age gap between them: Tom was engineering the first Genesis album, *From Genesis to Revelation*, in 1969 when Andy was busy being born! And yet, something told us it might work.

We were right. Andy knew all about Tom and had a huge respect and admiration for his previous work. Tom wasn't so well versed in Andy and his career, but as soon as they teamed up in Glenn's home studio, they clicked from the off.

They were exchanging ideas from day one. "If you move that there, old chap, *this* will happen!" Tom would say, pushing a fader.

"Oh, my God!" Andy would marvel. "I never knew that!"

Ten minutes later, it would be Andy's turn. He'd conjure a ferocious roar out of the mixing desk, and Tom would be equally astounded: "Good Lord, dear boy! How *did* you do that?"

They became thick as thieves and it was lovely to see. Most important of all, their alchemy drove us to make *Firepower* the incendiary, brutal document that its name suggested, and that we knew it had to be. And I know they will repeat the trick on our next album.

If you asked me right now, I'd be happy for Tom Allom and Andy Sneap to remain Priest's production dream team for the rest of the band's life.

But you should never say never in metal and rock. Never say never to a new hookup that might lift you to fresh creative heights.

Is there one producer left that I'd love Priest to work with? There is, and he is one of the undoubted masters of his craft: Rick Rubin.

It's amazing now to think that Rick started out as a hip-hop producer, working with LL Cool J and the Beastie Boys. He moved on to metal bands like Slayer and Danzig and, since then, he has helped so many artists to reinvent themselves, from Johnny Cash to Neil Diamond.

Despite this, stupidly and naively, I had thought it was probably a bad idea for Rick to produce Black Sabbath's 13 album in 2013. I figured they would just be musically too far apart. Our old coproducer, Mike Exeter, also told me some mad stories about their studio sessions.

Mike has always worked with Sabbath's Tony Iommi, and he said that before they began work on 13, Tony gave Rick Rubin a load of material that he had written for the album. Rick listened then told him: "Start again! It's not good enough! Go away and listen to the first two Sabbath albums again!"

Bloody hell! You need balls of steel to talk to Tony Iommi like that! Tony was shocked, but he did it. Then, during the sessions, Rick would lie on the couch with his eyes closed as Sabbath played. He'd look like he was fast asleep, like Rodger Bain as we finished *Rocka Rolla* in 1974!

Then, at the end of the day, Rick would tell Sabbath exactly what they needed to do: give *this* song more attention, lose *those* drum fills, move *this* track on the running order so it's after *that* one. And out of it came a great album and a fitting recorded high note for Sabbath to end on.

I started this section talking about record producers being our closest parallel to prophets and, come to think of it, Rick Rubin does look a bit like Moses! Will Judas Priest ever work with him? I haven't got a bloody clue! But I've certainly heard worse ideas . . .

ALBUM TITLES

Rick Rubin may be Moses, and record producers may be the prophets who carry artists' psalms and testaments to the masses—but that's not all. As I said, they're also the midwives who coax our albums, our *heavy metal babies*, to life in the delivery room of the studio.

And, as any proud parent will tell you, one of the hardest first decisions that you have to make when you have a new bab is what to call it.

Album titles can be—and this is a technical term—tricky buggers. You are always trying to think of something that sums up the overall feel, the *mood*, of a record. Sometimes, inspiration strikes early on in the recording process. Other times, it doesn't come until right at the end.

As the words-man, the lyricist, in Priest, I generally come up with most of the album titles. Not all of them, but most. It's part of my general job description of being the singer, and while some birth names prove easier than others, it's a task that I enjoy.

Priest album titles can simply be the name of the most important, and representative, song on the record. It's what they used to call the title track, and that's what we did on *Screaming for Vengeance*, *Defenders of the Faith*, and *Painkiller*, just to mention a few.

It doesn't always work like that. We don't have a song called "Sin After Sin" or "British Steel" or "Point of Entry." They're examples where I had an initial idea and then discussed it with the band (although I *still* can't remember coming up with bloody *Point of Entry*!).

Words and titles are my department, but I'm not a dictator. I couldn't force a title on Priest that nobody else liked: we're democratic and we talk things over. If it comes to a vote—well, there are five of us, so three votes win.

We certainly didn't get the luxury of a vote when we made our debut, *Rocka Rolla*. In fact, we weren't even consulted on a title! Gull Records simply told us: "That's what the album is called." That was how the record industry worked, back in those Old Testament days.

I *did* think of *Sad Wings of Destiny* and, nearly fifty years on, I'm still proud of that title. It means a lot in the Priest story. It's poetic, and a bit melancholic, and I think it says something about the human condition: *that's where we all lie, in the sad wings of destiny.*

Sin After Sin was one of mine, as well. It was obviously riffing off the themes of Priest, and faith, and religion, as we have always done as a band, but it was also referencing the lyric of "Genocide," an important song for us on *Sad Wings of Destiny*:

> *Sin after sin I have endured,*
> *Yet the wounds I bear are the wounds of love . . .*

When we got to *Stained Class*, that was Glenn's brainwave. As I recall it, Ken wasn't very keen. He thought it would confuse fans and we should just call it *Stained Glass*. But Ken got outvoted, and I liked Glenn's nifty little twist. I've always been partial to a spot of clever wordplay.

Album titles can be contentious. Sometimes, you can come up with the perfect title, but then it causes ructions. That was certainly the case in 1978 (our second album that year, after *Stained Class*) when we called our fifth LP *Killing Machine*. Or, rather, tried to.

We were defining our music as a heavy metal killing machine, but our US label hated the title, saying it conjured up images of electric chairs or psychopathic, murderous mass-shooting sprees. They insisted that we change the name of the record in America to *Hell Bent for Leather*.

Huh? I couldn't understand what they were on about, and I remember Glenn was particularly pissed off—*surely it was bleeding obvious what we meant by it?* But the label was adamant, so we had to just suck it up (and, in fairness, *Hell Bent for Leather* wasn't a bad title, either).

You can get inspiration for titles from the weirdest places. *Defenders of the Faith* in 1984 was obviously about keeping the faith of heavy metal. Yet I got the idea from the picture of Britannia on the back of a British 50p coin, looking like she was armed and set to defend the realm.*

Record titles mean different things to different people. Some folk can get the hump and the wrong end of the stick for no reason whatsoever, as I saw spectacularly when Priest released *Ram It Down* in 1988.

I came up with the title because I liked the idea of a massive steel fist smashing down on top of Earth—the fist of heavy metal dominating the planet. Well, that was *my* interpretation of the title, but I soon found out that it wasn't everybody's.

Our manager, Bill Curbishley, had by now opened a small management office in New York. It was run by a lovely lady named Ann, and she and I had become good friends. I happened to be in NYC and called into that office just after we had wrapped up making *Ram It Down* in Denmark.

I mentioned to Ann in passing what the title was so be—and she hit the roof. She was *livid.* "That is outrageous!" she yelled at me. "It's disgusting, it's offensive, and it's anti-feminist! That title is a total assault on women and on women's rights!"

Eh? I was utterly bemused. "What are you on about, Ann?" I asked her. "What do you mean? It's nothing to do with women's rights!"

Ann saw the title as gratuitous, misogynistic sexual brutality. She was so upset that she stormed out of the office. I was left with my jaw hanging open. I mean, why would I, a gay man, attack women via a

---

* My inspiration for the song "Heavy Duty" off that album was reading that phrase on my washing machine in my house in Phoenix. I suppose it's lucky I didn't call it "Spin/Dry" or "Mixed Fabrics."

record title full of lewd sexual connotations? The whole thing beggared belief.*

There again, album names can come from anywhere. *Painkiller* is a serious title. It describes a fearsome, mythical creature that obliterates all before it, and which is sent to Earth to destroy all evil. But where did I get the name for this monster? From reading a pack of aspirin!

I like it when album titles stretch back and forth across Priest's career, and cross-reference it. When I rejoined the band, after my unfortunate hiatus, in 2003, I wanted an album name that both tied in to my return and looked back to the terminology of *Sad Wings of Destiny*.

That was why I came up with *Angel of Retribution*, which I knew worked on both of those levels. Glenn loved it, but Ken didn't: he wanted to call it *Judas Rising*, after the opening track on the album. We had one or two heated debates about it . . . but Ken got outvoted. Again. Poor Ken.

Firepower was one of those titles that just chose itself. It references the gun violence and weaponry rampant in America, but our interpretation is a positive one: the firepower of heavy metal. In a way, it's *Killing Machine* all over again, but luckily, we escaped any daft record-label fuss this time.

It occurs to me that we've never done what a few major bands have—released an eponymous album relatively late on in their career. We've never named an album just *Judas Priest* and put it out in a plain sleeve or, worse, with our ugly mugs leering off the front.

The Beatles, Genesis, and Metallica all did that. If it's good enough for them, it's good enough for us, right? But I doubt we'll ever do it. Why? Because lots of Priest fans excitedly await our album titles, then pore over the artwork. It's all part of the new-album ritual for them.

I understand it, because I was exactly the same as a kid. So, why should we let them down and put out a lazily titled cop-out? Read

---

*Ann seemed to believe that *Ram It Down* was as offensive an album concept as *Smell the Glove*. Maybe we should have gone the whole hog and released it in a plain, none-more-black sleeve . . .

my lips: We. Will. Never. Release. An. Album. That. Is. Just. Called. *Judas. Priest.*

Never! Unless I change my mind. Because Metal Gods can do that . . .

ALBUM COVERS

When you buy a new album, the sleeve is the first thing that you take in about it, before you've even heard a note. It's your visual introduction to the concepts and the ideas that lie within it—so you have to make it count.

I can think of so many sleeves, over the years, that blew my bloody mind the second I set eyes on them. David Bowie's *Aladdin Sane*. That image of Bowie with his Ziggy stripe just seared into your memory and you knew it would never leave. It was instantly iconic.

That twisted face on the sleeve of King Crimson's *In the Court of the Crimson King* is a fantastic cover. And, while it's a completely different style of music, so is the Sex Pistols' *Never Mind the Bollocks*. That one image seemed to sum up the whole sound and spirit of punk rock.

Bat Out of Hell by Meat Loaf isn't actually a metal album, but it has an all-time-classic metal-looking cover. I like covers that make you think, like Pink Floyd's *Animals*. I love the story that their giant inflatable pig blew away so they photographed it flying over Battersea Power Station.

As I say, I don't usually care for sleeves with just a photo of the band on the front, but that Mick Rock shot of Queen in a diamond formation on the sleeve of *Queen II* is an exception to the rule. They weren't even famous at the time, but that image drilled the band into your mind.

Metal has produced some belting covers. Korn's first album, *Korn*, from 1994, had a disturbing sleeve. It's a little girl on a swing, in a playground, with the shadow of a man standing nearby, hovering over her. You don't know exactly what's happening, and you're not sure you want to.

The cover of Ozzy's *Blizzard of Ozz* is an absolute metal classic. It's Ozzy, kneeling down, in robes, his eyes ringed with kohl, waving a crucifix in the air, with a skull and a goat horn behind him. It's amazing—but what does it all mean? Your guess is as good as mine (and probably Ozzy's!).

In metal, or rock, or whatever, the most important thing about album artwork is that it should convey the content of the music. That's how the greatest covers work. As soon as you look at the album sleeve, you can *feel* the music.

Priest have always been very hands-on with our album covers. We brief the designers to get their imaginations working. We often have the first briefing meeting very early in the recording process because it can take a while, and lots of back-and-forth, to get to the final sleeve design.

We've *never* let a label say to us, *"This* is your cover. Like it or lump it!" . . . except for once. Our first inkling as to what the cover of *Rocka Rolla* was to be came when Gull Records presented it to us as a fait accompli. And we couldn't believe our eyes. It was fucking horrible!

It was just a stupid bottle top, with *Rocka Rolla* written on it in a parody of the Coca-Cola logo. *Huh?* It couldn't have been less heavy metal! We protested, furiously, but Gull just said, "Tough titty!" They'd never get away with it nowadays—Coca-Cola would sue their arses off.

Because Gull still own the rights to *Rocka Rolla,* they have re-released it once or twice. We can't stop them. They retitled it *Hero, Hero,* and the irony is they gave it a much better cover—a metal warrior, his sword drawn, emerging from a mist. Why couldn't they have given us *that* in 1974?!

Because *Rocka Rolla* was such a dud, a false start, we didn't really get going with our artwork until the follow-up, *Sad Wings of Destiny.* But we sure made up for it then. I still think that particular sleeve is one of the most powerful and iconic images in Judas Priest's history.

The designer, John Pasche, did such a great job. There is a lot going on. Look at the central figure, of the angel—is he a fallen angel, a good angel, a bad angel? Is he abject and defeated by the forces of evil, or is he gathering his strength to fight back?

There was so much to consider. The cover of *Sad Wings of Destiny* had motivational power, it was all about the battle of good versus evil, and it established visual and musical themes that overarch Priest's entire career. Those themes are still going strong today.

By the time of *Sin After Sin*, in 1977, we'd signed our major-label deal and the chief art director at CBS, a cool Polish guy named Roslaw Szabo, began designing our sleeves. Roslaw was a genius who produced some total belters for us—but *Sin After Sin* was not without its issues.

The central image of the sleeve was an Egyptian mausoleum in London, and it had a woman sitting at the base of the tomb. I didn't really take much notice of her (I mean, naked women have never really been my thing!), but she was nude and in high heels.

Priest signed the artwork off and it was all ready to go off to print when somebody at the record company saw the naked woman and had an attack of the vapors. They said that it was sexist. Well, as the great Nigel Tufnel famously asked, "What's wrong with being sexy?"

We were a bit bemused by the whole thing—after all, we hadn't asked for a bloody naked woman in the first place!—but Roslaw had to move quickly. He yanked the offending floozy off the sleeve, leaving only her eerie silhouette behind. Which actually looks loads better.

That *Sin After Sin* cover was also cited as evidence of Priest's supposed moral depravity in the short spell when evangelical Christians, offended by our band name, began picketing our shows in America. They claimed the picture depicted "satanic worship," which properly made me lol.*

Why? Well, for one thing, the Egyptian mausoleum was in Putney. *I ask you—satanic worship? In Putney?*

Roslaw was still on board and gave us the great picture of the guy in the studded headband and blood-red smashed sunglasses on the sleeve of *Killing Machine*. It's an image that just *exudes* heavy metal. Yet his most famous contribution to the Priest narrative is the cover of *British Steel*.

---

*Priest have never had anything to do with Satanism, and thankfully the protests died down pretty quickly. There were never too many of those Holy Rollers outside our US gigs. They were like that mad family you see nowadays—you know, the Westboro Baptist Church. Complete nutters.

The striking image of a leather-braceleted hand tightly clutching a razor blade was the perfect representation of the uncompromising, sharp-edged music that lay inside that sleeve. Initially, when Roslaw presented us with the idea, the hand had blood oozing from the fingers.

I've told this story many times, but I never tire of relating the response that Priest gave him. "We love it, mate!" we told him. "It looks amazing! But lose the blood. We're a heavy metal band! We're so hard that we don't bleed . . ."

In fact, *British Steel* was such a brilliant, unforgettable sleeve that it's a shame we followed it up with one that was bloody rubbish.

Our *Point of Entry* album in 1981 fell short on a few levels. The music wasn't all it could be because, as I say, we were too focused on getting hammered in the pubs and clubs of Ibiza. And the sleeve that it came wrapped in was a complete debacle.

We were stuck for inspiration for a cover image, time was running out, so when the label showed us a suggestion for the British edition, we said, "OK, that'll do." It was a photograph taken out of the window of an airplane, showing the tip of the plane's wing framed against a sunset.

What did it mean? Was the wing a point of entry? Er, a point of entry to *what*? It was all a bit weak and ambiguous. I mean, I had no idea what it was supposed to represent, and I was the singer in the bloody band! It was our fault: we never said "OK, that'll do" to an album cover again.

Yet even that looked like a Peter Blake special compared with what our label foisted on us for the American edition of *Point of Entry*! It was a print-out of white computer paper stretching across a desert setting into the distance and sun-dappled mountains.

It was real sub–Pink Floyd shit, a bad Floyd copy, like something Storm Thorgerson might have knocked off in ten minutes on a bad day. The US label hadn't told us in advance and we went ballistic—but what could we do? Nothing, except to make sure it *never* happened again.

When we're lucky, the idea for a cover image comes to us fully formed. For *Screaming for Vengeance*, I told our designer, Doug Johnson, that I had an image in my head of a screaming eagle swooping out of the sky. That was all that he needed and he brought it to life brilliantly.

It was an amazing sleeve, and yet at about this time in the eighties, the impact of all cover art was being reduced by the record industry moving wholesale from vinyl to CDs. Suddenly, the music might have sounded better (*maybe* . . .), but it came in a package that was a quarter of the size.

That gave designers less space to play with and made it impossible for them to dream up the kind of visionary, intricate covers like *Houses of the Holy* or *Sgt. Pepper's Lonely Hearts Club Band* that fans pore over for weeks. I hated the introduction of CDs partly because of that.

I've never really gone for old-fashioned, sexualized heavy metal imagery of women with big tits (as I said, why would I?) but our cover for *Turbo*, in 1986, was pretty phallic. It was a woman's hand grabbing a gear stick that clearly represented a cock. In truth, I didn't like it very much.

The ideal for any rock or metal band is to find a designer who is totally on your wavelength, and whom you can trust to always find the perfect visual representation of your music. For the last thirty years, Priest have been lucky enough to have that relationship with Mark Wilkinson.

Before he came to us, Mark had done a lot of work with Marillion, and then with Fish. He is not a heavy metal maniac, but that doesn't matter. He is so astute that we can explain the basic concept for a cover to him and he will say, "OK, lads, I've got it." And he invariably has.

Mark designed the giant metal fist of *Ram It Down* then really came into his own on *Painkiller*. I wanted a sleeve that both nodded to the futuristic themes of the album but also harked back to that important, seminal sleeve of *Sad Wings of Destiny*.

I told Mark that I wanted to take the very human-looking angel from that cover and make him more robotic, and that I'd also like to acknowledge the Harley that I ride onstage at every show. It was a hard concept to explain, yet Mark *got* it, brilliantly. He drew exactly what I was thinking.

Mark understands how pivotal that angel from the *Sad Wings* cover is to Priest visuals. On the *Redeemer of Souls* album, I asked him to merge it with the famous image of Mel Gibson, in his leather gear, bestriding a highway like an avenging angel in *Mad Max*. He nailed it, yet again.

Mark gets our creative vision, but he isn't the only person who is bang on Priest's wavelength. On *Firepower*, we worked with a Chilean-Italian digital artist and photographer, Claudio Bergamin, whom Richie knew and had recommended to us.

Claudio designs covers for books about the paranormal as well as metal album sleeves. He got it in one. We were in Glenn's studio wrapping up *Firepower* when his first-draft design arrived. I'll never forget opening the envelope and seeing his vivid, spectacular artwork. *Wow!*

"This is it!" I said. "We don't need to change anything. It's everything the album represents. It's perfect!" Those moments when everything falls into place are so rare—in music, lyrics, sleeve designs, *whatever*. But they're what bands dream of, and what they never stop striving for.

CONCEPT ALBUMS

Some people, even in metal and rock bands, are horrified by concept albums. They regard "a good concept album" as a self-contradiction, an oxymoron, like "a good fatal accident" or "a good dose of the clap." I am not one of those people.

I've always enjoyed a great concept album. I love a record that tells a story, like a book or a movie, with characters who change and plots that develop. You can kick back, crack open the popcorn bag, and immerse yourself in the storyline as the album unfolds.

So much in rock began with the Beatles, and there is a strong argument that they made the very first concept album, *Sgt. Pepper's Lonely Hearts Club Band*. This album told a story that intrigued me from the second I heard Kenny Everett play it on Radio 1 in 1967.

An album of amazing songs based on a fictional Edwardian military band? *Cosmic!* I also think their White Album had conceptual elements to it. I spent many teenage hours poring over the music and the poster that came with it, trying to decipher it. *What does it all mean, man?*

The seventies were a great decade for concept albums. I remember listening endlessly to Mike Oldfield's *Tubular Bells*. It was revolutionary—

an instrumental album, with just two very long tracks, that you had to listen to all the way through. It blew my mind.

It became one of the biggest albums of all time. Apparently, Mike was miffed that you had to take the record off to flip from side one to side two because it disturbed the flow; the *concept*. Not that I had a bloody clue what the "concept" was, because it was all instrumental!

There were some classic concept records around then. Yes's *Tales from Topographic Oceans*. Rick Wakeman's *The Six Wives of Henry VIII*. Genesis's *The Lamb Lies Down on Broadway*. Jethro Tull's *Aqualung*. Rush's *2112*. I was a sucker for the lot of them. I thought they were ace.

Concept albums fell out of favor when punk rock came around. The punks thought they were bloated and pretentious and too far from the everyday life that they were singing about. Johnny Rotten said, "I hate Pink Floyd!" and a generation of music fans fell in line with him.

I never agreed with that school of thought. I think it's weird to accuse musicians of being pretentious, like it's some sort of crime. Aren't we *supposed* to be ambitious, and audacious, when it comes to making records? Isn't it our job to have outrageous ideas and *dream big*?

The other body blow for concept albums was *This Is Spinal Tap* mocking overblown bands recording jazz odysseys and introducing ludicrous Stonehenge-themed stage sets. But *Spinal Tap* is brilliant satire and you can only satirize great events. Which many concept albums are.

I think that I'd probably always had a subconscious hankering for Judas Priest to record a concept album. But the idea didn't come bubbling to the surface of my mind until 2005, when our manager, Bill Curbishley, flew out to join us in Estonia during the *Retribution* tour.

Bill had quite some history in concept albums, as the manager of The Who, who had helped Pete Townshend to realize both the *Tommy* and *Quadrophenia* projects. So, when he suggested it was time for Priest to dip our toe into that water, I was all ears.

Bill had a couple of suggestions for possible subjects for us to tackle. The first was Rasputin, but that didn't really float our boat. The second was a different matter: "Have you heard of a guy called Nostradamus?" he inquired.

BOOM! The second that the words left Bill's lips I was transfixed by the idea. You just know that some ideas are *right* the instant that you hear them, and this was one of those epiphany moments. It was obvious to me that this was perfect subject matter for Priest.

I knew a bit about Nostradamus, and I quickly researched and learned a whole lot more. He had a fascinating life, this sixteenth-century French seer and astrologer who wrote *Les Prophéties*, his historical masterpiece seemingly predicting major world events awaiting mankind.

More than four hundred years later, I wanted to get inside his head on *Nostradamus*. He was a clairvoyant, perceiving the future—but how did that *feel?* When did he realize that he had this extraordinary, mystical ability? Was it a pressure? Did he think he was going nuts?*

Writing *Nostradamus* felt different from anything Judas Priest had done before. We knew we were out of our comfort zone, but we absolutely loved that. It felt like a real band effort, all of us pulling together to make this crazy, weighty metal opus work.

We wrote highfalutin songs called things like "Revelations," "Shadows in the Flame," and "Future of Mankind," and we made them mysterious and *dark.* Don Airey from Deep Purple joined to play keyboards on easily the most orchestral and symphonic record Priest have ever recorded.

We didn't know how it would go down. We guessed a few of our more traditional, headbanging fans might see *Nostradamus* as poncy. At the same time, we felt our forty years in the metal game had earned us the right to experiment and, well, be a little bit poncy.

In any case, and this is the important point—the album was still *metal.* The sounds and instrumentation were a long way from *Painkiller*, but *Nostradamus* was still definitively a heavy metal album. Today, it's the only Priest album I ever sit down and listen to from start to finish.

---

*I tackled this topic in the song "Visions" on the album: "Visions in the night / Show me what is right / Help me through the maze of mystery . . ."

It came out to a mixed response, but we expected that. Some fans said, "Why make a concept double album? Why not just give us two *normal* CDs?" At a press conference in Mexico City, a journalist asked us, "Why make an album this long when people's attention spans are so short?"

We got some flak like that, but other people loved it for the classy piece of work it is. Even today, some fans will tell me, "I hated *Nostradamus* when it came out, but now it's my favorite album you've ever made." I love it when that happens.

We talked of taking the album on tour with a full theatrical production—after all, Rick Wakeman did *The Myths and Legends of King Arthur and the Knights of the Round Table* on ice!—but we never did it. We did a normal tour instead. And, to me, that's still a box to be ticked.

I have a bucket list in my head of things I'd still like Judas Priest to do. One of them is that I'd love us to go out and perform *Nostradamus* in its entirety. (Although maybe not on ice! My knees aren't up to it!) Or, if we don't do that, I'd like it to get an alternative staging that it deserves.

I'd love to see it performed classically by the Birmingham Symphony Orchestra. Why not? Metallica did that fantastic concert with the San Francisco Symphony that became their *S&M* [*Symphony & Metallica*] album. There are loads of precedents like that.

I'd get together with the orchestra director beforehand and discuss the instrumentation: Should we lead this section with a cello? Or an oboe? Then, I'd sit in the front row of the symphony hall and nod my head (or even bang it) through the performance. *Nostradamus* belongs in the classical world. I want to hear it on Classic FM in Britain.

I'd like to go further still. It would make a great opera, to be staged at the London Coliseum. Or it could work brilliantly as a ballet. Really, the sky's the limit! If you are going to think outside the box, and make a fantastical concept album, just fucking go for it!

Will it ever happen—*Nostradamus* on the South Bank, or at Carnegie Hall? I genuinely believe that it will, one day! I might be eighty, or even ninety, years old by that time. But that's OK. I can wait . . .

LIVE ALBUMS

"Good evening, London! Are you ready to rock?!"

There are no more exciting words to hear from a singer when you are crammed into a club or an arena, about to lose your mind. But do you *really* want to hear them when you are slumped on your sofa in a vest, scratching your arse, on a rainy Tuesday afternoon?

Well, the answer is *Yeah!*—if you love the artist enough and the gig is good enough. There are a select few live recordings that I enjoy just as much as the best studio albums that band ever made, because they capture the sound of that band right at the top of their game.

The Rolling Stones' *Get Yer Ya-Ya's Out!*, recorded at Madison Square Garden in 1969, is a phenomenal live album. So is Deep Purple's *Made in Japan*. And in the seventies, it appeared compulsory for everybody in the world to own a copy of Peter Frampton's *Frampton Comes Alive!*.

No Sleep 'til Hammersmith is the only British number-one album that Motörhead ever had. The Who's *Live at Leeds* is fantastic, a historical document. And when you listen to *Johnny Cash at Folsom Prison*, you can hear the inmates going wild with total fucking excitement.

There's a line of thought with live albums that *you had to be there*, and it's true that they gain an extra edge if you were actually at the gig. It means that you are on the album. Every time the crowd cheer, you can think, *That was me! I was there!*

That's a bonus, but attendance isn't essential. We've all been to enough gigs to be able to imagine ourselves there once we hear the roar of the crowd. Yet the weird thing is that, although I can enjoy listening to live albums, I'm not all that keen on recording them.

Priest have done a few now, and I'm still of two minds about the process. Whenever we play a gig, I always want to give our very best for the fans who are watching us, right there and then. Knowing that the night is being recorded for future use introduces a bit of a mental curveball.

When we have to have meetings with producers and engineers before recording a show, it can put my mind in a different place from usual. It can be an intrusion, and I hate that because I just want to focus on what I'm doing as a singer.

At worst, it gives me a thing going on in the back of my head while I'm performing. It makes me feel self-conscious, although that tends to pass a couple of songs into the show, as I get into it and I half-forget that the bloody recording is happening.

Back in the day, the routine used to be that once you'd released three or four studio albums, your record label would want to whack out a live record. This process led to Priest's first, best-known, and, to some, most *notorious* live album.

I think *Unleashed in the East* is still one of the all-time seminal heavy metal live albums. People still rave about it today. It was recorded at two shows at the Kosei Nenkin Hall and the Nakano Sun Plaza, both in Tokyo, during our second tour of Japan in 1979.

Or, at least, *most* of it was.

I was pretty whacked on that tour. Jetlag had kicked in and triggered my insomnia, which is never a hard thing to do. When I haven't slept, I am out of sorts and, try as I might, I knew that my voice at those shows was strained and well below its normal level.

I didn't realize how badly until Priest came to mix the record, back in England, at Tittenhurst Park with Tom Allom. I winced as I heard my knackered voice dribbling out of the studio speakers. *Christ! Had those poor sods in Japan really paid good yen to listen to that?*

Nowadays, sound-editing software like Pro Tools can make that kind of problem go away. In 1979, that wasn't an option, but I knew there was no way we could release me sounding so shit. It would have been bad for the band and worse for the fans who had shelled out. So I came to a decision on the spot.

"I'm going to take a mic and go to the sitting room," I told Tom. "You press 'Record' and I'll sing the entire show now. I'm not going to stop. I'll do it all in one take. Then we'll see what we've got."

And that's what I did. I put my headphones on and re-sang the whole gig in one go. In its own way, it was a proper live performance. The only difference was that the rest of the band were Live in Tokyo, Japan! And I was Live in Ringo Starr's Sitting Room, Berkshire!

It sounded great and, when we put *Unleashed in the East* out, it sold well, and fans loved it. It wasn't until I let the secret of my rerecorded vocals slip in an interview that some people started taking the piss and calling it *Unleashed in the Studio*. But I still think we did the right thing.*

The sleeve photo wasn't from Kosei Nenkin Hall or Nakano Sun Plaza, either. We never thought to arrange a photographer at the Tokyo gigs, so we piled into our van one sunny afternoon and drove to... St. Albans. Well, we had always gone down well there!

We set up our gear in the empty City Hall that we'd sold out so many times. It felt weird, posing away with no one there, as the photographer, Fin Costello, snapped away. Look closely at the sleeve pic: there's no drummer on it. Les Binks had just quit and we didn't have one.

Priest have released seven live albums now, including a couple while I was out of the band. I don't mind them, but if I am honest, I don't listen to them. Why would I need to? *I was there* ... and also, like I say, I just can't stand listening to my voice.

My favorite is *Priest... Live!* from 1987, as much for the cover as for the music. We recorded it on *Turbo*'s *Fuel for Life* tour, and the gatefold sleeve, with a giant picture of the robot's hands holding Glenn and Ken up in the air, captures what a crazy, spectacular stage set that was.

Live-album sales have never compared to studio albums. Record labels don't expect to make a mint off them. But they are cheap for them to make, and the main intention used to be to keep the band in the fans' minds if, for example, they didn't have a studio record out that year.

There also used to be a cottage industry in making bootleg albums of live gigs. Priest would play a show and a small ad would appear in the back of the music press the next week, flogging vinyl or cassette recordings of the show via a PO Box number.

It was a busy, flourishing industry. Whenever I was in Tokyo, I used to go to a poky little music store on the fourth floor of a tower block,

---

*Ironically, apart from *Unleashed in the East*, we've always tried to keep our live albums authentic. If there's occasional feedback or bum notes, we leave them in. Rock and roll's not supposed to be perfect.

and they would have bootlegs of every metal and rock band imaginable. I used to poke through ours: "Oh, they've got *this* gig, and *this* one . . ."

I admit I bought bootlegs there myself—not of Priest, but of other bands. The sound quality differed hugely. Some were crackly and crap. Others were perfect, clear evidence they had been recorded straight off the mixing desk. The crooks would slip someone at the venue a couple of hundred quid to do it for them.

Bands could go after bootleggers with lawyers—but what would be the point? As soon as you got one, another would spring up. It would be like whack-a-mole! Pearl Jam took a different tack and tried thwarting bootleggers by releasing vinyl albums of all of their gigs as soon as they finished playing them.

The whole palaver was a big deal for years and yet now bootleg albums, and even bands' official live albums, are dying out. And the reason, like everything else that has changed in the music industry, is the internet.

Bootlegging has moved from vinyl or cassette to YouTube. No matter how hard promoters and venues try to stop it happening, anyone who buys a ticket for a gig can turn up, hold their phone or iPad up all night to record the show, get home, and stick it on the internet. And there are thousands of people doing exactly that.

Some are fans who just want to share their souvenirs of the gig. Others are more professional. Two people might work in tandem, filming the show from different angles. They'll send their footage to a guy who can edit it, and the slick footage will be up on YouTube a day or two after the gig.

It always happens. In August 2020, Priest played our first big gig back after the COVID-19 pandemic lockdown at the Bloodstock music festival in Derbyshire. The next morning, I woke up, did a bit of googling, and within a minute found an HD-quality video of the entire set on YouTube.

They don't sell the footage, but they don't need to. Algorithms bring thousands of fans to their site. Clicks mean advertisers, and every few minutes an advert for some major corporation or High Street giant such as Pepsi or McDonald's will spring up.

Ker-ching! The guys running those sites make thousands of pounds off the backs of bands, and what can we do about it? Fuck all! There's no real point in getting het up about it. It's just the way of the world now, for better or worse (for what it's worth, my money's on "worse").

It means bands, and record labels, can't compete with websites giving gigs away for nothing. In fact, the only way I can see Priest ever making another live album is if we put on a special show in Walsall, record it, and stick it out as *Get Yer Yam-Yam's Out!*

Because, let's face it, that would be a cracking title.

RECORD COMPANIES

The only negative point about going to a studio and crafting your metal and rock psalms and testaments is that, when you've finished making the album, you have to hand it to a record company.

I'm joking. *Sort of.* Record companies have never had a good press. It's easy to view them as the straights, the suits, The Man, always trying to squeeze money out of the bands and the fans alike—and, to be honest, there is a lot of truth in this viewpoint. But they're not all bad. *Not quite.*

Like lawyers or bankers, record companies are a necessary evil. You will never love them, but you need them. It's their job to get the maximum return out of your music, your *product,* and they *are* like a bank in that you are always in debt to them. Always. Whatever happens.

Unless they're very lucky and get signed by a major straightaway, most bands will start out on a little independent label. They are often run on a shoestring, a wing and a prayer, as Priest found out in our early days when we were signed to Gull Records.

It's well known that we were so skint with Gull that we had to record our first album by night, and to take part-time jobs when they refused to sub us even a fiver a week. We all longed for a major-label deal and assumed that it would be the keys to the Promised Land.

Which, in a way, it *was.* But as all decent-sized bands learn, dealing with major labels presents its own challenges and problems. Plenty of them.

Major record labels now are not the force they once were. Streaming and the web have taken their toll, and now there are only three of them left. Back in the day, though, they were all-powerful and bossed the music industry. That was how it was in 1976, when we signed to CBS.

Back then, A&R men ruled the roost.* They decided who the record companies should sign and, once you were on board, they were your first point of contact with the label, choosing studios and producers, overseeing your development, and giving you (often unwanted) advice.

A&R men would spend every night propping up the bar in clubs like the Marquee in London, looking for new talent. They'd form a critique in their mind: *This band could be great, but they definitely need to change THIS one thing!* Then, once they'd signed you, they'd try to mold you.

They never got very far with Priest, because we had a lot of confidence and self-belief from day one. We wanted to control our own destiny, and once we had an idea for what we wanted to do, it was very hard to shift it. I believe the technical term is "stubborn buggers."

God knows what A&R men do nowadays, in this digital era when major labels are hanging on by the skin of their teeth. Do they still exist at all? If they do, I guess they are on their laptops all day long, like the rest of us, trying to dig out new talent on TikTok and YouTube.

The good thing about signing to a major label back then was that they made a commitment to you. When they signed a band, they realized that it could take three, four, or even five albums for them to break through. It was a nice contrast to now, where it's all about overnight success.

When we first signed to CBS, though, we didn't feel well treated. It all seemed very impersonal and distant. Our main, consistent complaint was that we were slogging our guts out playing loads and loads of gigs, and nobody from the label ever came to watch us.

It was frustrating. We felt like they needed to come to our shows, and to see our fans, to understand what Judas Priest and our music

---

* A&R stood for Artist & Repertoire, but a lot of those guys took so long to make a decision that musicians called them umm & ah men.

were all about. But they never did. We never got any feedback from the label, and they didn't seem to care.

I'm pretty sure some CBS senior executives hadn't even heard of us. I always imagined the top dogs in the boardroom, scrutinizing share prices, spreadsheets, and sales figures, while having conversations like this:

"What's this name—Judas Priest? Who are they?"
"They're on our label, sir. They've made three albums . . ."

That general indifference towards us only really vanished when we had our commercial breakthrough. Because nothing turns heads, and wins the money men's attention, like success.

Oddly enough, we got more interest and feedback straightaway from the US wing of the label. They seemed to sense that Priest had the potential to do well in America and, unlike CBS in London, they got proactive in thinking of ways for us to realize it.

Our record company in America knew the importance of radio play, but they also understood that we were not a band who wrote singles—we wrote albums that were heavy, weighty pieces of work. So, how could they translate what we did into snappy, radio-friendly music?

They hit on the idea of us doing a cover version of a well-known song per album, in the hope of gaining the attention of radio programmers. We were open to that idea. We didn't see it as selling out, because we knew a higher profile would let us get our music across to millions more people.

At their behest, we covered Spooky Tooth's "Better by You, Better than Me" on *Stained Class*, and Fleetwood Mac's "The Green Manalishi (With the Two-Pronged Crown)" on *Hell Bent for Leather*. Neither were hits, but they maybe opened a few doors for us on US radio.

Instead, CBS America came good with one of our own songs. When we gave them *Screaming for Vengeance* we had, as usual, front-loaded the strongest tracks at the start of the record. We thought "Electric Eye" would be the most effective lead-off single from the album.

To us, "You've Got Another Thing Coming," buried down on side two, felt musically simplistic compared to the rest of the record. In fact, it only just made the cut for the album. So, we were quite pissed off when CBS America stuck it out as the lead single in the US.

How wrong we were. The American execs had realized that the song's very simplicity—that *chug-chug-chug* rhythm—was a huge asset when it came to radio play. Put simply, it was a song that would sound great blasting out of your dashboard as you sped down the freeway.

You could say that again! "You've Got Another Thing Coming" went top ten in the US rock chart. It was the song that fully broke Priest in America, and we never looked back. And it made us realize, "OK, our record label *does* know something after all!"

It's human nature, though, that sometimes you forget the leg-ups you get like that and instead focus on the times that your record company fucked things up. And, every now and then, they certainly have. For every bit of help, there's been at least one resounding cock-up.

Sometimes, it's a failure of vision and an unwillingness to think outside of the box. When we first began writing *Turbo* in Spain, we were inspired by our new synth guitars, and we came up with a wealth of great material that we wanted to put on the album.

Bingo! A light bulb came on over our heads. "Let's do a double album! We can call it *Twin Turbos*! It will be brill!" Our management passed the idea on to the record label. They didn't share our enthusiasm. In fact, we got a very straightforward reply: "No."

We didn't understand why and persisted, with a second brainwave: "Why not make a double album and sell it for the price of a single one?" We were offering CBS an album's worth of extra material for free. They should have bitten our bloody hands off!

They didn't. Instead, the suits at the label told us that they weren't a supermarket doing two-for-one specials. Our plan didn't fit their strategy and marketing plan for the band. I still think it was a simple lack of imagination on their part.

That was essentially a difference of opinion, though, where the label could still defiantly argue that they were right. Far worse is the kind of unmitigated fuckup that record companies occasionally make, and in those cases they simply haven't got a leg to stand on.

Record labels' most basic function is *distribution*. It's their job to make sure that your music is out there on all platforms and particularly, back in the day, in record shops. And if they fail to perform that most basic function of all, I think that is fucking unforgivable.

Priest were incredibly proud of the *Painkiller* album that we recorded in 1990. It was a creative rebirth for the band, and when we had finished we knew it was very special. It was deeply frustrating when we had to postpone its release to go through the charade of the crazy court trial in Reno to explain that we didn't really want our fans to kill themselves.

That long delay meant that CBS had all the time in the world to press and distribute *Painkiller* so that it would be in the stores when we finally came to tour the album later that year. They failed to do so. When we launched the tour in North America that October, the nation's shelves were bare.

No *Painkiller*.

We were fucking furious! Everybody was yelling at everybody. Bill Curbishley was yelling at the very top dogs of CBS America, because this was an utter disaster. *What was the point in us spilling our souls onto an album, then touring it around the world, if nobody could buy it?!*

CBS knew they had made a monumental fuckup. It took them weeks to sort it out, and we brooded and stewed as we played sell-out show after sell-out show to fans who were loving our new album but weren't able to buy it. We weren't inclined to forgive our label quickly.

Nor did we. CBS attempted to give us a peace offering when the tour reached New York. The label guys came backstage with plaques they had made, representing the silver and gold discs they were certain *Painkiller* would accrue now that it was finally available.

We didn't bite. We turned the gifts down flat. "Where we're from, we get awards like this when *we've actually sold the records!*" we snapped at them. "How about you apologize to us, instead of stupid gimmicks like this?" And, in fairness, they did. Often, and abjectly.

The problem is that, even if you grow to like individual people at your record company—and we *have*, over the years—you can never trust the music industry as a whole. It always seems to be trying hard to find a new way to screw the artists over.

A few years ago, the record companies introduced their latest sleight of hand, known as the 360-degree business model. The idea was that the labels would invest in bands and in return they would take a cut of every bit of income the artists generated—records, publishing, gig tickets, merchandise, the lot.

The thinking was, because bands were a "risk" for record companies—*what if an album doesn't sell?*—they deserved to share in all of their rewards. The 360-degree fad didn't last all that long, but it was ubiquitous for a bit. Madonna signed a 360-degree deal, as did loads of metal and rock bands.

Priest never got involved in that crap, and I hope that nobody would have dared offer it to us! I thought it was utter thievery from the first second I heard about it. I am not a violent man, but I think if I met the guy who invented the 360-degree model, I might punch him on the nose.

Given the ruthlessness with which the music business looks to exploit artists, it's no surprise that bands have sometimes tried to opt out and form their own record labels to release their own music. It's a brave and audacious project, and it usually ends in failure.

Even the biggest band in the world ever, the Beatles, made a mess of trying to run Apple Records, and Led Zeppelin didn't do much better with Swan Song. The problem was they still needed distribution—and the majors have that sewn up. The music industry is a global machine.

I even had my own indie label for a while, Metal God Records. I still love that name and I thought the project had great potential, but it didn't go well. However, as I wound up in a major court case with the guy who ran it, I'd better zip my lip on that one!

One of the few good side-effects of the internet destroying the music business is that record companies have to treat their artists so much better. The whole perspective has changed. For decades, the bands needed the labels. Now, it's the labels that need the bands.

I read recently that record companies now make something like 90 percent of their profits from catalogue, which means albums that are at least twenty years old. It means they've got no choice but to keep us so-called "heritage artists" sweet.

In fact, veteran bands like Priest are now effectively the cash back-bone of the record industry. The record company has no choice but to value us, which is great: our relationship with our label, both in the US *and* in Britain, is currently the best that it has been in years.

We want the same thing from them that we always have: *distribution*. There are hardly any record shops left now, but we want CBS to make sure Amazon has plenty of stock and our videos are up on all the social media platforms. As long as they're doing that, we're happy.

Priest are fortunate because our management negotiated us good deals with our record company a long time ago. We are also lucky because, when it comes to music-purchasing habits, metal and rock fans tend to be decidedly old school.

It's very hard for pop artists to make money from albums now because their fans only want streams and downloads, which earn them buttons. But the bulk of heavy metal fans still want to buy albums on vinyl or CD. Priest fans still want to hold our psalms and testaments in their hands and cherish them as physical objects.

And thank God for that.

THE BOOK
OF PILGRIMAGES

T he time comes for every band when they must make an Exodus from the Chosen Land of the studio and journey out into the wilderness to meet their disciples. They must make a pilgrimage to take their holy scriptures to their true believers.

When we go on tour, we travel far and wide to many corners of the globe for as long as two years at a time. It's a blessed chance to meet our followers and it's always an exhilarating experience: everything I dreamt of as a lad in Walsall, boggling at the Beatles or Led Zep.

Having said that, tours also have their downsides: the hours and hours of travel, the anonymous hotel rooms, the intra-band frictions, the dodgy promoters and backstage catering, and, most of all, the aimless waiting and hanging around. Touring can make a band—or it can kill them.

Thankfully, I've picked up a few good survival tips in fifty years on the road with Judas Priest. So, how do we ensure that our Exoduses lead to heaven and not to hell? Read on, gentle pilgrim . . .

SETTING OUT ON TOUR

When a big, arena-filling rock or metal band goes on tour, it's like taking a city on the road. That may sound dramatic, but it's what it's like.

An army of musicians, management, and support staff packs up, takes off, and becomes its own little world for the next year or more.

But, no, it's not a city—it's a *factory*. Because it's a place of work, and you've got singers, tour managers, lighting men, sound men, and truck drivers all putting in a shift and slogging their guts out, night after night. You clock in, and you don't clock off until eighteen months later.

It's not as simple as just turning up on the first night, strolling onstage, and letting rip. You have to roll up your sleeves and put the groundwork in before the circus gets to roll—and it starts with pre-tour rehearsals.

As I said earlier, Priest hate rehearsing nowadays, but we also know just how crucial pre-tour rehearsals are. We'd never skip or skimp on them. We get together at least five times in a fortnight before the first night of a tour and rehearse the fucking arse out of the show.

We'll have a set list to work out and a new stage set to get used to and, most of all, we need to lock into playing together again; find our mojo and our rhythm so we're a well-oiled metal machine. We need to get to the point where playing the songs is as natural as breathing.

We start off honing the music, and then we go into the full production where we are basically playing the full stage set with the full light show but no audience. We will run through it again and again until we get to the point where it feels like clockwork and we're totally happy with it.

Martin Walker has been our production manager for donkey's years. He oversees the whole rehearsal process, and there is a lot to think about: guitar changes, the set, the lights, pyro, special effects, the big video screens by the sides of the stage. They all need to be perfect.

I'm totally involved in these rehearsals, yet I'm not always singing. As I've got older, I find that I can't sing day after day after day because my voice gets worn out. The guys can rehearse OK without hearing me, so some days I just listen and run through all the songs in my head. *I sing in my head.*

Pre-tour rehearsals are a chore, but, like all chores, they're necessary. Any production, whether it's an opera, a pantomime, or a heavy metal show, has to go through them. You rehearse and rehearse until you know the show off by heart. Then you rehearse a little bit more.

We're not quite on autopilot during them, but we're going through the motions and we can feel a little distant from the process, even bored. But then we do exactly the same show on tour, in front of thousands of screaming metal maniacs, and it all becomes *real*. We *connect*.

All through rehearsals, I know that on the first night, with our fans going crazy, it will mean so, so much more. That's the joy and thrill of playing live tours and it's what keeps every—and I mean *every*—metal and rock band going.

There is a lot of preparation before you go on tour. In the early days, I used to try to be part of all of it. I'd worry about how the lights would look; the show security; if the mics would fail. I'd call our management to check up on ticket sales: "How is London going? Birmingham? Hull?"

Now, I've learned to let go. I've accepted: I'm *not* a lighting man or a sound engineer. It's not down to me to make sure the drums are set up OK or the merchandise stall is well-stocked. All that my job is, is making sure I give the best possible performance on the night.

It's a question of confidence and having the best people around us. If I know that our management are taking care of everything that needs to be taken care of, and the band are going to sound fantastic, then I can relax and focus on me. Focus on my voice. Focus on the *now*.

If all those things are in place—and they always are—I don't even feel nervous the night before the tour starts. I don't have a sleepless night.* I know that something big is about to happen, but I also know that we are rehearsed and ready. And that means I can go into the tour feeling calm.

I feel calm, but I also know that the thrill of playing live always carries an element of risk and danger. My microphone might pack up. Richie's guitar strings might snap mid-solo. I might fall off my motorbike

---

*Well, I probably *will* have a sleepless night, because of my perennial bloody insomnia! But that's the same whether we're about to go out on tour or not.

again, or crash it into the drums. Anything can happen ... and you know what?

It's that anything-can-happen feeling that I love the most about going out on tour, *out on a pilgrimage*, with Priest. *So, let's have it! Fire up the fucking tour buses! Let's roll!*

GIGS

Bands always talk about "getting their tour legs." That means getting the first four or five shows of a tour under your belt and growing used to being out on the road again. You fall into your rhythm of daily roadwork and the tour quickly becomes its own all-consuming little world.

You might play a warm-up show in a small venue first, and you might need a couple of nights to get fully on top of your game, but the shows feel fucking fantastic from the off. I have always said this: playing live is the very best bit of being in a rock or metal band, bar none.

Getting up onstage, opening my mouth, and pouring out my heart and soul is an amazing feeling. It's an honor and a privilege to be allowed to do it. Singing with Judas Priest nourishes, stimulates, and satisfies me. It's the only time that I feel whole: when I feel *most alive.*

The very best gigs are magical. If everything is in place—the band, the songs, the fans—that show can be transcendent. No, scratch that: it *will* be transcendent. Yet you can't predict when those special nights will come along. It's not an exact science. It's written in the stars.

Gigs are always a subjective experience, though. Nobody sees them the same way. Priest have played shows where we've come offstage and said to one another, "God, we were shit tonight!" All through the set, I'll have been thinking, *Oh no, I'm singing bollocks! I'm useless!*

We sit in the dressing room, disconsolate, then friends and family and fans come in and lavish us with praise. They tell us, "That's the best show you've ever done!" and "Rob, I've never heard you sing so well! You were like a bird!" And I'm sitting there, thinking, *Are you sure?!*

Over fifty years with Priest, we've played gigs in intimate venues to small audiences and others in huge stadiums to massive crowds. I enjoy them both, but I'd be lying if I didn't admit that, like any band, I love playing enormous arena and stadium shows. The more people there, the bigger the thrill.

We've played to some *preposterous* audiences. It gets silly when you're onstage in front of more than three hundred thousand people, like we were at the US Festival in 1983. Or playing Live Aid in Philadelphia, two years later. You can't help but think, *Is this really happening?*

It can become an out-of-body experience to stare out at such a mass of humanity. *Are they really all here for us?* It can mess with your mind and you start going into strange, random thought processes: *Oh no! How can I reach the guy right at the back?*

I'd far rather have that than empty seats, though! In 1991, Priest went straight from our mega-successful, sold-out *Painkiller* jaunt to a multi-band traveling-festival tour, *Operation Rock & Roll*, with Alice Cooper and Motörhead. It was a mistake; a lot of the dates were half-empty.

It was deflating to walk out and see the gaps in the crowds. That didn't change our approach, or mind. Those people had bought tickets, so we tried to give them the show they deserved. We'd do that even if it was one bloke standing on his tod.

When you've been in a big band for years, though, you get used to thousands of fans turning up and to sold-out signs. You don't take it for granted but you grow accustomed to it. It's like a drug and you can get addicted to it very easily.

Like any addict, you don't realize the depths of your dependence. Any band's popularity waxes and wanes, and there have inevitably been times we've got a bit Spinal Tap. I've been sent an itinerary of upcoming tour dates, and called our management in a state of high indignation:

"Oi! How come we're not playing Chicago Enormodome? We played it last tour!"

"Well, people have moved on, Rob. This album's not done as well as the last one and you're not as popular as you were back in the day."

"*Back in the day?* What do you mean by that? We're not back in the bloody day—we're still here!"

Priest are lucky. We've always had super-loyal fans, so apart from the odd blip, our popularity has been pretty constant. Over the years, I guess I got to feel that the arena circuit was my home. When it got taken away from me (or, rather, I took it away from myself), it hit me hard.

Having left Priest in 1992 and formed Fight, our first tour, playing the sort of poky club venues that Priest had left behind fifteen years earlier, was a shock. I'll never forget walking into our first gig, in a provincial nightclub in Germany, looking around the small, empty room, and thinking:

Rob! What the FUCK have you done?

Really, my naivety and presumptuousness were ridiculous! What was I expecting to happen when I formed Fight? That I'd carry on playing to the same ten-thousand-people crowds that Priest had?! We were a brand-new band. I had to prove myself, and pay my dues, all over again.

It fucked with my head. I found myself getting stupidly angry at the modest venues we had to play, changing in the toilet because there was no dressing room. It was Dudley JB's, Redcar Top Deck, and Lincoln Drill Hall all over again. It took me a long time to come to terms with it.

In fact, I'm not sure that I ever did.

It was a relief to get back to Priest and playing major venues and arenas again. I appreciated it all the more for my decade away, *my pilgrimages in the wilderness*, and that wake-up call made me grateful for our big crowds all over again.

I'm only human, and there have been times I've ogled a hot bloke in the crowd, especially if he's down the front and crushed against the security barrier. I've been yowling "Electric Eye" while gazing around for our tour manager, thinking, *Quick! Give that guy a backstage pass?!**

---

* As I detailed in *Confess*, I even met a long-term romantic partner via that route! But that's a different story . . .

That was always a rare self-indulgence, though. When I go onstage, I am hyperaware that I am singing, and performing, for everyone. The guy up the front, the girl at the back, the couple to the side. That's the only way to describe it: *I'm singing for everyone.*

I see the crowd as one giant, heaving mass of metal maniacs and yet I still notice individuals. It's impossible not to. From the corner of my eye, I'll see a guy going crazy and smashing his head against the crash barrier . . . and someone behind him, yawning and eating a bag of crisps.

That used to do my bloody nut in. As I said earlier, it killed me whenever Priest did a pub gig and some guy had his back to us, supping his pint: *Why isn't he into us? What's wrong with us?* Now, thankfully, I've managed to let that obsessiveness and insecurity go. *Mostly.*

Naturally, as a, ahem, Metal God, I'd love everybody in the venue to give me their undivided attention! But they've paid their dosh, and if they want to spend all gig on their phone checking the football scores, it's up to them. I accept it. It's part of my maturity as an artist, and a person.*

At our gigs, I don't talk much between the songs. I never have. Over the years, Priest management, or even other band members, have said, "You should chat to the crowd more, Rob!" I don't agree. I think the fans want to hear Judas Priest playing, not me flapping my lips.

If I do speak, I sometimes stumble over my words or I don't know what to say. I'm not very good at standing and bantering away. I like to let the music speak for me. I mean, make small talk with the crowd? What am I bloody supposed to say?

"Ooh, that's a nice coat, love. Where did you get that?"

"Hey, you! Looking good—did you do your own hair tonight?"

It's *just not me,* any more than would be reading out requests: "This is 'Breaking the Law' and we'd like to play it for Mr. and Mrs. Johnson from Boise, Idaho, who've been married twenty-five years today!" I'll save all that cheesy stuff for my Las Vegas years, when they come!†

---

* So I hope, anyway. But I still have lapses . . .

† And they will—see my Book of Revelations for details.

The other danger is that if I *do* start talking onstage, I won't stop. In everyday life, I love a good natter. It's a Halford gene. If anybody in my family talks about something, we tell you every tiny, unimportant, microscopic detail. As they say in Walsall, *We gew on a bit.*

I'd love it if I could sing a song and then just say, "It's great to be back here in Stoke-on-Trent! I remember playing this very stage in 1974!" But I know that wouldn't happen. Once I'd started gassing, the problem is that I'd go on and on:

"Yeah, I remember after that show, we went to the fish-and-chip shop down the road! They did a really nice pickled egg! Then we stayed at a hotel around the corner—do you know the place? The rooms were nice, but the night trains going past kept me awake . . . blah blah blah . . ."

So, trust me, it's best if I stick to singing. For *all* of our sakes.

A confession: I've done the classic idiot front man thing of marching onstage and greeting the wrong town. It's dumb and embarrassing to yell, "Hello, Newcastle!" when you're in . . . Sheffield. I've fucked up on both sides of the Atlantic, and I've noticed I got a very different reaction.

If you cock up in Britain, people just laugh and give you the "Wanker!" sign, which is fair enough. In America, if you accidentally say, "Good evening, Denver!" when you're in Dallas, you either get silence or boos. They react like it's a hanging offense.

So, on the whole, I always keep my between-song patter to an absolute minimum. We play two or three songs, then I say, "It's Saturday night in Birmingham, and the Priest are back!" The fans will cheer, and I'll say:

> "Look at all you metal maniacs out there! Are you ready for some Judas Priest–style heavy metal?"
> *More cheers.*
> "Are you ready?"
> *More cheers.*
> "Are you ready? Then let's go!"

It might be a bit formulaic, but at least it avoids me complimenting people's coats or hair, or going on about chip shops and pickled eggs.

Things can always go wrong at live gigs. It doesn't happen so much now that we're a slick metal touring machine, with an extensive on-the-road support system, but in Priest's earlier days, we often fucked up at our shows.

Our dodgy cheap speakers were always blowing up. I remember that happening at one show at Birmingham Town Hall. The fans cheered because they thought it was a special effect, like confetti bombs. They stopped cheering when they realized how shit the sound had gone.

On our early tours of America, we used to get grief with the sound because there are so many radio frequencies out there. In the middle of a song, we'd suddenly get radio stations or local minicab controllers broadcasting through the guitar amp or the PA system.

Me, singing: *"You think I'll let it go, you're mad / You've got another thing coming . . ."*

Our PA: *"Crackle . . .* OK, are any drivers free? I need a taxi on the corner of Twenty-fourth Street . . ."

It's funny now, but, God, it pissed us off at the time!

We couldn't control *that*, but some early gig mishaps were completely our own fault. I used to like a good prop, and I remember one seventies show—I think we were in Nottingham—I was mooching around the venue after the soundcheck, looking for anything I could use onstage.

I came across some cardboard tubes, and a light bulb came on over my bonce. I asked one of the crew to spray them with silver paint so they looked like scaffolding poles. Then, I collared Glenn to tell him my big idea.

"We'll leave these leaning at the back of the stage," I said. "Halfway through, I'll suddenly pick one up and start lamping you with it! It will be great! The fans will think I'm clobbering you with a scaffolding pole, but it won't hurt because it's only a paper tube!"

Glenn gave me a look that said *Christ, another mad Halford idea,* but he went along with it: "Go on, then!" So, when we got to the agreed point of the show, I picked up a silver tube and started belting him with it. The crowd were going wild so I hit him more, and harder.

I had to hand it to Glenn—he was being a surprisingly good actor! I was bashing him as he played a solo, and he was flinching and wincing really convincingly. I got carried away in the frenzy of the moment, and by the time I broke the tube in half over his shoulders, he was bent double.

"That looked fucking brilliant!" I said to him as soon as we got backstage after the show. Glenn looked daggers at me, whipped his shirt off, and turned around. His back was a purple mess of welts and bruises.

"You nearly broke my neck!" he yelled. "It really fucking hurt! Didn't you hear me, yelling at you to stop?"

Oops! "I'm sorry, I thought you were just getting into the part!" It turned out that the cardboard tubes had been especially reinforced for heavy-duty industrial use. We didn't use the fake-scaffolding-pole trick again.

Even in today's super-slick-gig age, things still go wrong. For all of our rehearsals, we can still crash into each other during a song, or go arse-over-tit over a monitor. I took Ken's eye out with a guitar string once, and I've famously fallen off my bike a couple of times.

In fact, if you have a look, YouTube has loads of fan-recorded videos of metal and rock bands having onstage mishaps. Kiss seem to be leading the slapstick league table. I think it must be because of those big boots they wear.

When Priest are doing a long tour, night after night for a year or more, it's super-important that we stay on top of our game and don't get sloppy. We have to keep our heads in the right place. Touring can get on top of you, but the gigs have to stay special.

Even if we are fifty or sixty shows in, it's crucial to remember that the fans watching us might have waited two years for that night and are seeing the tour for the first time. We have to play for them like it's the first night—or like it's the last gig we'll ever play.

It's a psychological thing. I remember reading Brian Eno say that during a Roxy Music show, while he was playing keyboards, he found himself thinking about doing his laundry. He was so horrified that things had got so routine that he quit the band at the end of the tour.

Yet I know what Eno meant. I might be screaming my tits off during "Painkiller" at a show, giving the song absolutely everything, while at the same time, in the back of my mind, I'm mulling over what I want to have for dinner: *Do I fancy Chinese? Or Indian?*

It's not like I'm not concentrating, or I'm short-changing the crowd: I'm totally into the song. It's just the weird way the human mind works. The important thing is to focus, ignore distractions like that, and ensure the show is fresh and vital every night.

The great thing is that for us, or for any rock or metal band, no matter how long in the tooth, playing live is *never* a routine. It's still a thrill to me. The smell of the greasepaint and the roar of the crowd first got me when I worked in the theater, aged sixteen, and I'm still hooked.

I'll never forget going to a gig as a kid. I'd be so excited, running home to get washed and changed, having chips on the way, then getting to the venue early to squish my way to the front. I know how it feels and *that's* how I want our fans to feel, every time that we play.

I'll say it until I'm six feet under: playing live completes me not just as a musician but as a *person*. Singing onstage is the most comfortable I will ever feel. I missed it so much during the never-ending Covid pandemic, and so did every metal and rock band in existence.

Because, yeah, gigs *are* a subjective experience . . . but when you play a great one, there's nothing else like it in the world.

TOUR MANAGERS

If a big metal or rock tour is like taking a factory out on the road, then I suppose that the tour manager is the foreman—the hapless sod who has to make sure that everybody puts a shift in, and whom none of the workers like all that much as a consequence.

But that's not the whole story. There's more to it than that. At heart, a good tour manager is more like a school teacher overseeing a very, very long class trip. It's a particularly appropriate analogy because it's hard to deny that most bands are basically a bunch of kids.

Tour managers have to make sure you get your wake-up call, get fed, get on the tour bus, and make the venue on time. They don't *quite* make band members hold hands, wear hi-vis, and walk in a crocodile file to the stage, but there've been times it might have been a good idea.

At other times, they have to be sergeant-majors. If a band are pissing about, and about to miss a crucial deadline, it's the tour manager's job to shout at them to get them into line. This has been known to cause musicians to bridle: "Oi! Fucking shut up! *You* work for *us*!"

"Yeah, but if you don't listen to me, there'll be nothing to work *for*!" the tour manager will yell back. "Because you're going to miss the flight/the tour bus/the gig/the rest of your career . . ."

Yet another function is that they have to be a relationship expert. If a record producer is a therapist in the studio, soothing bruised egos, a tour manager, trapped on the road with fractious, warring musicians for months, needs the full skill set of a marriage-guidance counsellor.

If a band has, ooh, I don't know, two guitarists who aren't getting on,* the tour manager will try to calm them both down separately. Also, I've been to chew a tour manager's ear about a drummer before, unaware the drummer was whinging to him about *me* twenty minutes earlier.

And that's the key. A good tour manager *isn't* the foreman that you all hate—he may be a disciplinarian, but he's also a friend and confidant who you grow to trust, like, and maybe even love. Given that musicians are kids, he is basically the tour parent. And he is bloody needed.

At the start of every tour, the tour manager produces an itinerary for each band member covering the entire jaunt. Back in the day, when we were basically lads on the piss, I'd chuck mine on my bunk on the

---

*I don't know *what* made me think of that example!

bus and forget it. Now, I read it closely from cover to cover. It's all part of getting old!

The itinerary includes details of every single flight we will catch on the tour, every hotel we are staying in, and any contact number we might need. There are photos, quips, and funny sayings. "Please note: reduced air pressure causes flatulence" advised our *Firepower* tour booklet.

Unlike band managers like Colonel Tom or Peter Grant, tour managers don't get famous. The sole exception is probably Richard Cole,* who got well-known for his antics with a mud shark and a groupie with Led Zeppelin. Not that that's really a great thing to get famous for!

When bands first start out, they can't afford a tour manager, and Priest were no exception. We'd have to phone each other up (*"Wot yow doing still in bed? Gerrup!"*), call for each other in the crappy Transit, and put the pedal to the metal to make it to the gig on time.

When we got a major deal and our tours went up a notch, we got given our first tour manager, a bloke named John Blackburn. John was OK—in fact, we got on so well that we ended up spending a lot of time taking the piss and playing pranks on each other.

It was in John's time that I got into my unfortunate habit of setting off fire extinguishers. I fired one under John's hotel room door in Japan—except that it wasn't John's hotel room door. The Japanese bloke in the room didn't find it too funny. I eased off on the fire extinguishers after that.

Yet the tour manager who was so closely associated with Priest that he was virtually a member of the band was Jim Silvia. Jim entered our lives on the *World Wide Blitz* tour, promoting *Point of Entry* in 1981, and was to become our "Fearless Leader" on the road for nearly forty years.

Jim started off as our security man before quickly being promoted to tour manager, and he was quite a character. He was a diminutive

---

*I think it's important not to confuse him with Richard *Coles*, the gay vicar and former member of the Communards, who is always on Radio 4. I doubt *he's* ever done anything with a groupie and a mud shark.

BIBLICAL

but tough-as-nails Italian-American guy and absolutely nothing could throw him. He had seen everything.

Jim had the best stories. He had been in the US military and was posted to Germany at the same time as Elvis. He told us that he'd bump into The King when he filled up his car at the local gas station ("I'd ask him, 'Hey, Elvis, how you doin'?' Just being friendly to the guy, ya know?").

After going to Vietnam, Jim joined the Secret Service and did loads of undercover work. Then he became a New York cop and did stuff like dress up in drag for armed drug-sting operations in Central Park. All in all, he was a pretty unshockable bloke.

When he joined Priest, Jim knew absolutely nothing about heavy metal or tour management. He was a very quick learner. I guess when you've guarded US presidents on trips that are timetabled to the second, you can handle turfing a bassist out of bed and onto a bus in Wisconsin.

Jim would micromanage every aspect of Priest's tours and make sure they ran like clockwork. He'd get us from hotels to radio stations to soundchecks to gigs. Under Silvia, I would wake up each morning and know every minute of the day ahead was planned. Whether I liked it or not.

Jim would meet the head of security before every gig we played, and he'd tour the venue with them. He'd check backstage, entrances, exits, and the all-important crush barriers, and give the in-house security team helpful advice on what would happen during our set:

"Listen up, youse guys! During the second song, Rob will run over *here*. The song after that, K. K. and Glenn will be headbanging together right *there*. So, make sure you station some guys *here* to keep a lookout on the fans in case there's a crush . . ."

It was a great talent of Jim's, almost like a sixth sense. From his years in shades and a walkie-talkie, working on presidential motorcades, he just knew everything about crowds and how they behaved, and he knew how any sudden excitement in the throng could lead to disaster.*

* Sadly, this topic is still very relevant at music gigs.

110

For Priest members, Jim's most important task was dishing out our per diems, or PDs, at the start of each week. This is the personal allowance, paid in the currency of the country you're in, for your day-to-day living expenses. We'd queue up like kids waiting for their pocket money.

We wouldn't always get all of it. Jim ran a very tight ship, and if we fell out of line we got punished by fines. His main bugbear was lateness, especially if we were checking out of a hotel in the morning or getting on the tour bus for a gig.

Jim would increase the fines by increments of $10. If you were five minutes late checking out at the front desk, you'd get fined $10. Five more minutes would be another $10. It used to hit Dave Holland the worst. Our drummer was so slow to check out. He was like an old granny.

We'd all be getting our per diems, and a moan would go up from Dave: "Ay, Jim! Yow've med a mistek! I'm $50 short on me PDs!"

"That's because you were twenty-eight minutes late leaving the Philadelphia Hilton!" our tour manager would snap back at him. And there was no arguing. His word was final.

One of Jim's primary tasks was stopping Priest fans getting too close to us at inappropriate moments. We love our fans to death, and we always try to make time for them, but sometimes—especially around gigs—we are in the zone and we need to focus.

Jim threw himself into this area of his job with his customary zeal and efficiency, and maybe sometimes he was a little *too* zealous in the way that he carried it out. I'll never forget the morning that he phoned me up in my hotel room, hardly able to speak for laughing.

"Rob, Rob, are youse up?" he asked, between guffaws. "I've got to play you something, man!" He turned up at my door a minute later, still cracking up and with tears of laughter running down his face. "Here!" he said. "Listen to this!"

Jim always carried a microrecorder around with him. He would use it to record reminders and messages to himself: put so-and-so on the guest list, check on airline baggage limits, whatever. And the previous night, it had made an unintentional recording.

Unknown to Jim, the device had been switched on when he had a post-gig encounter with a fan insisting that he had to meet Priest and get all of our autographs. The guy had shoved a pen into Jim's hand and told him to go find us: "I need to see them! Now!"

Jim politely explained that it wouldn't be possible, but the guy kept on and on. Years of military training meant Jim nearly always kept his cool, but this aggressive fan got under his skin and he went ballistic—as I was about to hear.

When Jim turned on his recorder, I heard that initial conversational exchange—and then Jim yelling at the top of his lungs, sounding more than ever like a *Sopranos* hitman: "I fucking told ya! I told ya! Youse don't get anywhere near the fucking band!"

"Sorry! I'm sorry!" came the shocked reply, the guy suddenly sounding a whole load less cocky.

"I kept fucking telling ya, but you kept coming back!" Jim screamed.

"OK, OK, but can I get my pen back?"

"YOU WANT IT? YEAH! HERE IT IS! HERE'S YOUR FUCKING PEN! TAKE IT! HERE'S YOUR FUCKING PEN!"

In between Jim's shouts, I heard muffled yelps, as if he were simultaneously kicking a small puppy. "Eh? What's that weird noise?" I asked.

"Ah, that's when I was stabbing the guy with his pen!" explained Jim, by now doubled over with laughter. Jim got his comeuppance, mind you: virtually every time the band saw him for the rest of the tour, we'd yell at him, "SILVIA! HERE'S YOUR FUCKING PEN!"

Being a tour manager can be a laugh, but it has its serious side as well. I said earlier that it's like being a parent. Well, one of the most important jobs of parenting is being there for your kids if they go off the rails. And, let's face it, I *certainly* went off the fucking rails.

When I was deep in the shitpit of alcoholism on our early eighties tours, and doing enough coke to stun a rhino, Jim was always there to heave me onto the tour bus or into bed. He pulled me out of *so* many scrapes in dressing rooms, hotel bars, clubs . . . you name it.

In fact, if I am honest, I can't remember most of those scrapes because I would usually black out. I can't remember them—and, if I'm honest with you, I don't *want* to. But I know Jim Silvia was always there for me.

He was never off duty. He'd come out with us for a drink after a show and he had serious stamina. Priest would all get hammered and Jim would match us drink-for-drink, all night long, and still be alert enough to chaperone us back to the hotel. Our foul-mouthed guardian angel!

In fact, Jim Silvia and I would butt heads on tour on one thing and one thing only—and that was days off.

As I've got older, days off on tour are sacred for me. If we have a rest day in a hotel, I like nothing more than to spend the day in my room doing some reading, looking at metal websites, checking my socials, and ordering up room service. Bliss!

Jim Silvia had a totally different approach. Whether it was his gung ho, get-go military background, or whether he just liked a nice day out on the Priest shilling, I'm not sure, but every time we had a tour day off, he'd arrange a Band Activity. *Every. Bloody. Time.*

We would play an arena show in Seoul, South Korea, and I'd be just offstage and still dripping with sweat when Jim would collar me in the dressing room.

"Rob!" he'd say. "Band trip tomorrow morning! Meet at eight o'clock in the hotel foyer!"

"Huh? What you on about, Silvia?"

"We've got a one-hour coach journey, then we're going to walk through a tunnel to see the Demilitarized Zone, the DMZ, between North and South Korea!"

"I'm not doing that! I can see it on YouTube if I want to! Which I don't!"

So, the band would go off early the next day without me. Richie would come back and say, "Rob, it was amazing!" And I'd tell him, "Whatever, Richie. I had some *lovely* room-service sandwiches!"

Or we'd be in Norway on tour, and Jim would tell us, "Right. On the day off tomorrow, we're leaving at seven in the morning to get a ferry to a remote island. We'll have lunch there and then we'll sail back."

"You might be, but *I'm* not!" I'd tell him. "Have a nice time! Don't forget your brolly and a jumper, because it'll be wet and a bit parky!"

I used to call them Jim Silvia Excursions and they just kept on coming. The band all had different attitudes towards them. Glenn and Richie were normally up for whatever was going on. Ian blew hot and cold. I was always adamant: "I'm going nowhere! *It's! A! Bloody! Day! Off!"*

Jim would go spare at me sometimes: "What's fucking wrong with youse? Just want to sit in your room all the goddamn time?" And I'd sigh, and I'd tell him: "Mate, I've been around the world a hundred times! I just want a bit of rest! And, in any case . . .

"It's. A. Day. Off."

Jim's other indulgence was organizing tour-party meals for everyone to go on, either after shows or on days off. His main accomplice was Glenn. Glenn was always suggesting that we all go out for a meal . . . or, as he always insisted on calling it, "a nice meal."

That phrase used to do my head in. It still does. What does it even bloody mean? It's so English, isn't it? "Let's all go for a nice meal." I mean, who is going to say, "Let's all go for a *shit* meal?" But there it was, every time. *A nice meal.*

I just don't get it. Those "nice meals" can take three hours, once you factor in getting to the restaurant, waiting to get served, and working through three courses. Once you factor in the booze, they cost $100 per person, which adds up to a $1,000 meal—all out of band money.

I'd say all this to Jim Silvia. He'd listen, and then he'd just say, "Ah, youse is a fucking dick! Just let the guys go out!"

Well, I don't think I'm particularly tight, but I don't want to spend $30 on a posh-restaurant green salad, then sit around watching people get pissed for three hours! I'd rather my partner (and tour PA) Thomas goes out and gets us a Subway or some spaghetti and we eat it in my hotel room.

Trying to be a team player, I will go to a "nice meal" or two with the band on each tour, and . . . *I hate every minute.* I think Jim always saw them as bonding experiences, but, to my mind, we're *already bonded,* by heavy metal and by being in Judas Priest. You can stick your nice meals up your arse!

OK. Rant over.

Jim Silvia could be the last guy out of the gig at night, and then he'd be up at 6 a.m. to get a ferry to a Norwegian island the next morning. This was because he never slept. Or he never seemed to. But sadly, time catches up with all of us, even hyperenergetic, action-man Vietnam vets.

During shows, I'd normally see Jim prowling his beats of the photo pit, side stage, and the mixing desk. One night on the *Painkiller* tour, his last tour before he retired, I couldn't see him anywhere. I collared him after the show.

"Silvia, where were you?" I asked him. "I never saw you once!"

"Ah, youse weren't fucking looking hard enough! I was standing right by the mixer!"

A minute later, the local promoter wandered over. "Ah, there you are, Mr. Silvia!" he greeted him, innocently. "I need to speak to you. I saw you asleep in the dressing room during the show, but I didn't want to disturb you . . ."

Cue gales of laughter. Even Jim saw the funny side. *Eventually.* But that was nowhere near his most comical moment in nearly forty years of shuttling Judas Priest around the globe. That came the day that he innocently agreed to do me a favor.

On our *Fuel for Life* tour in 1986, we had a two-week break after a show in Oklahoma. I decided to take a mid-tour beach break and refresh my batteries in Cancun. As Jim, like me, lived in Phoenix, I asked him if he'd mind taking a small bag home on the plane for me.

"No problem!" he replied. He never even bothered to glance in the bag as I handed it to him. We went our separate ways.

The next morning, Jim was heading through security at the airport in Oklahoma. As he tells it, as my bag passed through the X-ray machine, the female security guard gave it a quizzical look, paused the machine, and then turned her attention to Jim.

"Is this *your* bag, sir?" she asked him.

"Yes, ma'am, it is."

"Can I have a look in it?"

"Of course!"

The guard picked up the bag, turned it upside down, and tipped the contents onto a metal table. With no idea what was in there, Jim's blood ran cold as he heard my possessions hit the table with a *clang*!

Out fell a set of handcuffs, followed by a whip with a sharpened end. Two spiked metal wrist bands were next to emerge, then a leather motorcycle cap. It was all rounded off by a black, double-ended dildo, which hit the table, switched on, and then lay there, vibrating gently.

The customs woman did a double take at the small, dapper, and suddenly excruciatingly embarrassed middle-aged man in front of her.

"Are you *sure* these are your property, sir?"

"Yeah!" insisted Jim, wishing he were dead. Actually, no—he was wishing *I* were dead. He made his way to the plane through the sniggers and stares of the airport staff and fellow passengers, and spent the flight home plotting his revenge on me.

He got it. For months after that, whenever Jim had to book a solo flight for me, I seemed to have a lot of two-hour stopovers in the middle of nowhere. Jim busted my balls and he made me pay—but it was all worth it for the mental image of his horrified face as my dildo rolled down the airport table!

Jim Silvia was such a master of both the light and dark arts of tour management that he made the job look easy. That was misleading. It's not easy at all—but you don't realize how difficult it is until you endure somebody well and truly cocking it up.

While I was out of Priest and fronting the Halford band, we did a mini-tour of South America. Somebody I was working with decided to save the expense of paying a tour manager and do the job himself. Against my better judgement, I went along with it. It was a complete disaster.

We were turning up in countries to find the hotels weren't booked and meeting promoters at venues to learn that contracts weren't signed. We'd arrive at airports with no visas, or there'd be nobody to meet us and we'd have no idea where to go. It just went on and on.

We got to one venue and our "tour manager" was having a screaming argument with the promoter within five minutes about fuck-knows-what. Money, I guess. We never played the show, and we ended up freezing our nuts off in the local airport at four in the morning.

The moral of the tale? For any rock or metal band, a good tour manager is worth his weight in gold—even if he does try to march you off to the Korean DMZ, and gets pissed off at having to carry your double-ended dildo through airport customs. Thank God for Jim Silvia.

ROADIES

There is a perennial, clichéd image of a rock roadie as an overweight, hairy, unshaven bloke in a faded band T-shirt, his arse hanging out of the back of his jeans as he bends double onstage to fix a dodgy amp lead, or grunts "Two! Two!" into a feedbacking mic at soundchecks.

Now, I'm not going to deny that, over the years, I've met one or two characters like this. Like most clichés, it has some truth about it. But most roadies—or, to give them their full name, road crew—today are skilled professionals a long, long way from this unflattering caricature.

How important are roadies? Here's a basic fact: not a single major rock or metal gig would take place without the band's road crew working flat-out behind the scenes. They are our unsung and hirsute heroes, the (sometimes) merry band of men who keep the whole show on the road.

When Priest are on an arena tour, every morning at the crack of dawn our fleet of trucks will pull up at that night's venue with our stage set and all of our gear. Around the same time, our road crew will arrive on a tour bus after an overnight drive from the previous night's show.

The venue will generally have built the stage already. If our roadies are lucky, the manager will also supply an in-house crew to meet them and help to *hump the gear*: unload all the lighting, sound gear, and flight cases into the arena. Then our crew's work begins.

It's their task to get all the equipment onto the stage. The riggers will go up to the ceiling to hang the lights and the sound equipment.

The stage managers oversee everything being brought onstage and make sure it is put in the exact place that it needs to be.

It's a very specific process: the drums go *here*. No, not there, *here*. The stage monitors go *here*. The guitar amps go *here*. After the first one or two nights of a tour, our crew will be a meticulous machine who make what is actually an extremely challenging task look absurdly easy.

Then, at the end of the night, even as the crowd are still filing out, they start to dismantle the stage and get ready to do it all again the following night. I mean, Priest flounce about, posing and getting cheered for two hours a night. But it's these guys who are the *real* grafters!

We realize this, and so Priest have always been very close to our road crew. Because of their negative image, there can be a certain snobbery from bands towards roadies. It seems to happen more in America. I've seen certain bands over there treat their crew really badly.

We would never do that. Every tour, we make a point of taking the road crew out for a meal—yes, a *nice* meal—at least once. Our US roadies have been amazed at that, but why wouldn't we? They're important team members with the same goal as us: to put on a flawless show.

We've worked with some of our road crew for years. Martin Walker has been with us for twenty years and is the acme of production managers and mixing guys. We have total trust in him as our sound guy and that is crucial, because a bad one can so easily fuck up a gig.

Any time Priest are onstage, there are fifteen guys working unseen alongside us through our performance. When Richie or Ian goes behind a curtain to switch out a guitar or bass, their tech is waiting with the strings changed, the instrument tuned, and their amps on the right setting.

Of course, when you're first starting out, you don't have the benefit of a slick, professional support team like that. You're on your bloody own. We used to have to get to working men's clubs early and hump our own gear out of the van and up flights of stairs to the function room.

It was grueling physical labor but that wasn't my main objection. My biggest fear was being seen by somebody from the crowd. There was nothing worse than taking the stage at a pub gig, ready to give it your all, and some big gob at the front saying:

"Oh, am yow the singer? I thought yow was just a roadie!"

Then we started getting friends to help. Our good mate, Nick— now sadly long passed—would come along. We had no dosh to pay him, but, as I said, he'd help himself to anything not nailed down in the club: cutlery, glasses, tables, chairs, radios. God knows how he got away with it.

Another occasional roadie, whom I'd better not name, also had very light fingers. He always knew where the unlocked back doors to pubs and clubs were, and where things were likely to fall off a lorry. He supplied good weed to some of the guys. Frankly, he was an asset to our Transit.

Even in this era of greater professionalism you get some real characters being roadies. A guy called Jude has worked with us forever. He always wears shorts, no matter the weather. Just for a laugh, he'll wander onstage during soundcheck in a mankini. You've got to love him.

Roadies often seem to go by weird nicknames. We have got one at the minute called Carrot. Carrot hasn't even got ginger hair. Over the years, we've also had a Chapstick, a Spider, and a Goat.

Some road crew are very talented musicians in their own right. Scott's drum techs are really good drummers, and we've had guitar techs who are excellent guitarists. It makes you wonder, are they a bit like music journalists—frustrated musicians at heart?

Some of them might be—maybe the right band never came along for them?—but others simply don't want the limelight. They just love guitars: taking them apart and putting them back together again. And they know they are absolutely crucial to our show.

We have got close to, and become friends with, many of our road crew over the years. But there was one guy I never got as close to as I longed to be. I'll spare his blushes and keep his real name to myself, but to me he will always be "Teutonic."

I met Teutonic when I was with the Halford band. We were playing a tiny club in Oklahoma City, and a massive guy with a chiseled physique, blond hair, and blue eyes was going wild down in the front of the crowd. I couldn't take my eyes off him. My reaction was untrammeled lust.

He was a muscle god: the perfect physical specimen. Between songs, I ran over to the side of the stage and to my partner, Thomas, who as usual was on tour with me as my companion and PA. "Wow! Have you *seen* that guy in the crowd?" I asked.

Thomas *had*: "Yeah! He looks so Germanic! Superhot!" On the spot, we nicknamed the guy Teutonic. When we left the club after the show, he was hanging around the stage door, with a load of other fans. "Get him on the bus!" I hissed to Thomas as I posed for selfies.

Teutonic and his equally hot brother came with us on the coach back to our hotel. I chatted to him. He was a competitive bodybuilder and a highly qualified civil engineer but also a complete metal freak. "Man! I can't believe I'm talking to you!" he repeated every five minutes.

We walked around the dark streets of Oklahoma City for yonks, looking for food. Over burgers, Thomas explained what he did on tour. "You have the coolest job in the word!" Teutonic exclaimed. "You think so?" sniffed Thomas. "You can have it, if you want it!"

He meant it. Playing club gigs with the Halford band could be a slog. Thomas was feeling disenchanted with life on the road and fancied a break. "Would you *really* give up your well-paid engineering job to be my tour PA?" I asked Teutonic. "In a heartbeat!" he nodded.

We kept in touch with Teutonic, he quit his job, and by the time the Halford tour picked up after a break, he had replaced Thomas. I was excited but not quite sure what to expect: if I am honest, I was a bit infatuated (or, at least, still perving over him).

It quickly became clear nothing physical would happen between me and Teutonic. He was resolutely, 100 percent straight (not that that had stopped me chasing blokes in the past!). But he knuckled down well to road-crew life, and, well, he was still good eye candy!

Like a lot of roadies, even fresh recruits, Teutonic was eccentric. His only, and I mean *only*, interests in life were heavy metal and bodybuilding. His ambition was to grow so huge that he would have to be buried in a piano case because his body wouldn't fit in a coffin.

I fancied Teutonic—well, that was how he had got the bloody job!—but I was respectful to him and didn't try it on. *Not too much*, anyway. And it didn't stop me insisting that he pulled his considerable weight on the road, like every other crew member.

When Halford were in Tokyo, Teutonic got chronic food poisoning. I went to his room and found him lying groaning on the bathroom floor next to the toilet he'd just been throwing up in. "I'm sorry you feel so shit," I told him. "But you've still got to do the show."

That's just how I am. As I said in *Confess*: the Walsall factory workers I grew up among didn't have a day in bed if they had a dicky tummy. They just *got on with it*. I am a firm believer in an old showbiz dictum that is as true of metal and rock as it is of anything else:

The show must go on.

Teutonic worked with me for a year or so and toured South America, Asia, and Europe with the Halford band. He's an engineer again now: we keep in touch. He had the time of his life with us, and he learned the home truth known by every metal and rock band:

Roadies aren't just overweight, hairy, unshaven blokes with their arses hanging out of their jeans. They're crucial, skilled professionals: without them, there is no show.

VENUES

When you assemble your workforce and take your rock or metal factory out on the road, you take a deep breath and accept that you'll be away from your home for more than a year. And yet, in another way, you are going to a whole series of home-from-homes. Hundreds of them.

Out on tour, you inevitably revisit many venues, all around the world, again and again and again. You get acquainted with their every strength and weakness, get to know their every quirk and foible. In a funny way, it gets to feel like you're calling in on bricks-and-mortar old mates.

There have always been venues that have a legend and a stature way greater than their physical presence. They loom so large in music history that you're quite taken aback when you finally get to the place and discover that it's actually a bit of a shithole.

The classic example was the Marquee in Wardour Street in London. I spent my youth reading articles in *Melody Maker* and the *NME* about Hendrix or The Who playing triumphant gigs there. In my fevered teenage imagination, it was a palace that reeked of rock history.

I was so excited when Priest were booked to do a support gig there, in 1974, but then I found the Marquee didn't just reek of rock history. *It reeked full stop.* It was a grotty dim cave with a cupboard for a dressing room. Not that that stopped us loving playing there!

It's the same story in America. CBGB was a legendary venue, played by thousands of punk and metal bands since the Ramones were the house band in the seventies. I went there with Fight. It was a dump the size of my kitchen, yet its rock heritage oozed from every corner.

In Los Angeles, all the action used to be on the Sunset Strip. Every decent-size rock or metal band in existence has played the Whisky a Go Go. I remember what a thrill it was to gig there and feel that we had arrived: we were playing in the heart of the West Coast rock world.

Priest went back to the Whisky just a few years ago to perform with campers at the Rock 'n' Roll Fantasy Camp. The venue has had a bit of a facelift since its scuzzy days. There again, it was never as scuzzy as the Starwood next door, which was another milestone gig for us in the seventies.

Whatever stage of your career you're at, it's always great to play an iconic venue. It just gives the gig something special: extra buzz. In recent years, I've always looked forward to, and absolutely loved, playing the Fox Theatre in Detroit.

If you've never seen the place, google it! *Now!* It's a beautiful art deco theater originally designed as a cinema in 1928 by the same American architect who designed Earls Court in London. It's got a giant classic Wurlitzer organ and ornate balconies. What a place!

I suppose the nearest equivalent in Britain is the London Palladium. Priest have never played there, but I'd love to. It's not even all that big inside, but to me it will always summon up *Sunday Night at the London Palladium* and huge TV stars like Bruce Forsyth and Jimmy Tarbuck.*

There again, when you're talking metal and rock venues, nowhere in the world is more iconic than Hammersmith Odeon. God knows how many times we've played there! The dressing rooms are mouse-holes, but the place has so much history and character.

It has had so many poxy corporate rebrandings that I had to google to find out what it is called at the moment—apparently, the Eventim Apollo. *Well, bollocks to that!* For me, it will *always* be the Hammersmith Odeon, the finale to every British metal tour back in the day. As the great Lemmy said, *No Sleep 'til Hammersmith!*

When we were on the midsize venue circuit, which we were for years, Barrowland in Glasgow was one of my favorites. We went back on the *Redeemer of Souls* tour in 2015, and the place hadn't changed a jot in thirty years. I love how not just the carpets but even the wooden *walls* smell of beer.

Belfast City Hall was another good one. Priest always tried to go there. We figured, why should Northern Irish kids not get a chance to see us, just because of the Troubles? They needed cheering up! First time we went there, our hotel had recently been bombed by the IRA.

The nature of Priest's tours changed more than thirty years ago and, since then, we've mostly been strutting our stuff in the world's arenas and sports halls: what Spinal Tap called enormodomes. These venues present their own rewards and challenges.

The main issue with arenas is that they can all merge into one. They're bland spaces that accommodate not just gigs but basketball games, ice-hockey matches, and theatrical spectaculars. You can fit a lot of metal maniacs into the O2 in London, but it's a pretty sterile place.

---

*I suspect another reason that I love the Fox Theatre and London Palladium is that, deep down, they remind me of Wolverhampton Grand Theatre, where I worked the lights when I was a spotty oik.

BIBLICAL

One problem with playing aircraft-hangar venues is they can play hell with a gig's acoustics. Front-of-house guys hate playing certain venues because the ceiling is too high, or the room's too wide, or the sound is bouncing off glass. It makes it really hard to mix the sound right.

It's not an issue for me personally now because I wear in-ear monitors, or "in-ears," when I'm singing, but Richie and Scott don't, which means they can suffer from the acoustics of a building. Richie says he doesn't want to wear in-ears because he wants to hear everything.

Hear everything? That makes me laugh—I'm surprised he can hear *anything*! He has everything blasting out of his monitors: bass, drums, me, the lot. Like Lemmy used to be, he's so loud onstage that I don't know how he makes anything out. *Richie? How are you not deaf?!*

Of course, big venues also have their plus points. I like that we can fit our entire production in. I hate when arena tours call at smaller venues and we have to cut down on our stage set or lighting. If the fans have seen the full production on YouTube, they'll feel short-changed.

Everybody knows by now about Priest's little local difficulty at Madison Square Garden in New York. The second time we played there, in 1984, our fans did a spontaneous rethink of the venue's decor by ripping out all the seats and hurling them onstage. We're still banned from there.

Would I like to play there again? I'm not sure. My heart says yes, but my head says no. It's a world-famous, iconic venue, for sure, but we have been there, seen it, done it, and there is a problem of economics: it's an extraordinarily expensive place for bands to play.

A huge chunk of money from playing Madison Square Garden goes to paying union fees. I've got nothing against trade unions, far from it, but it's hard to make a profit from playing MSG. Given the choice, I'd rather do the PNC Arena in New Jersey or Jones Beach Theater out on Long Island.*

* I don't exactly think that I've got tighter with money as I've got older. I've just got more careful.

124

Just occasionally, a metal or rock band gets lucky and gets to play a big venue that also has lots of character and personality. One that ticks a lot of boxes for me is the Microsoft Theater in Los Angeles, right next to the humungous Staples Center (currently called the Crypto.com Arena—yuk!).

The Microsoft is huge, but it's a great building with lots of levels, which I love, a gigantic stage, and the crowd isn't too far away. A lot of awards shows are held there, and it feels like a real show business, Hollywood venue. I always walk in feeling good, knowing it's going to be a brill show.

Oh, and the Microsoft Theater also has one more very good thing going for it—its dressing-room door.

Over the years, Priest have got changed in every kind of dressing room imaginable. We've pulled on our stage clobber next to working men's club urinals, in plush suites, and in backstage caravans at festivals. But only the Microsoft has a star on the dressing-room door.

And that *has* to be good. Because, whether you're Liza Minnelli, Brad Pitt, or just some old Metal God from Walsall, *everybody* likes a star on their dressing-room door . . .

PROMOTERS

Writing these heavy metal scriptures has emphasized to me just how much the worldwide music industry has changed during Priest's lengthy career. For better or worse, it has got far more professional in all areas—and gig promoters are a very good case in point.

When we first started out, the whole concert promotion area was the Wild West. There were more cowboys at play in the pubs and clubs of Britain than in the O.K. Corral. We never felt in danger of getting shot, but we were certainly scalped a few times.

Our dealings with promoters would begin with Corky phoning them up to try to get us a gig. Our wide-boy manager would give them earache for twenty minutes about us being "the best new rock band in Britain" and maybe haggle our price up from £5 to a princely tenner.

Corky wouldn't always come with us to the gigs, so it was sometimes left to John Hinch, our first drummer, to go off and find the promoter after the show to get our dosh. Hinchy would sometimes return to the dressing room looking very downcast.

"He said that we only pulled fifty people, so he's only giving us half of our money," he'd report. We'd be left with the grand total of £1 each. Which wouldn't even cover the petrol to get home.*

Concert promotion became a more refined and acceptable profession partly due to the efforts of people like Bill Graham in America. We first met Bill in 1977, when he promoted the Day on the Green festival in Oakland at which Priest miraculously got to support Led Zeppelin.

Bill was a proper gentleman and a true music fan. As a teenager, he'd hang around outside rock shows in the afternoon waiting for the bands to arrive. He'd ask them if he could go in with them and help to set up the stage in exchange for a free ticket.

Bill then managed to get a job as a runner, or gofer: an all-round dogsbody sent on various menial errands before gigs. It all gave him an insight into how badly promoters treated touring artists, and he vowed that if he ever got to put on shows, he would do things differently.

He was true to his word. Both in his San Francisco venues, the Fillmore and the Winterland Ballroom, and at his huge festival productions, Bill treated bands with respect. He paid well and made sure the backstage facilities were classy. It made you want to work with him again.

Bill revolutionized gig promotion in the US, really. We played one of his venues and worked with him at the US Festival in 1983 and at Live Aid, two years later, and it was always a joy. When he tragically died, aged only sixty, in a helicopter crash in 1991, I was really upset.

Britain's nearest equivalent to Bill was Harvey Goldsmith, who ruled the London live scene for years and put on the Wembley leg of

---

*No wonder Chuck Berry used to demand his payment in full, in cash, before he even set foot on the stage! Chuck was still doing that in his eighties, right up until his death.

Live Aid. Harvey knew the music business inside out, and he knew all about money, but you could trust him. He always kept his side of a deal.

Priest have worked with some legendary international promoters. Ossy Hoppe was Mr. Concerts in Germany and every metal and rock bands' go-to guy. Ossy is retired now, but he still turns up backstage at our shows with his big grin and never-ending supply of rock-and-roll war stories.

His equivalent in Japan was Mr. Udo, who promoted Priest's gigs for decades. He would always give us the very best flights and hotels, put Michelin-level sushi in our dressing room, and spend thousands of his own yen taking us out for high-end Kobe beef dinners.*

Sadly, Mr. Udo has passed now, but I have such fond memories of band nights out with him in Tokyo. He was a keen angler, and I bought him a high-end fishing reel as a gift. He was so touched: "Rob! Bands never do this!" But they should have. Because Mr. Udo was worth it.

It used to seem like gig-promoting attracted charismatic, larger-than-life personalities like Bill, Harvey, Ossy, and Mr. Udo. But the landscape is totally different today. The global concert-promotion industry is dominated by two behemoths: AEG and Live Nation.

They are slickly efficient corporations and they have made putting on tours exactly that: *corporate*. They get the job done, but bands don't form the close personal relationships with them that they did with the maverick, personality-plus characters back in the day.

It works like this. If, say, Priest want to do a thirty-date European tour, our manager, Jayne, calls our booking agent, Rod MacSween, whom we have worked with for many years. Rod gets in touch with a promoter, very likely Live Nation, who begin lining up the venues.

The promoters offer Rod a fee for the dates. It varies from venue to venue according to their size. Rod goes back to Jayne. Jayne says we want more. Rod goes back to the promoters. The business haggling goes on until they've settled on a sum that everyone is happy with.

---

* These meals were a bit wasted on me as I don't eat beef, but they were still a lovely gesture.

The band don't get involved at all: the negotiations are a triangle of management, agent, and promoters. The system works and they reach a solution. But I can't help feeling that something has been lost. I doubt I'll ever buy anybody from AEG or Live Nation a high-end fishing reel.

RIDERS

There's a major misunderstanding about Van Halen. In 1982, their tour contract stipulated that their dressing-room rider had to include a bowl of M&M's with all the brown ones removed. If they saw a single brown sweet, the band reserved the right to pull the show.

It sounds daft, and the story was presented at the time as an example of a major metal band getting so up themselves that they had totally lost touch with reality. In fact, as David Lee Roth later explained, they had a far more cunning plan.

On that tour, Van Halen were taking 850 massive lights with them—the biggest rock-show production ever, at that time. Some venues weren't equipped to cope. If the band spotted a brown M&M, they'd know the promoter hadn't read the contract properly and thus might fail to meet their technical specs. *Clever, huh?*

Riders are important. They help the mood in the dressing room before the show, and a happy band means a good gig. That said, Priest have never asked for anything bonkers on our rider. We're not Kanye West asking for a barber's chair, or Janet Jackson demanding an Arabian tent.

Our requests for pre-gig food and snacks are modest. Before a show, we like some hot soup and a deli tray of meat and cheeses (Ian and I love our cheeses). I like some Evian water and a Red Bull to have just before I go on. Scott likes his protein drinks for energy.

I ask for a bit of chocolate to nibble on and loads of tea bags. I'm a true Brit Abroad in that respect. I like English tea: PG Tips or, my favorite, Yorkshire Tea. Our crew always have sacks of tea bags to hand to make sure that I can get a nice brew.

The others have a bit of booze: no hard liquor, just beer and wine. Richie likes a drink before a show and Scott and Ian will have one after we've played. If we come offstage at 11 p.m., we eat at 11:30. I'll be nibbling at the cheeses and swigging my cuppa. It's hardly rock-and-roll Valhalla!

One reason we don't have a lot of food backstage is that we're paying for it! One of my favorite parts of The Comic Strip's *More Bad News* British TV show from the eighties, about a spoof metal band, comes when the group have a massive spread laid out at a video shoot.

One of them casually asks, "Who's paying for all this, then?" When the band learn that *they* are, they immediately start trying to eat the whole spread! They stuff their faces, and slap the hands of any crew members who try to take a sandwich: "Get lost! *We* paid for this!"

Of course, it's hard to discuss riders and not reference the classic spoof metal movie, *This Is Spinal Tap*. If Priest ever have any issue at all with backstage catering, we'll go straight into deadpan Nigel Tufnel mode: "What's this mini-bread? I can't work with this! It's a catastrophe!"

When a band is starting out, they're lucky if they get a rider at all. I remember at Priest's pub and working men's club gigs, on a good night we might get given five bottles of beer and five bags of salt-and-vinegar crisps. "That's yer lot!" we'd be told. "Tek it or leave it!"

Maybe that's why, when we moved up the ladder a little bit and got proper riders, we went slightly mad. We didn't ask for food: we weren't fussed about that.* We just wanted every kind of booze going: crates and crates of beer, wine, champagne, the strongest spirits, the works.

At my peak, or rather my nadir, on the *Metal Conqueror* tour in 1984, I would have sixteen cans of Budweiser and a bottle of Dom Pérignon set aside for my personal after-show consumption. Then I'd head out to a club to drink more. Happily, that's a distant, very fuzzy memory now.

On our world tours, the backstage catering in different countries can be interesting. I might be a Brit Abroad when it comes to tea bags, but I'm not the kind of bloke who flies to Benidorm and eats egg-and-chips every night. I like to dip my toe into international cuisines on the road.

---

* Come to think of it, I'm not sure Judas Priest ever *ate* in the eighties.

I love the sushi that we get given backstage in Japan. Priest used to get into a dressing room in Tokyo, see a huge platter of fresh sushi that would cost £1,000 in Britain, and demolish it. It would be a free-for-all. We'd be hurling that food down our necks. The worst culprit? Scott!

Our polite Japanese hosts would be looking at us quizzically, smiling. *Ah, these poor guys must be really hungry!* Then, the sad realization would dawn on them. *Oh, no, they are just animals! Pigs . . .*

Some of the guys love the riders in Brazil because you get great steaks and beef. That's not my thing, but I like their chicken, pork, and fish. In the States, backstage catering varies across the country. We get given Cuban food in Miami, Mexican in LA, and fish up in Seattle.

When we go down into the Deep South, we often get given grits. My partner, Thomas, is from Alabama, so he loves that stuff, but I'm not really into it. It always tastes to me like having a mouthful of sperm. I mean, there's a place for that, but it's not the dressing-room rider!

No, we're fairly low maintenance when it comes to riders. We are straightforward blokes and we'll eat most things. There has only ever been one time when we got into a major palaver over our backstage catering. It was The Unfortunate Romanian Fish Incident.

Let me set the scene. It was 2018 and we were in Romania. We had flown into Bucharest from Bulgaria and were not too impressed when we arrived at the gig to find that our dressing room smelled of paint, with flies buzzing around the food that was lying uncovered on the table.

Ah, well, the show must go on! I used to do this thing where I posted a little preshow video to Instagram to whet fans' appetites for the gig, so I got my phone out, pressed record, and went on a wander around the dressing room.

I was doing a running commentary as I went: "OK, metal maniacs, we're in Romania! Here's my gear all laid out, ready for tonight's show. Oh, and here's Ian! All right, Ian, how are you doing?"

"Sound, yeah, great!"

It was all going fine until I came to Scott. "Hey there, Scott! What are you up to?" I asked him.

"I'm just dealing with this fish! Have you seen this shit?" he asked.

"Pardon?"

"Follow me!"

Scott led me and my phone across the room to a giant microwave. He pinged it open and pulled out a plate that had the biggest, strangest-looking fish I had ever seen cooking on it.

"What are we supposed to do with *this* crap?" Scott said, and began to thump the fish. "How are we meant to eat this shit?" I thought it was funny, stuck the video up on my Instagram before we did the show, and thought nothing more of it.

Until the next day. It turned out that the fish that Scott was laughing at and ripping to bits was a local luxury and pretty much the national dish of Romania. Our mocking it quickly became a big news story and was all over social media in the country. They wanted to lynch us!

It sounds funny, but the Romanians certainly weren't laughing. We didn't want to insult our hosts and offend an entire nation, so I went on our social media and made a diplomatic apology for our behavior and for disrespecting their big-fish platter.

It defused The Unfortunate Romanian Fish Incident, but since that day, I've stopped filming backstage Instagram videos. I also make sure that Priest never go online and slag off national dishes. I mean, we have to remember: there's a time and a plaice . . .

STAGE SETS

The Crazy World of Arthur Brown never troubled the charts too much. In fact, they were classic one-hit wonders with their 1968 British number one and US number two, "Fire," which singer Arthur Brown performed on *Top of the Pops* with a flaming helmet on top of his noggin.

Yet they made a big impression on me as a teenager when I went to see them play a club in Walsall. Not only did Arthur stick on his burning headgear, but his road crew donned pirate hats and a big papier-mâché Spanish galleon costume to weave in and out of the fairly sparse crowd.

It gave the fans something to natter about on the way home, and that's what I like Priest to do. I love theatrics and a good stage set. Any metal or rock gig is 90 percent about the music and that's how it should be, but that extra 10 percent—lights, sets, *gags*—is so important.

I don't say "gags" in a flippant way. I mean dramatic tricks or scenes that woo the crowd, whether it's a metal gig or the pantomimes I used to work on at Wolverhampton Grand. I used to love scenes where we'd explode a flash pot.* *POOF!* The wicked witch would appear!

I remember seeing Alice Cooper do a great gag on his *Welcome to My Nightmare* tour. At the start of the show, Alice was running around in a film that was being projected on a white screen at the back of the stage. Suddenly—*BANG!* Alice burst through the screen and there he was, on the stage!

I love stuff like that because it's all part of the illusion, the *escapism* you are after when you go to a metal or rock show. Stage sets and lighting and costumes are all added dimensions to help you get away from the crap of what-can-be-boring everyday life for just one night.

Obviously, like everything else I've talked about, when your band is first starting out, you have nothing at all. If you're lucky, you might be able to scrape together enough cash for a backdrop with the band's logo or the title of your latest album on it.

For a metal band, the next stop is probably a bit of pyro for that *Wow!* factor. You can't beat a nice explosion to back up a guitar solo. But pyro is not just a metal thing. I've seen Lady Gaga using loads, and Cher, and Madonna. Even country artists go big on the flames nowadays.

Of course, fire can be dangerous, kids! I remember one Priest show in America where someone threw a cherry bomb onstage, and it blew up in Dave Holland's bass drum. That was nearly a Spinal Tap moment: drummer spontaneously combusts during show!

The first visual accessory, the first *gag* we introduced to Priest gigs, was the motorbike, of course. It was a pure on-the-spot whim of mine

---

* A flash pot is a small container of pyrotechnic powder that produces a bang, flash of light, and cloud of smoke when ignited. It's a little magic box that works as well for *Aladdin* as for an enormodome metal gig.

to ride a Harley onstage in Derby in 1979. The crowd loved it, so did I, and now it's a centerpiece of any Priest show. I'll never tire of doing it.

For years, metal bands always performed in front of banks of amps and speakers. It just seemed like how things had to be. Fans loved to see a guitarist soloing and headbanging in front of a mountain of speakers. Well, that's great—but there's so much more that you can do.

The first time Priest had the dosh to put on a proper big production of a stage show was probably the *Metal Conqueror* tour in 1984 to promote *Defenders of the Faith*. We gave the tour that name because in the center of the stage we had a re-creation of the giant metal head from the album sleeve.

It was my idea to try to re-create the album artwork like that, and it looked bloody great. At the start of every show, I'd emerge from the mouth of the metal monster—the Metallian—surrounded by flames, then walk along its arm towards the crowd, singing "Love Bites."

It was brill, but not everybody in the band was so enamored of it. The Metallian was so big that we had no room onstage for Dave Holland's drum kit. So we had to put Dave and his kit on the creature's head, fifty feet in the air! He bloody hated it.

Dave first became aware of our daring concept at the full production rehearsal. "Well, where am I going to be?" he asked, as he surveyed the stage set. "You're up there," I said, pointing up in the air.

"Up there?! I ay fuckin' gewin' up there!"

He had no choice in the matter, so before every show he'd be making his way up the ladder at the back of the Metallian, grumbling away to himself. "You all right, Dave?" I'd call over.

"No, I'm bloody not!"

Poor old drummers, eh? They always get it in the neck!

We were one of the first metal bands to take stage sets as far out as that. I suppose you have to be careful not to go too far and tumble into self-parody, but ultimately if some people sneer, so fucking what? I don't care. I'm far more concerned with giving our fans a great show.

Priest upped the ante again when we did the *Fuel for Life* tour after we released *Turbo*. This time, it wasn't just a monster's bonce: we had a whole giant robot at the back of the stage, seizing and lifting up me, Ken, and Glenn at various points of the show.

It was a massive contraption and it took a lot of carting around. Bands used to brag in those days about how many buses and trucks they took on tour. We had about six buses and fifteen trucks on that jaunt. Well, great—but it meant that our overhead expenses were stupidly high.

We ended up, between ourselves, calling that jaunt the *Arm and a Leg* tour, because we didn't make a penny profit. We sold out every show, but spent the lot lugging our ginormous stage production from arena to arena. Ah, well, at least the robot looked cool!

We tried something different on the *Painkiller* tour, with a set that had loads of levels and runways, and skyscrapers of speakers towering over everything. Intentionally, the whole stage resembled the inside of one gargantuan set of speakers. Our message was simple. *VOLUME! NOISE!*

That set nearly finished me off, mind you. One night I was yowling away and a piece of the lighting rig snapped and came swinging down. I felt a rush of air on the back of my neck as a gigantic girder covered in lights missed me by inches. That could have been curtains for me.

Special tours deserve special sets. When it came time to plot Priest's *50 Heavy Metal Years* anniversary tour, we knew we wanted to pull out all of the stops. Not many metal or rock bands survive for fifty years, and it is a landmark worth celebrating in style.

Our planning always starts with me sending my ideas to our production manager, Martin Walker, who gets the ball rolling. I love being involved in the creative side of stage design, and Martin has the logistical and economic know-how to understand what will work and what won't.

The fiftieth anniversary tour acknowledged where, and *what*, Judas Priest came from, half a century ago, so the set is all machinery and chimneys, like the inside of a Black Country factory. That's ace, but I knew that I wanted a couple of visual spectaculars as well.

Fans always remember the opening sequence of a show more than anything else. We wanted to present something visually spectacular, so

I got on Snapchat in my bedroom, I gave myself a Viking filter to help and inspire myself . . . and I wrote a speech.

"In the beginning, all Earth languished in cold, empty darkness. A vast, silent void waiting to be brought to life. Far, far away, out in the deepest depths of the universe, a flame ignited, heralding forth a light and sound so immense it shook the very foundations of this world . . ."

I knew the fans would need something to gawp at while they listened to these words, so we commissioned an absolutely massive version of the Priest metal pitchfork symbol to tower above the stage. And then I had my light bulb moment of inspiration:

The Giant Inflatable Bull.

Birmingham has always been famous for its Bull Ring. In medieval days, it was a setting for cruel animal-baiting sports. Nowadays, it's a massive shopping center. So, we asked a Dutch design company to make us a huge inflatable bull that would blow everybody—*everybody*—away.

I told them: "We need it to have the *Wow!* factor. We don't want a poxy thing like Spinal Tap's eighteen-inch Stonehenge!" And they rose to the challenge. They made us a gobsmacking twenty-foot bull that inflates to its full, jaw-dropping size in just ten seconds. And it cost us £80,000.

You know, I'm funny like that. I hate paying over the odds for after-show band "nice meals," but when it comes to spending money on our shows, I never bat an eyelid. It's dosh well spent. Anyone who saw our giant bull inflate on Priest's fiftieth anniversary tour will never forget it.

When you present something like that to your fans, it makes them feel even prouder to be attached to you and to have been attached to you for years—fifty years, in some instances! They've supported us for so long and it's their reward. We're saying, "Thank you."

Priest have had some amazing stage sets over the years and I'm proud of all of them. There's still one thing left that I'd like to do, though, one box to tick—I'd like to fly.

I had an idea of making my entrance on the anniversary tour via the roof of the stage. We didn't do it in the end, not *this* time, but I still hope to go swooping over the crowd's heads one day. Yes, I will don my Mad Wings! It just feels like my Destiny . . .

SET LISTS

On our *50 Heavy Metal Years* tour, Priest decided to play the first single we ever released, "Rocka Rolla," back in 1974. Now, heard through 2022 ears, it's quite an unusual song that could easily sound very dated now, so it wasn't a decision that we took lightly.

Glenn wrote the lyrics to it, which tell the story of a mean metal mutha who *"takes no messin, all-in wrestlin' / Is one of her pride and joys."* She is a *"bar-room fighter / Ten-pint-a-nighter."* It's a curious tale, and it's fair to say that Glenn had the strongest misgivings about disinterring it.

"What about 'Rocka Rolla'?" I asked in the pre-tour rehearsals, as we put the set list together in Glenn's studio.

"No!" said Glenn. "Just, no!"

But we had a trick up our sleeve. We changed the texture of the song, upped the tempo, made the guitars and drums heavier, and suddenly it sounded great and contemporary. It was as much of a thrill for us to play it on tour as it was for our longest-standing fans to hear it again.

Set lists are absolutely critical to any metal or rock gig. They can make—or break—the show. They have to strike a balance and be very carefully thought out to hit the right dynamics, tempo, content, moods, and emotions. There is a real science behind getting it right.

You have to include certain songs in the set. They are your lifeline to your fans. If someone comes to see Priest and doesn't hear "Breaking the Law," "Hell Bent for Leather," "Living After Midnight," or "Victim of Changes," they will feel cheated. We call those songs our *chestnuts*. They have to go in.

I've heard of bands who get bored of their chestnuts and stop doing them. They announce in interviews, "We're sick and tired of playing those songs and we're not playing them again!" Well, fair enough, but that's not Priest's way. Because we've never got bored of playing them.

The dynamics of a set list are vital. At the start of a show, everyone has their eyes and ears locked on the band, so you have to start full-on and smack them around the head. *BANG! BANG! BANG!* The opening three or four songs need to be full-on energy and adrenaline.

It's a manic metal attack, so we have to think about guitar changes. We don't want the momentum of that opening blast to be disrupted by us having to wait while Richie takes off one guitar and straps on another. Richie helps me compile the set list to ensure that doesn't happen.

Once the set is well underway, we can put in the occasional ballad and tracks where the tempo is a bit slower. That's also the place for our epic, longer songs that are six or seven minutes long. We'd never open or close the set with one of those.

On the *50 Heavy Metal Years* tour especially, we tried to include songs from all points in our history. I've said before, our gigs are like a time machine for our fans. They might hear a track from 1978 or 1982, and be transported right back to their school days or a specific moment in time.*

Priest generally do ninety-minute sets and that feels right to me. Any longer might be too long. I'll take quality over quantity every time. You get some bands playing three-hour sets. I hear the Grateful Dead used to do six hours. Well, try bloody doing *that* night after night for a year!

Most of our chestnuts come at the end of the set and in the encore. There are good reasons for this. The front end of our set is very tight and full of skilled musicianship, and when we're worn out at the end of the night, it's nice to throw ourselves into those old favorites.

It's also great to finish the set with a big singalong with the fans which, let's face it, ain't gonna happen with "Painkiller"! That's why we generally close with "Living After Midnight." Everybody can belt that one out and it's a great celebration to end on.

We all contribute to the set list. I'll ask everyone to send me a list of songs then I put it all together. I sit in my kitchen, write a set list, put it on the wall, and stare at it. I can hear the whole set in my head: how it starts, how it ends, and the connection between all the songs.

---

* I first heard "Eleanor Rigby" on a family holiday in Devon when I was fifteen. Even today, whenever I hear that Beatles classic, I'm back in my bunk in a four-berth caravan. Musical memory is a powerful thing.

Obviously, Priest have to agree on what we're going to play, and there are certain songs that some band members are more attached to than others. This can lead to droll conversations in pre-tour rehearsals:

"Oh, no, not *that* one! We car do *that* one!"
"Why not?"
"I dow like it!"
"Well, we recorded it!"
"So what? I dow like it!"
"Eh? What was the bloody point in recording it, then?"

Positioning new tracks and deep cuts in the set is a balancing act. There is a cliché that when a band says, "Now, here's a new song!" half the crowd vanishes for a pint or a piss. But Priest are lucky in that respect. Our fans are loyal and they tend to stick around and listen.

Having said that, we did do a couple of tours back in the day when our new album was only just out, or even not quite out yet. We'd play three or four new songs that fans had never heard before and it led to a bit of a dead spot in the show. That's a thing to avoid.

Some fans love it when we play obscurities—old album tracks or songs we've not done in years. Richie plays the first chord of "Bloodstone," say, and cheers go up here and there in the crowd. I long ago accepted that we have fans who know a lot more about our music than we do.

We will keep a set list intact for a whole tour and just occasionally slip in an extra song or move a couple of them around. It helps keep us on our toes and stops us from slipping into a rut, and it also introduces an element of surprise for the fans on that night.

Some of them don't *want* to be surprised, mind you. Before the show, they'll have memorized the set from the website setlist.fm and that is what they want to hear. If we vary it, I normally get a few grumbles on my social media afterward:

Dude! You played "Exciter" in Detroit and Cleveland but you didn't do it for us in LA! What the fuck?!

Well, that's showbiz! You can't please all of the people all of the time! Ultimately, Priest play gigs for our fans and we always want them to go away happy at the end of the night. But when it comes to set lists, we don't just give them what they want—we give them what they *need*.

GUEST LISTS

There is a scene that is as old as rock and roll itself that I can absolutely guarantee will happen a few times outside every single show that Priest play. A security gorilla will be standing in front of the venue in a hi-vis jacket, holding our guest list. A fan will run up and give him his name.

"I'm on the guest list, plus one!" he'll say, excitedly. "Rob/Glenn/Richie/Ian/Scott/Andy put me on!"*

The security guy will examine the list, purse his lips, and shake his head. "Sorry, son," he'll tell him. "Your name's not down. And if you're not on the list, you're not coming in!"

It's not that Priest are particularly mean on handing out guest passes. Far from it. It just happens to every band. Guest lists are both a great opportunity for metal and rock bands to welcome friends, family, and loved ones to their shows, and the absolute bane of their bloody lives.

At any gig, the promoter will generally give every band member about twenty complimentary tickets, or "comps." The band manager will also get some, as will the record company to share among its executives and the media. The numbers soon add up.

It's more of an issue in some places than others. At big shows like New York, London, or Los Angeles, *everybody* seems to ask for comps. The guest list will stretch into the high hundreds. It can feel like there are more people poncing around backstage than there are in the crowd!

Everybody loves being on a guest list. You feel special, privileged, and, well, you get in for nothing! People get very excited about being on the list, but, if for any reason they've been left off, they can get equally disappointed. Sometimes, they lose their minds about it.

*Mark as applicable/guilty.

I must admit I'm to blame for a lot of Priest's guest-list disappointments because I have a very bad habit. Thomas, my partner who also doubles as my PA when we're out on tour, goes spare at me about it. I've tried to mend my ways but, well, *I just can't help myself.*

I will be doing a load of Zoom interviews with journalists to promote a show. The interviewer will comment that he loves Priest and has been into us forever and I always, *always,* say the same thing:

"Oh, that's great! Tell you what—come down and see the show! I'll put you on the guest list and give you backstage passes!"

"Really? Wow! Thanks, Rob!" the journalist will say.

The problem is that the second the interview ends, and the screen goes blank, I forget that I've said it. I don't tell Thomas, and the poor guy fetches up at the venue only to get turned away by the gorilla in the hi-vis jacket.

If Thomas and I go out for a quiet pizza in Chicago, say, the night before a gig, there will always be Priest fans who spot me and come over for a chat and a selfie. "We'd love to see you play tomorrow!" they'll say. And Big Mouth strikes again: "Yeah, come on down! I'll put you on the list!"

The fans will be beside themselves with excitement. Thomas will look daggers at me because our list is already full, but he'll give them his email address and manage to squeeze them in. That's all lovely— but the problems start the *next* time we come to Chicago.

Those same fans will have held on to Thomas's email and, in the weeks leading up to the show, his inbox will light up. "Hey! You know how you got us into the Priest show last time? We'd like to come again, with a load of friends—can we have six tickets and backstage passes, please?"

If we say yes, the demands get more and more outlandish. "Great, and I see you're playing Nashville. My cousin lives there and is a big metal fan: Can he come down with four friends? Oh, and I've got an old high school buddy in Detroit who needs tickets for that show . . ."

It's an extraordinary process. A lot of fans are respectful when they get in touch again, but others email Thomas wanting the moon on a stick: "Yeah, can you give us VIP passes this time?" If he says no, they get well pissed off and tell him they're going to ask me to give him the sack!

Because we've given these guys—whom we might only have met once in our lives—tickets for a previous show, they think they can have them forever. They assume the band get countless tickets for free and can dish them out, but it doesn't work like that. *Nothing* comes for free.

Somebody has to eat the cost, whether it's the band or the promoter. Priest have to pay for any extra guest tickets. If they cost $50 each, and somebody emails requesting five freebies, they are basically asking us to give them $250!

I'm surprised poor Thomas isn't as bald as me because he'll be pulling his hair out trying to deal with these entitled guys. Sometimes, he will call in Jayne Andrews for support because, like all great band managers, Jayne is very good at saying no.

I think the ultimate example of guest-list freeloaders came deep in the Midwest on one recent tour. We have an ex-military friend there, and when he asked us if he could come down and bring his family, we said yes. We didn't expect that to mean *twelve members* of his family!

I was in the dressing room before the show when Thomas appeared and said, "You *have* to see this—follow me!" I did. Somehow, our ex-military guy and his extended family had blagged into artist catering, and were demolishing our pre-gig food like pigs at a trough.

"Hmm, honey, this cooking is so much better than yours!" our friend's father was saying, saliva drooling down his chin.

"Yep, it sure is!" his wife agreed, gnawing on a chicken bone.

It was funny, and it made us laugh at the time, but is also made one decision pretty easy for us. The next time we play that particular Midwest town, that hungry family will be hearing those dreaded words from the guy in the hi-vis jacket: "You're not on the list. And you're *not* coming in!"

TOUR BUSES

When a metal or rock band graduates from a battered Transit or even a glorified bread van to a proper slick tour bus, it is truly an upgrade of *Biblical* proportions. In fact, you feel as if you've died and gone to a heaven on wheels.

It's all about personal space. When you're piled on top of each other in a Transit van, you have none. In Priest's first days, I used to try to bagsy the front passenger seat, next to the driver. You'd get your own little cocoon of space. It wasn't much, but it was something.

For British tours, we had a couple of years where we gratefully exited the Transit and the band drove to gigs in a car while the road crew took our gear separately. We started off in a Ford Granada and then upgraded to an orange Volvo.

We were in the Granada one cold, dark midwinter evening in about 1975. We were on our way to a show somewhere up north and Glenn was driving us through a near-blizzard of heavy snow. I seem to remember we were on the A1M . . . when we hit the black ice.

It all happened very quickly, and in slow motion. I was sitting in the back of the car, Glenn had us going at quite a lick, and I sensed the danger even before the back end started to go and we went into a full 360-degree spin.

Shit! This is not going to end well! My life flashed before me as the whole band yelled out in fear and panic. We smashed hard into the motorway's central barrier, slid back across the three lanes of tarmac . . . and came to a halt.

We appeared to be all still alive, and we scrambled out to survey the damage. It could have been worse, but steam was hissing out from under the Granada's buckled bonnet. It was clearly going absolutely nowhere else that evening.

Shit! What to do? This was *long* before mobile phones. We all stared at each other . . . then a vehicle slowly appeared over the snowy horizon and pulled up next to us. A grinning, wizened face peered out from under a peaked cap: "You lads had a bit o' bother? You alright, are yer?"

It was a farmer, in a knackered old Land Rover. The old chap was also a saint. He towed our Granada to the hard shoulder, piled us into his stinky farm vehicle, and drove us to the venue. Heavy metal warriors? We felt more like the bloody Wurzels!*

In America, by then, we had been upgraded to our first proper tour bus with bunk beds. It felt like luxury, absolute fucking bliss. *Oh my God*, I thought, *where have you been for all of my life? This is the way to live!*

Thinking back, our first American tour buses weren't really all that. They were basically old Greyhound buses with the seats ripped out and bunk beds and a few facilities added. They were pretty bare bones, even rickety, but to us they felt like mobile palaces.

Sophisticated, top-of-the-range tour buses can cost millions of dollars nowadays. Our primitive early models were nothing like that, but, even today, the layout largely remains the same. It's basically this:

At the front, the driver is cocooned away, protected from any mayhem that might unfold behind him. Next is a lounge area, with couches, sofas, a fridge, and a microwave. Nowadays, there'll be a big-screen TV. Back in the eighties, we were plugged into Sony Walkmans.

Next up on the bus are the bathrooms, with toilets and a shower. In the center section are the bunks: there are normally four or six on each side of the bus. At the back there will usually be a second socializing area, maybe with books and games.†

When we graduated to tour buses, for me the key factor was the bunks. Your bunk was only just big enough to fit in, and it could feel like lying in a coffin, but you could squeeze in, put the light on, pull the curtain . . . *and relax*. It gave you some privacy; a place for a tiny bit of "me" time.

---

*The Wurzels were a seventies British novelty band who recorded joke versions of pop hits in country-bumpkin accents. They were never really going to break in America.

† I am describing the *band* bus here, of course. The road crew's bus will have one small social area, at most, and up to twelve bunks crammed on each side of the aisle. Not for nothing is it nicknamed the "slave bus."

Once we were settled in, we'd be on the tour bus for many weeks and months. We would all live, breathe, eat, drink, pee, and party together. But there was one golden rule, as true today as it was then:

YOU. NEVER. SHIT. ON. THE. TOUR. BUS.

The reasons are obvious, really. Buses are confined spaces and with six or seven sweaty, belching, hairy-arsed blokes cooped up on them, they can get rancid. You don't want to spend the morning speeding down a US freeway with your nostrils full of the drummer's breakfast dump.

The etiquette is that if you need a crap on a tour bus, you have a word with the driver. He'll pull over at a truck stop or, if it's the middle of the night and you're desperate, by the side of the road so you can run and drop one behind a tree. *Ah, the glamour of touring!*

In theory, the tour bus is a vehicle to get you from A to B: to transport you between your various places of work. In practice, in the early years of Priest, this function was eclipsed by a far more pressing concern: full-on, raging, heavy metal partying.

We would all pile off the stage and back onto the bus, high on adrenaline and the buzz of the show, and the madness would begin. Drink, drugs, groupies, and scores of people running around screaming and going mental, me included. Random strangers everywhere. It would go on all night.

Sometimes we'd be driving—to a club or to a hotel or overnight to the next show. Sometimes we'd be static in the gig parking lot, with female fans lining up to introduce themselves to the band. The tour bus would be a mobile Sodom (well, none of that, sadly!) and Gomorrah.

Like most young metal or rock bands, we went to town. We filled our boots. Groupies would stay overnight on the bus with some of the lads, there'd be drug-fueled mini-orgies, the police would pull us over and come on with sniffer dogs . . . you name it, we did it!

It sounds great, right? Well, some nights it *was*. You're a young British bloke, in a band, in America, and you're living the life. You're the all-drinking, drugging, hard-partying rock star that you dreamt of being. *Whoa!* We had some amazing tour bus nights that I'll never forget.*

But you can only live that life for so long. The party always ends and the morning always comes. And as you get older, you get tired of waking up with a killer hangover, on a trashed tour bus, feeling as shit and grumpy as the bandmates scattered around you.

As I've said more than once in this book: *it's a young man's game.* You grow tired of the aftermath of the parties—and the hangovers, and the pissed-off mornings accelerate the tensions that inevitably build up as you spend months living on top of each other.

It creeps up on you. You hardly notice the mood changing. You start a tour full of excitement and enthusiasm, then a few months in you'll be lying in your bunk, at 3 a.m., listening to a stupid pissed argument, or people having drunken sex above you, and you find yourself thinking:

Fuck! I've had enough of this!

Bad feelings can incubate on a tour bus. There'd be nights when Glenn and Ken would have a full-on row in the lounge. One of them would storm off to the back of the bus and they wouldn't talk for days. You'd feel like you could cut the air with a knife.

I just couldn't sleep on the bus. There'd always be noise, whether it was all-night parties or someone bloody snoring their head off. With my lifelong chronic insomnia, I had no chance of nodding off. Eventually, I realized there was only one solution: I needed my own tour bus.

It wasn't me catching LSD, or Lead Singer Disease (more on this ailment later!). The rest of the band understood: if I was arriving at a venue low and knackered from no sleep, it did *not* equal a great Judas Priest show. I began renting my own bus, and my on-the-road life improved no end.

I kept my bus immaculate, as well! Tour buses are like hotel rooms: if you trash them, you pay. On my tour bus, you'd normally find me in

---

* Well, except the ones where I was so pissed that I'd forgotten them by the next morning.

my Marigolds, sleeves up, scrubbing the sink or cleaning out the fridge. I turned into a heavy metal housewife on wheels!

Nowadays, though, I hardly ever get on a tour bus, whether it's the band's *or* my own solo vehicle. Because Priest always tour by private jet.

It sounds swanky, and it's true that private jets cost a fucking fortune, and yet both economically and practically, it makes sense. I'm not in my twenties and able to go all night without sleep any more. I'm an old guy in my seventies and I need looking after.

We have to face the fact that none of Priest are spring chickens. If we're to put on a good show for the fans, we need our TLC. I think it's no different to a football team or an NBA basketball squad. They travel by jet so they can arrive fresh to the game.

Without (I hope!) sounding like a spoiled rock star, it's still exhausting. Some nights we fly out straight after the show, cross various time zones, and arrive at a hotel in the early hours. *If it's 4 a.m., this must be Chicago!* My poor old body takes a right battering.

Ultimately, it's worth it. Judas Priest wouldn't be able to do huge tours nowadays if we were still spending eight hours a day inching through traffic on tour buses. Now that the travel is less grueling, the promoter can stick on an extra six or eight dates per tour. And that's what counts.*

I must admit the expense of the jets is eye-watering, though. Often, we don't pay the extra cost of hiring a stewardess. On one European tour, the band got my partner, Thomas, a stewardess hat to wear on the jet. We have photos of him in it. He doesn't like them much.

So, now we're just one more poncy band, zooming around in a private jet! Besides the cost, the only other drawback is the same as the Transit van—you don't have any personal space. Sometimes, I even sit there, at 35,000 feet, and find myself missing my bunk on the tour bus.

But not very often.

---

* Some people might question how green swanning around the world in private jets is. I see their point, but we're not spewing out fumes in a tour bus all night long. I know some bands whose members all have their own jet! At least we don't do that . . .

PRE-GIG RITUALS

If a tour is a pilgrimage, then the venues that we play are temples of worship to the God of heavy metal. And, like any priest about to deliver a sermon, I have my little preparations that I have to go through before I can recite my scriptures.

I probably have more pre-gig rituals than most. I'm a creature of habit and I need to know everything is just how I like it before we can take our service. I have my routine and I follow it, well, *religiously*. It probably sounds a bit OCD, but I don't think it is. It's just how I am.

Any band will tell you that, when you're on tour, from the moment you wake up in the morning until you go onstage at 9 p.m. is dead time. You just have to keep yourself occupied. Some bands do interviews, but I hardly ever do those on the road because I like to save my voice.

In an ideal world I'd get to a venue an hour before we go on, or less, but that's not possible because Priest travel as an entourage and some people have to get there earlier. So, we generally arrive two hours before showtime and I set about distracting myself and killing time.

There's always something to talk to management or production about. I might go for a wander backstage. I check my social media, which is fun, because there are normally fans already at the gig posting photos and saying, "We're here!" I feel the excitement starting to build.

The dressing room will be set out *just so*. We'll have a food and booze room, as outlined in the contract rider, and I'll have a table with all my little knick-knacks laid out. It has my stage jewelry and makeup, photos of my mum and dad in little frames, and a picture of Elvis Presley.*

I don't go to watch the support act, even if it's a band that I really like. I might have a sneaky peak at one song through the curtain, but that's it. It's a superstition: I don't really like to see the stage until I'm about to walk out on it.

---

*People might be surprised I have a photo of Elvis, but he's the guy who started this whole rock-and-roll / showbiz thing rolling. Elvis was larger than life and, in a funny way, he's a bit of a focus for me.

By the same token, Priest don't do pre-gig soundchecks anymore. We used to but, my God, they're boring! With technology nowadays, we can do our soundcheck in pre-tour rehearsals, set the levels, and our sound guys and road crew can finesse it on the day.

I don't do preshow vocal exercises. I know some singers do their scales beforehand, but I never have, at any stage in my career. I don't need to. I hope it doesn't sound arrogant, but I know if I'm in the right mental place, I can hit my notes.

Our stage manager, currently a guy called Rick Benbow, watches the clock for us. Rick will keep popping in the dressing room and giving us time checks to count us down to showtime:

"One hour to stage time, lads!"

"Thirty minutes to go!"

"On in ten minutes!"

I'll have music going on my Bluetooth speaker in the dressing room before the gig. It's metal: *always* metal. I play Ronnie James Dio—"The Last in Line" and "Holy Diver"—and Sabbath, probably "Paranoid." Maybe a bit of Slayer. I play it to psych me up for the gig, and it always works.

Thirty minutes before showtime, I put on my stage gear. I could do it all myself—I'm not quite too old to get myself dressed yet!—but all my jewelry and my in-ear monitors can be a right palaver, so I enlist the help of our wardrobe girl, who takes care of our costumes and laundry on tour.

She's a lovely lady called Heather, whom we naturally call Hell Bent for Heather. For a while, Heather put new underpants for me on our gig rider, so they'd always be waiting for me. But it felt a bit daft . . . why should the band pay for my undies?! So, we stopped doing that.

I know some bands do inspirational pre-gig huddles and pep talks, but Priest never have. It's not the yam-yam way. Instead, the rest of the band all mooch off ten minutes before the start and go to wait side stage. Ian always grins at me as he leaves and says: "See you on the dance floor!"

Left alone in the dressing room, I'll have a last-minute piss. There is nothing worse than getting onstage and needing the loo. Usually, I'll have a Red Bull before I go on, but sometimes I have a bit of a mental wrestle about it. *Is it OK to have this, or will I need the toilet?*

I have a superstition that I always have to be the last person onstage. Rick Benbow leads me to it right before the start. It's always an exciting moment. The backstage area will be empty by now, and I'll hear the crowd screaming and Martin Walker playing our preshow music.

Rick takes me to my stage man-cave.* This is a little area behind Richie's speakers where I keep my other stage gear and my costume changes. It has to always be laid out in exactly the same way. I hate to see any changes or anything out of place.

There is a little table with a Union Jack and the Black Country flag on it. Also on the table are my Vicks inhaler, my packets of Airwaves gum, and a container of hot honey-and-lemon drink. There will be a can of Red Bull (*do I dare?!*), paracetamol, and some eye drops.

The last warm-up song before we go on is always Sabbath's "War Pigs": *"Generals gathered in their masses..."* The crowd goes wild when they hear that and, in my man-cave, I say the Serenity Prayer, the same one that I recite in bed every night before I go to sleep:

> *God, grant me the serenity to accept the things I cannot change,*
> *The courage to change the things I can,*
> *And the wisdom to know the difference...*

Before a show, I might be a little nervous. Actually, *nervous* isn't quite the right word. You might say I'm in a state of heightened awareness. But after I've said the prayer, I'm very calm. I'm acutely aware of

---

*I vanish into my man-cave during the show for costume changes, a swig of honey-and-lemon, or just a minute's rest. Some fans ask, "Why does Rob keep wandering off?" but what am I supposed I do when Richie or Scott are doing their bit: Stand there with my arms folded, like a spare dick at a wedding? *Bugger that!* I'm onstage when I need to be.

the gig that's about to happen, and I also know that I'm totally ready for it:

This is it! This is the moment! This is what I live for and what I'm about. I'm about to do something that means the world, everything, to me. So, let's do it!

Rick appears again at the entrance to my man-cave and gives me the thumbs up. "Are you ready, Rob?" ·

Yep! Too fucking right, I am! It's showtime!

AFTER-SHOW PARTIES

Nowadays, when I come offstage at the end of a gig, I'm done for the night. *Goodnight, Vienna!* Give me a cup of hot cocoa, tip me into bed, and read me a bedtime story.

But it didn't used to be that way.

All through the seventies and the early eighties, a show didn't mark the end of the night for Priest. *It was the start.* I'd run from the stage into the dressing room, shower and clean up, come out swigging Dom Pérignon from the bottle, and start raging. *Seriously* raging.

After-show parties were a huge thing back in the day. Particularly in America. We'd lurch out of our dressing room to find the rest of the backstage area packed with hundreds of people schmoozing, drinking, drugging, and going mental. We might even know a couple of them.

In the seventies, when bands like the Stones or Queen played London, New York, or LA, they'd compete to throw the wildest after-show party. They'd throw tens of thousands of dollars at them. Themes, costumes, dwarves with bowls of coke on their heads . . . the works!

Priest never went to those lengths, but we were always up for a full-on party. Not in our dressing room, though. Even when I used to come offstage already pissed and high (that is, every night), I didn't want anybody in our dressing room.

A band's dressing room is their inner sanctum; their sacred space. I don't want anybody to see me with my head still buzzing from the gig. Even today, we still have a strict rule: the dressing room is for band, crew, and management only. Even our families are not allowed in.

So, after gigs, hangers-on used to pile into our separate food-and-booze backstage room and wait for us. Guests, groupies, record company guys, agents, promoters, radio DJs, journalists, competition winners. At least half of them looked like Artie Fufkin from *This Is Spinal Tap*.

When we emerged, somebody from the record label would grab hold of us and maneuver us around the room:

"Hey, you *must* meet Dirk Tempest from Radio XKRY!"

"Rob, this is Mike Meteor, the rock journalist! He's a *huge* fan!"

I'd nod, mumble a few pleasantries, and offer one hand for shaking while continuing to swig Dom Pérignon from the bottle with the other.

It was a ritual we had to go through and, to be honest, I never loved it. The drinking was brill but yam-yams like us aren't good at schmoozing. It can all feel a bit false. And the worst thing about those backstage parties was people ladling me with bloody compliments.

"OhmyGod that was the best show I ever saw!"

"That was awesome! You are the most amazing singer in the history of heavy metal—of all music!"

"You're the greatest—don't you know that?"

No, I bloody don't! As I've said, I have never been good at taking praise, no matter how sincerely meant. It doesn't sit well with me. I'd normally cope by finishing off the Dom Pérignon and starting on the sixteen cans of Budweiser I also had carefully lined up.

After-show parties could last deep and long into the night. They might move from place to place. We'd jump into cabs to a club and then, hours later, back to the hotel bar. I'd often black out and wake up in my room, at midday, without a clue how I'd got there.

Ah, fuck it! Who cares? Which city are we in, anyway?

They were the wild days of music-industry excess—but like all golden ages, they came to an end. Around the end of the eighties, as grunge kicked in and rock hedonism was seen as passé, excess gave way to austerity. Crazy after-show parties were no more.

I didn't mind, personally. I was sober by then, so meet-and-greets and glad-handing felt like a chore. In every city, there would usually be one or two old friends or allies I was happy to see again for a minute or two. But at most parties, I'd be thinking, *Get me out of here!*

Today, record labels are more likely to throw album-launch parties. They're fairly muted affairs, often inside the record company itself: a playback of the album, a few nibbles, some beer and wine for media bods, and home by teatime. Which is just how I like it.

On the road, we come offstage, wind down in the dressing room, and eat together in the rider room. We don't hold an inquest on the gig. In fact, we often don't even talk about the show. We just share a bit of banter and relax.

On the *very* rare occasions nowadays when the record company tries to get us to an after-show party, I react with absolute horror. It's the *last* thing I want to do. I feel like saying to them:

"Are you kidding me? I've just screamed my tits off for two hours, and now you want me to go and make small talk and chin-wag? Forget it!"

After-show parties aren't enjoyable for me now. Parties are meant to be relaxing, but I'm the singer: if I go to our own party, every eye is on me and everybody wants a chat; a selfie; a piece of me. It's wearying. Plus, I'm sober. Watching everyone else get drunk is no fun.

It's one of the many things that change as you get older. I used to love after-show parties. Now, I'll do anything to avoid them. My alarm bells go off and my internal monologue goes something like this:

Eh? I've done my show and I've clocked off, mate! I'm finished for the night! Now it's my "me" time! You want to go and party? Great, knock yourself out! Right, where's my cocoa mug . . . ?

FESTIVALS

Back in the day, Priest would play one-off festival shows even if we weren't on tour at the time. Why not? All that we needed was our van, our gear, and the clothes we were standing up in. It was an innocent, uncluttered experience and there was a real purity to it.

We can't just rock up and play like that nowadays, now that we've transformed into a traveling behemoth of trucks, rigs, lighting, enormous stage sets, and scores of road crew. That world has gone. But if we're already out on the road, we love to squeeze a festival or two into our itinerary.

Playing a festival is not like doing your own gig. The biggest difference is that not everyone is there to see you. The festival may be a celebration of our genre, of metal, but some fans won't have ever seen us before. There might be a degree of indifference, or even hostility.

Nowadays, we're in the lucky position that we'll usually be the festival headliner. This removes the hassle of playing halfway down a bill, but it adds a new kind of pressure. We have to smash it, to be so strong that the crowd instinctively think: *Yep, THAT'S why they're headlining!*

The first festival I went to as a punter was a biggie. It was the Isle of Wight Pop Festival in 1970, the famous landmark event with the Doors, The Who, Family (I used to bloody love that band!)—and Jimi Hendrix, who took the stage in the early hours of Monday morning, just weeks before he died.

I was blown away by the whole thing. It was such an adventure. I twigged straightaway that it wasn't just about the bands but the whole festival experience. It wasn't so much "Bloody hell, I'm watching Hendrix!" as "Bloody hell, I'm at the Isle of Wight Festival!"

It felt a pretty wild event. It was primeval, primordial. Fans were literally rolling around in the mud. There were more than half a million people and, at some point, the fences got pulled down and everyone poured in for nothing. The thinking was, "Music should be free, man!"*

Priest's first festival as a band was the Reading Festival in 1975. As I said in *Confess*, we lucked onto the bottom of the bill via a casting-couch route, when a mate of the band allowed one of the bookers to give him a blow job. But once we were there, we were determined to make it count.

---

*I might even have been into that hippie ideal then. Now I figure it a bit different: *You've got to pay the bands! Because we ain't gonna play for free!*

We opened the whole festival, gave it our all, and I stalked round stage in a red jerkin like a mad marionette. If I look at it now, on YouTube, I just think: *Who are those guys? Huh? Is that REALLY me?* But it was such a big deal for us at the time and I think it opened a few doors.

I remember doing a festival in Finland, in free-love Scandinavia, in 1976. The first thing we saw when we got on site was couples openly fucking in ditches. Ken boggled out of the van window and said, "Ar, *she'd* be a bit of alright!" He wanted to line up a shag before we'd even played a note.

It was the height of summer, we got bombarded by mosquitoes, and we had to go onstage in broad sunshine. It was exciting, but it disoriented me. If I had my way, there'd be no such thing as daytime gigs. Heavy metal is meant—destined!—to be played in the dark.

Priest have had landmark festivals in our career. One of the biggest was Day on the Green in California in 1977, supporting Led Zeppelin at the end of our first tour of America. *At the express request of Robert Plant.* Forty-five years on, it still feels mad to me to write that sentence.

Probably an equally significant festival for us was Monsters of Rock in 1980. It was momentous because it was the first time that a promoter* had set up an event that was purely rock and metal, and held it in the birthplace of metal: the Midlands, at Castle Donington.

We were on with Scorpions and Saxon, and Rainbow headlined. We got changed in a crummy little caravan, but it was a fantastic day. I still have a photo of me backstage with Rudy Schenker that I will always treasure. I've got a pint in one hand and a whip in the other.

Priest were just starting to get big and we decided to let off fireworks at the end of our set. We bought a handful of rockets—then learned that Rainbow were setting off £10,000 worth of fireworks for their climax! It would have made ours look feeble, so we abandoned the plan.

Instead, Ian and I decided to let them off at my house on Bonfire Night. We had a couple of mortars but we had no idea they were

---

*Oddly enough, that promoter, Maurice Jones, later lived next door to me in Walsall for years before he died in 2009. It's a small world . . .

heavy-duty industrial fireworks for professional displays only. In my back garden, we ignited them with a nine-volt battery, like the instructions told us to.

WHOOSH! BANG! CRASH! FIZZ! They shot miles into the air, exploded, and turned the skies above my quiet residential area into a riot of lurid colors and what sounded like war-zone gunfire. *Fuck me!* Ian and I gawped at each other. It felt like Krakatoa was erupting over Walsall!

We could hear doors opening everywhere and people saying, "What the bloody hell was that?" So we scarpered back in the house. We later learned that one mortar shell landed on the roof of the local cricket club and set it alight. *Oops! Maybe we would have upstaged Rainbow, after all!*

I have some crazy festival memories. The US Festival in San Bernardino in 1983 was quite corporate, but it gave us the chance to fly in by chopper and play to 330,000 metal maniacs. And, of course, Live Aid, two years later in Philadelphia, wasn't the kind of experience that you forget in a hurry.

In the twenty-first century we've got involved in one or two traveling festivals. I like the whole idea behind that. To me, it's just the same as in medieval days, when parties of minstrels would travel from town to town. That's what a traveling festival is: a rock-and-roll circus rolling into town.

When I rejoined Priest after my time away, we went across America with Ozzfest in 2004. Sharon Osbourne had founded it in 1996, after the organizers of Lollapalooza sneered at her when she asked them if Ozzy could be on their bill.

Trust me, you do *not* sneer at Sharon Osbourne! Lollapalooza was dead by 2004 but Ozzfest was a major annual event in the metal calendar. We went on before the headliners, Black Sabbath, with Slayer, Slipknot, Lamb of God, and Dimmu Borgir also on the bill.

It was ace. The festival had a real sense of community and I loved that we bumped into our fellow metal minstrels in catering every day. We didn't see a lot of Ozzy, who gets very psyched up before shows, but Sharon was always floating around backstage and up for a chat.

Other metal bands have copied Ozzfest, like Slipknot doing Knotfest. We've never done a Priestfest, as such, but our *Metal Masters* tour in 2008, with Motörhead, Heaven & Hell, and Testament, wasn't too far away. We still occasionally think of doing something similar.

Today, there are well-established metal and rock festivals all around the globe. Wacken in Germany and Graspop in Belgium are huge. We have played Hellfest in France, and there are metal festivals in Asia, South America, and even in African nations like Botswana and Namibia.

In Britain, the prime metal events are Download and Bloodstock. If I am honest, I prefer Bloodstock. I like that it is family-run and has a nicely organic, honest feel; whereas, to me, Download has become all about the money and is very corporate.

Festivals can always get trashed by poxy weather. At the last Download we played, in 2015, it pissed down as soon as we went on. It was cold and miserable, and we were playing to a sea of drowned rats in plastic ponchos. You do your best, but it's hard work for the band *and* the fans.

In contrast, the last Bloodstock we played, in August 2021, was very special for me. For *many* reasons. I had just beaten prostate cancer, I'd just turned seventy, and it was our first gig after eighteen months of Covid-induced lockdowns and inactivity. *Yeah! Bring it on!*

I could have been nervous, but everything just felt *right*. A British metal band headlining the biggest and best British metal festival, on their own turf! *We were back!* The night was magical. The crowd roar when Glenn came out to join us for the encore is something I will never forget.

Priest are used to metal festivals, but I still wonder sometimes about playing more general events, alongside all sorts of music. Metal bands can do that now that we're no longer viewed as pariahs. Metallica head-lined Glastonbury in 2014 and nobody batted an eyelid.

I think I'd like to do it because it would be a throwback to the days we could just turn up, plug in, and play without a £500,000 stage set and lights. All that matter are the band and the songs. And Glastonbury now is like Isle of Wight in 1970: it sells out for the *event*, not for the artists.

So, would I like Priest to play Glastonbury, second from top of the bill, between Dua Lipa and Billie Eilish? Yeah, I would. We're not so up our own arses that we'd demand to headline, and it would be an adventure and a box to tick off.

So, who knows? Maybe one day you'll see us down on the farm . . .

HOTELS

When you're taking your scriptures around the globe, you spend a lot of time in hotels. You can be living on room service for more than a year. I know some metal and rock bands don't like this and see hotels as a necessary evil, but I don't. I bloody love them!

When we're on tour, my hotel room is my sanctuary. If we have a day or two off, I do my level best not to leave the room once. I don't want to see the local sights, or go out to dinner: I just want my bed, my TV, my phone, and my iPad.

At the point in our career that Priest are at now, we're lucky enough to be able to afford a bit of luxury. But it wasn't always like that. As I said earlier, in our early years we'd kip in the van or drive home after gigs or, if we had a few bob for once, we'd crash out in a local B&B.

Corky might occasionally book somewhere in advance but, nine times out of ten, we'd run offstage, climb into the van, and hare around the streets looking for B&B signs. There'd be six or seven of us, pissed, knocking on a door just before midnight: "Av' yow got a room, please?"

And it *would* just be one room. If they'd let us, we'd all squeeze into a double room to save money. Two or three lucky people would get to share the bed and the rest of us would pass out in chairs, on the floor, or in the bath.

These guest houses could be pretty rough and ready. I remember one night, somewhere up north, Corky got us a room. It was the middle of winter and we had no heating. It was so cold that none of us could fall asleep. Ken lay on the floor and rolled himself up in the carpet.

At another place, the landlady's teenage daughter was prowling around us, excited that we were a band. Nothing happened, but next morning, at breakfast, the landlady went ballistic at us: "I know what you're after, you bastards! Get out!" We had to leg it without any breakfast.

Once in a blue moon, we'd have a lovely B&B experience. I remember staying in a beautiful place in the Scottish Highlands. The location was idyllic, and the older married couple who ran the place could not have made us more welcome.

We were used to fleapits, but they looked after us so well. The rooms were immaculate, they gave us mountains of breakfast, and as we piled into the van to leave, they serenaded us: "Will ye no come back again?" I was half-expecting them to put on kilts and pipe us out.

When we could afford to stump up for more than one room, and pair up, Ken was usually my roommate. We clicked in that way and rubbed along pretty well. He was a horrible snorer but, then again, so am I. Luckily, we were normally both so pissed that we just passed out.

I'd always tuck into the B&B breakfast but Ken never would. He was so obsessed with his weight ("Look, I can still fit into these jeans, that I've had since I was fifteen!") that I never saw him eat. K. K. Downing was the Patsy Stone of heavy metal.*

When Priest got a major deal, our tour accommodation improved. When we weren't on tour buses, we graduated from crappy B&Bs to *actual hotels*. Mostly they were Holiday Inns, which were identical whether we were in Chicago, Orlando, Miami, Dallas, or wherever.

Occasionally, we'd stay elsewhere to break the Holiday Inn monotony. We went to the legendary Edgewater Inn in Seattle, where you can fish out of the window of your room. Unlike Zeppelin's road crew, we didn't get up to any mud shark–related shenanigans with groupies.

---

*Played by Joanna Lumley, Patsy Stone was the stick-thin, hard-partying, promiscuous, fashion-mag-editor best mate of Edina Monsoon (Jennifer Saunders) in the nineties BBC sitcom *Absolutely Fabulous*. Just picture Ken with a beehive and a cigarette holder. Actually, no. Don't picture that.

Although we'd gone up in the world, we still shared rooms and I carried on pairing with Ken. After our gigs, we'd hit the hotel bar, or bring booze from our backstage rider back to our room to carry on drinking. We never touched the minibar, though. It was *way* too pricey.

I made use of *some* of the facilities, though. After Priest finally started getting our own rooms rather than sharing, I began taking an interest in the XXX movies that you used to be able to get via the little box on top of your hotel TV set.

I never actually rented them out, because (a) they were all straight porn, which obviously wasn't of interest to me, and (b) I would have felt too mortified paying for them at reception when we checked out. But I did work out a nice little cheat shortcut to get myself off.

The XXX movies used to have a short preview feature before the screen pixilated and you had to pay for the goods. Well, *a cock is a cock*, wherever it is going, so I'd cruise the various fifteen-second previews, looking for something that took my fancy.

I'd plan it like a military campaign. I'd play with myself until I was ready—right on the edge—and then hit the best previews for some frenzied masturbatory action. Alone, in countless Holiday Inns across America, I perfected the art of the fifteen-second wank.

Talk about embarrassing! In fact, I can't believe that I've just told you that! But, as I've said before, sometimes it does your soul the world of good to confess . . .

I never got into the clichéd rock star thing of trashing hotel rooms. It just seemed stupid, someone would have to clean it up, and I knew I'd have to pay for it. This was just as well, as the one time that I tried to do it, I was bloody useless.

I can't remember where in America I was, but I was falling-down drunk in my room and suddenly, fuck knows why, I *hated* the TV. I could have just turned it off, but instead I suddenly visualized myself smashing it up and hurling it out the window, like a *real* rock star.

I picked it up, but the wires from the back of the set were welded to the wall—or, if they weren't, I was too pissed to be able to work out how to disconnect them! All I could do was stagger around my room carrying the heavy telly, still firmly tethered to the wall.

This made me totally livid. I just about managed to manhandle it to the room door and I shoved it outside. The power cable was blocking my door so it wouldn't shut properly and, worst of all, the TV was still on—I could hear it chattering away in the corridor.

Fuck knows what the hotel made of me! A *proper* rock star would have smashed up the set with a baseball bat and hurled it out the window. I just sort of humped it out of the room and left it safely in one piece, in the hallway, still turned on. *Pathetic.*

The bane of my life in tour hotels was—it still is!—early morning calls. I'd do anything I could to avoid them, but Jim Silvia would book calls for the whole band at eight in the morning without asking us, even if it was a day off.

After I'd had my beauty sleep rudely disturbed by the receptionist, I'd phone Jim's room and yell at him.

"SILVIA! WHAT DO YOU THINK YOU'RE BLOODY DOING? AGAIN?"

"I told youse! If we leave any later than this, we won't have time to do anything when we get to the next city!"

"I DON'T WAN'T TO DO ANYTHING! HOW MANY TIMES HAVE I GOT TO TELL YOU? IT'S. A. DAY. OFF!"

And repeat . . .

The reason I used to get so pissed off with Silvia is that my sleep is very precious to me. I never stint on it, or take it for granted, because I have suffered from chronic insomnia for my entire life. It's horrible and there is no cure for it.

It's always harder to sleep in hotels than in your own bed, and I think it is a miracle that I've gone on this long in Judas Priest. I'm not joking. I'm amazed at my own tenacity and that I didn't give up touring years ago and just say, "I can't do this any longer—this is fucking shit!"

You can go mad lying awake in the dark for hour after hour. Insomnia is an ordeal and all I can do is try to live with it. Nowadays, when Priest check into a hotel, I have a list of requests and rituals to try to ensure I can grab at least a little shut-eye.

I always want a room on a high floor at the very end of a corridor. This means I only have one shared wall with another room and I'm at least a little insulated from the noise and commotion of businessmen banging around their rooms at 7:30 a.m., getting ready for work.

Thomas and I can't share a bedroom because our snoring drives each other nuts, so he will take the next room to me. I also pull my bed away from the wall because otherwise it works like a soundbox. Headboards will pick up noise from the rooms next to, above, and below you.

I need six pillows on the bed, earplugs, a face mask, and the room to be as cold as possible: *The Exorcist* levels of freezing. I carry a flat box fan with me everywhere I go. I put it as high on the bed as I can, so when I am lying down, I can hear it droning and feel it vibrating the bed.

Even after all this palaver, there is no guarantee I'll get to sleep. I say my prayers and read my book of meditations, just like I do at home. I do the Kegels that I started after my prostate cancer. I've recently started deep-breathing exercises. They actually seem to help, a little.

I even take some pills, although they're not real sleeping pills: they're more like placebos. It's just a psychological thing. And then, of course, if I finally manage to drop off at about four in the morning . . . I wake up and have to go for a piss, because I'm a bloke in his seventies.

Because I've rarely had a good night's sleep, I never go down to the hotel dining room for breakfast. Well, that's not the only reason. The other one is that I bloody resent paying $25 for a cup of coffee and a couple of eggs over easy. As my dad would have said, what a rip-off!

Instead, Thomas goes out and finds the nearest Starbucks or 7-Eleven. He's like a homing pigeon for them! He comes to my room around midday with a carrier bag full of miniature cereal boxes, mini-cartons of milk, and a couple of little fruit juices, and we knock up breakfast there.

After fifty years on the road, I'm a fast and efficient packer. I don't even need a suitcase. I just carry a little roll-on thing with shorts and a clean T-shirt in it. I've never once had cause to use a hotel Corby trouser-press, probably because I rarely wear long trousers.

There are hotels around the world that I always look forward to staying in, because they are beautiful and they treat me so well. Sadly, I can't name them here, to protect my privacy! By the same token, I'd better not share the pseudonym I've been checking in under since . . . forever.

On pilgrimages with Priest, we stay in top-end hotels, but we don't look like typical top-end-hotel guests. We're not walking around in pinstripe suits or smart-casual leisure wear, and wearing our heavy metal gear in la-di-da places can attract snobbery—or even horror.

I remember going for lunch with Thomas in a Paris hotel some years ago. I was in my usual daily wear of shorts and T-shirt, and an old couple done up to the nines at the next table kept shooting me hateful looks throughout our entire meal. *Merde!*

After they had finished, and were on their way out, they stopped at our table. The wife looked down her nose at me, and asked, *"'Ow dare you come 'ere to eat dressed like that? You are . . . practically naked!"*

Blimey! I was quite taken aback. But that's the French for you . . .

HOMETOWN GIGS

Over the last fifty years, Judas Priest have ranged far and wide across the globe and played shows in more countries that I ever imagined I'd visit in my life. Yet I can't deny that, like any band, it always feels very special when we come to play a hometown gig.

It's just human nature. You feel so many emotions playing to your own people: excitement, satisfaction and, most of all, validation. In a way, you're completing a cycle that began when you were a lad living at home and dreaming of conquering the world through music.

It's not quite, "There you are—*showed you!*" That's too negative. It's more that there is truth in that classic phrase "Local boys make good." The *Express & Star*, the paper I read as a kid, calls us "Local legends Judas Priest" every time we come home. It always makes me smile.

Hometown gigs resonate even more when you play venues where you went to gigs in your teens. You look out, and remember standing in the crowd, wondering: *What must it be like to be up there, on that stage? What does it feel like?* Now you know. It feels bloody great.

I saw my idol Freddie Mercury and Queen at Birmingham Town Hall, so it was a huge deal for me when Priest first played there, with Budgie, in 1974. There again, that was a funny old gig: it was Glenn's first gig with the band, which we celebrated by accidentally blowing up the speakers.

It meant even more to me to play Birmingham Odeon. It was a funny venue: a cinema during the day, then they pulled the screen up and held gigs at night. I'd seen so many great shows there, such as Genesis with Peter Gabriel, that headlining the Odeon always felt special.

That was why it hurt us so much when Priest turned up hours late for gigs there not once but *twice*, after we'd been delayed recording *Top of the Pops* in London. I'm not kidding: the memory of being slagged off by our own, pissed-off fans at the venue still makes me wince, forty years on.

One local show with far happier memories is Priest playing Birmingham NEC on 2005's *Retribution* tour, after I'd just rejoined the band. I was back, after years in the wilderness, fronting the band that I loved in a sold-out hometown enormodome show. I mean, *what's not to love?*

When you play hometown gigs, you have a unique connection with the crowd. *They're your people.* You come from the same place and you talk the same. They may even be gawping at you, thinking, *If they made it, why can't I?* They don't feel like fans. They feel like family.

Often, of course, your own family is in the crowd! When they were still alive, my mom and dad came to tons of our local gigs. I used to wonder: *Do they actually enjoy my yowling and the deafening guitars?* I don't think it mattered. They were just proud of their boy, up there.

There may be a slight added pressure to playing hometown gigs. In a way, you feel a little more under the microscope than usual. You find yourself wanting to wrench the volume and the effort up past 11, just to prove to your people that you deserve to be where you are.

I sometimes wonder: Does my accent slip back into yam-yam a bit more when we play Birmingham or Wolverhampton? I suspect it

might. Having said that, I don't walk onstage at hometown gigs and say, "*Orlroight, there, babs? How am yow? It's bostin' to be back!*"
But maybe I should.

TOUR MADNESS

Every metal and rock band loves to set out on a pilgrimage. As I've said, playing live is the best part, the *main point*, of being in a group. And yet there is every chance that at some point on the jaunt, tour madness will set in.

When you're on tour, every day is Groundhog Day. Hotel. Plane or bus. Venue. Gig. Hotel. Plane or bus. Venue. Gig. Hotel. Plane or bus. Venue. Gig. If you're not careful, the identical days will merge into one, and, if you're not even *more* careful, it can do your head in.

The raison d'être of a tour is the two hours you spend onstage every night. They are always fantastic. But there are hours, *acres* of dead time every day leading up to that moment, and how you fill them defines whether (or when) tour madness sets in.

Hanging around for hours with nothing to do, you focus and fixate on the smallest, most unimportant things. You can start to notice your bandmates' characteristics and find them hugely annoying. That's when intra-band tensions set in.

Little things start to wind you up. It can be the way somebody in the band blows their nose, or even how they *sit*. Or you might find yourself sitting in catering, staring at them, getting wound up over nothing at all:

Jesus! Does he have to ALWAYS mash his spuds and gravy up like that? Every single bloody day? Fucking hell, he's eating with his mouth open again . . . and why does he have to LAUGH like that?

These things shouldn't matter, and they *don't* matter, but when you're living on top of each other 24/7, they can feel like they do. That's when you get irritated and start to peck at each other. If you're not careful, it can start to seriously rock the boat.

It's no secret that, historically, most of the friction in Priest used to be between Ken and Glenn (more of which in The Book of Lamentations), but they weren't the only culprits. Familiarity breeds contempt, and we've all had a pop at each other at one time or another. Nobody is a saint.

Ian Hill is the most placid of men, an oasis of calm in the band, but I once saw even him whang his room key at the head of a male receptionist in a French hotel who'd inadvertently given him the wrong key (luckily, he missed). Tour madness gets to the best of us. It creeps up on you.

I used to get as bored, vexed, and riled on tour as the next bloke, and I'd usually escape Groundhog Days via another slug of Jack or line of coke. I'd believe it was helping, but in truth it was helping grudges to fester in my mind and putting me in a downward spiral. It made things worse.

In fact, it wasn't until I stopped drinking and drugging and got sober that I understood the only way to cope with tour madness. And that is to remind myself of The Importance of the Show. Of *every* show.

Sidelined and distracted by booze and drugs, I lost track in the mid-eighties of just how important our music and shows are. It took getting sober to remind me of how important they are to our fans— and to us.

When you're playing the same songs night after night, it's easy to forget people in the crowd may be seeing you for the first time in ten years. Or they may never have seen you before! They've saved up, bought a ticket, ringed the date on their calendar, and counted down for weeks:

Only three weeks until I'm seeing Priest!

Only ten days to go!

Two sleeps to go!

Yay! Tonight's the night!

No longer performing while off my tits, I reminded myself that that was what I used to be like when I was paying to see bands. Well, people are exactly the same with us. And, crucially, that applies to every single show.

When you're a band crisscrossing America and ticking off dates on your tour schedule, it's easy to think of some shows as more important than others. You look at your itinerary and New York leaps out at you more than Cleveland. Los Angeles stands out over Biloxi.

Well, that's bollocks! Every date is as important as the next. Every show will have wide-eyed, super-excited fans who've played Priest albums to death but never seen us live before. And it's our job, our responsibility, our *pleasure* to give them the best show we possibly can.

Now that I'm a sober, seventy-year-old metalhead, every Priest gig means the world to me. A single show today can mean more than the weeks of dates that I dialed in in the eighties, when I was pissed and in my pits. I'm way more serious about gigs now.

The other reason I'm better at coping with tour madness is simple: I'm older. I have the wisdom of age. If I start feeling negative, or down, on the road, I can recognize it and I will know how to deal with it. Because I've been through it before.

Some people like to be on the road forever. A few years ago, at the end of a year-long tour, I overheard Richie and Scott on the tour bus talking about how they wanted to add on extra dates: "Man, we can do at least two more months yet!" It made me laugh, but I loved their enthusiasm.

Every time we end a tour, and I put my key in my front door in Phoenix or Walsall, I have the warm feeling of a job well done. It always feels great to get home—and yet I can guarantee that, within two weeks, I'll be wishing I was back out on the road again.

Well, that's musicians for you. We're never bloody satisfied!

THE BOOK
OF VESTMENTS

Much like Moses and the Israelites in that *other* Bible, metal and hard rock fans used to wander in the wilderness. For years and years, they were ridiculed and patronized. The music they loved was not afforded the respect given to other musical scriptures. The fans responded to this with defiance and by donning a uniform—garments of denim and leather that showed that they belonged to the cult gang of the metal community. These vestments showed they felt pride in that sacred music, whatever its mockers and detractors said.

Metal is no longer a mocked, belittled music, but its disciples still hold firm to its dress code. They still don the vestments. Anywhere in the world that you see a guy or girl in the street in a battle vest, you'll know they are a metalhead who listens to Motörhead, Iron Maiden, Def Leppard . . . and Judas Priest.

And more power to them!

DENIM AND LEATHER

The two defining vestments of metal and rock fans are denim and leather. Priest's Yorkshire musical mates, Saxon, celebrated these two venerated fabrics in 1981 in a great song and album title track:

"Denim and leather brought us all together . . ."

The Bible is not always that keen on mix-and-match fashion. In the Book of Deuteronomy, it advises, "You shall not wear cloth of wool and linen mixed together." Well, I'm sorry, Lord, but some clothes combos just *work*, and denim-and-leather is a lifelong metalhead classic.

As a youth, I found my way to denim pretty quickly. I had a couple of detours along the way. At the end of the peace-and-love sixties, I was swanning around Walsall in an anti-Vietnam olive-green US GI jacket with peace symbols on it. They were all the rage for a while.*

When the seventies dawned, I began the decade very partial to a three-quarter-length herringbone coat that I wore for absolutely everything. I accessorized it with very long hair and loon pants (stylish!) and took that look into my early bands and the very start of Priest.

Then I got bang into denim. I was seduced by the Marlboro Man, the classic American advert of a guy in double denim and cowboy boots smoking a fag on a horse. I could never afford Levi's, but I'd prowl the Oasis clothes market in Birmingham in search of knock-off Wranglers.

Metal fans really appropriated denim with the rise of the battle vest. This was—and is—a sleeveless Levi's vest with patches of the bands you love sewn on the back. As soon as Priest got big enough to have merchandise, a battle-vest patch was one of the first things we flogged.

In the same way that the Marlboro Man glamorized denim, Elvis and James Dean popularized leather. You only had to clock Marlon Brando in *The Wild One* to realize that *leather = trouble*. Put on a leather jacket and you were a rebel, on the fringes of society.

No wonder metal and rock fans fancied a bit of that! I got into both looks big-time and started to wear a regular black leather motorcycle jacket with a sleeveless denim top. I took that combo onstage on a couple of early Priest tours.

The only thing with the classic denim-and-leather get-up of the early seventies was that it could get a bit . . . whiffy. Metal and heavy rock fans in those days were not regular patrons of launderettes or

---

*That jacket was probably a precursor to a military uniform sexual fetish that I developed later in life. But that's another story . . .

dry cleaners. I reckon some jeans and battle vests could stand up by themselves.

I was no different. After my endless nights propping up the bar at my local, the Dirty Duck, my denim and leathers would reek—properly *reek*—of cigarettes and booze. You almost took pride in the authenticity of the stench. Ha! Hygiene was for squares, right?

At most, you'd cover up the odor of your metalhead uniform with Brut ("splash it all over, like Henry Cooper!"*), Old Spice, or a nice big dollop of patchouli oil. Ah, the smell of the seventies! It takes me back . . .

BAND IMAGES

Bands have always known the importance of a snazzy set of vestments. When I started getting into music, in my early teens, the groups I saw on *Juke Box Jury*, *Ready Steady Go!* or the early episodes of *Top of the Pops* all had a certain planned look, whether it was smart or hippie-esque.

Yet the first band whose look really spoke to me was the Beatles. When they ran out at Shea Stadium with their mop-top hairdos and matching Nehru jackets, they looked fantastic. The image represented the music. Next to them, the Rolling Stones were just a bunch of scruff-bags.

I've always said the look of a band, whatever type of music they play, is almost as important as the music. I loved the flamboyant clobber of the early seventies' British glam rockers like Slade and the Sweet, even if they *were* treading a thin line between glamor and panto.†

So, it's bizarre, and unfortunate, that in our early years Priest had no sartorial style at all. We never talked about how we should look and

---

* Henry Cooper was a British heavyweight champion boxer. He fought Muhammad Ali (then Cassius Clay) for the world title, knocked him down and very nearly beat him, but is still best remembered by some for saying "Splash it all over!" in a TV ad for cheap aftershave.

† Oh, yes they were!

we were totally at sea. Just look at the band picture on *Stained Class*. For some reason, I seem to be wearing a fucking schoolboy's tie. *And was I in AC/DC? No!*

Or, Exhibit B: a photo of us supporting Led Zeppelin in California in 1977. I'm in some kind of kimono, Ken's sporting red trousers, Ian's a vision in white satin, Glenn appears to be in an Irish jig band, and Les Binks is in a bloody rugby shirt! Frankly, we were a visual catastrophe.

Who'd have thought we'd go from that dog's dinner to inventing one of the most distinctive images in the history of heavy metal? Yet that was exactly what happened the following year, and the transformation was almost overnight.

Ken had the initial brainwave. He'd been playing around with wearing leather for a bit—there are old Priest photos of him in leather trousers, a leather vest, and a choker. I liked the look, so I went down to London with him to get measured up for some leather gear myself.

When I got it, I loved how it felt and how it made me feel, so Priest had our first ever discussion about our image. Glenn and Ian were up for it and, in no time, we were all decked out in black leather.

When we all got together in our new gear for the first time, it was an absolute epiphany. It felt perfect. We looked at ourselves and we thought, *Oh, THIS is exactly who we are, isn't it? The way we look is the way we sound. Why didn't we realize earlier?*

We weren't doing it for a laugh. We were deadly serious about our new image. I knew we were nicking elements of Marlon Brando, and macho biker wear, and S&M gay subculture, but we took them and turned them into a look that was totally Judas Priest. We reinvented ourselves.

Over the years, people have said our look is camp, but that's wrong. It was never our intention. Others reckon that I started wearing studs and leather as a means to express my repressed homosexuality at the time, but let me make it clear: *That. Is. Utter. Bollocks.*

To anybody who says, "Oh, Rob Halford was sending out a gay message"—*no, I fucking wasn't!* My leather gear was, and is, nothing to do with my personal proclivities or my sex life. Glenn, Ken, and Ian were all wearing that stuff, as well: are they all supposed to be gay?!

I've never been to a dark S&M, kinky-sex bar in my life. I mean, live and let live, but I don't have the slightest interest in them. I started wearing leather for exactly the same reason that I still wear it today. I look in the mirror and I think, *Yeah, that's exactly how I feel inside.*

Admittedly, I did take the look further than the others. I soon got well into studded wrist bands, bullet belts, chains, and leather caps. As for my whip and handcuffs—well, they're great accessories, visual gags for the fans to gawp at and talk about on their way home from the show.

Not too long after we adopted leather, we got our first ever stylist, and our only one to date. Ray Brown has dressed Priest for nigh on forty years now and he is brilliant. When we first began working with him, he was a revelation.

Ray and I sit down before each tour and discuss the general theme that we want, then he goes away and creates a bespoke look for each band member. He always intuits exactly what we need. Ray is totally part of the Priest family. He even lives in Phoenix nowadays, like me.

Ray isn't just a visionary designer: he's practical. Running around the stage in leather trousers for two hours makes you sweaty around the crotch, so Ray suggested I wear chaps instead. It gives you more room to spread your legs, *as it were*, and avoid gusset irritation.

Our leather look has occasionally proved controversial over the years. In 2001, the protest group People for the Ethical Treatment of Animals (PETA) wrote to us asking us to "use our mettle (and our metal) to riff against animal abuse" and to stop wearing leather.

The PETA people said that they were big Priest fans and, with tongue in cheek (I hope!), asked us to rename "Hell Bent for Leather" as "Hell Bent for Pleather"—the synthetic leather substitute. The irony was that we were a step ahead of them, as we had adopted pleather already.

Ray Brown had switched us on to this faux leather a few years earlier. As well as the animal-rights aspect, he pointed out that pleather is a better material to wear on the road because it will take all the rough and tumble of touring. It also washes and cleans up a load easier.

Pleather doesn't have the classic smell of leather ("Smell the glove!" as Spinal Tap famously said), but it's a lot more supple and flexible.

It gets the job done. I still have a few classic real leather things in my homes in Phoenix and Walsall, though. Just for old times' sake.

Priest's image has developed as we've played with it over the years, but some fans love our eighties era. They're hooked on that classic look of me in the black motorcycle jacket, chaps, boots, studded belt, biker cap, dark glasses, and whip, and they want me to look like that forever.

They see that look as the archetypal visual definition of heavy metal. I agree with them, it *is*, but I like to keep things fresh and mix things up a little. I love my Danny La Rue* costume changes during the shows, and some songs need a different look from others.

Priest have been all about leather for more than forty years now, but when we close our encore with "Living After Midnight," I come out in a full-length denim battle vest. It has loads of patches of metal bands I love: Sabbath, Maiden, Anthrax, Pantera, Black Label Society . . .

When I do that, I am saying to the fans, "I am one of you. OK, I may be the singer of the band you have come to see, but I wear the patches and the insignia just like you. I identify with you." I know the value and the importance of making that known to them.

For *50 Heavy Metal Years*, I am wearing gold leather. Or, rather, gold pleather. Fifty is always represented by gold, as in people celebrating their golden wedding anniversary, and I think Judas Priest getting to fifty is worth marking, visually as well as musically.

I'm proud of many things that Priest have achieved, and the heart and the soul of everything is obviously the music: the albums, and the gigs. But I'm also proud that we played a big part in inventing the style, and the design, and the very *look* of heavy metal.

Because I think that we did.

---

*Danny La Rue was a female impersonator and drag queen who was always on telly in Britain in the sixties and seventies. He was ahead of his time and (surprise!) I thought he was great.

HAIR

I talked at the start of this Book of Vestments about the uniform that metalheads don to show their allegiance. Well, no part of that uniform is more important than their hair. Hair is crucial in rock and metal, as it has been in music since Elvis's quiff and the Beatles' mop-tops.

The sixties was the first era that long hair on a male began to represent rebellion. The hippies sported shoulder-length locks to show that they were nonconformists, they were kicking back against the squares, and they didn't "fit into your bourgeois society, *maan!*"

Long hair in heavy metal and rock was initially a continuation of that attitude. It was still a pushback against the straights, but it became more accepted in the seventies. Men could go to work in offices and factories with long hair, as long as it wasn't too out of control.

As a confirmed music freak and trainee metalhead, I had long hair for yonks when I was a young bloke. It was swishing around my collar when I was selling non-tapered trousers at Harry Fenton's, and when I joined my early bands, then started out in Priest.

Ken, Ian, Glenn, and John Hinch all had their hair long as well, but I didn't always stick with that look. My sister, Sue, then a trainee hairdresser, gave me a bubble perm around the time of *Rocka Rolla*. Not many photos of this survive. I'm quite pleased about that fact.

Over the next few years, I veered around, looking for my own separate identity. I flirted with facial hair, both with sideburns and mustaches. In Priest's video for "Don't Go," from *Point of Entry*, I had a weird little 'tache halfway between Hitler and Blakey from *On the Buses.**

I had a full-on beard for a bit, and by the time Priest were playing the US Festival in 1983, my hair was cropped and dyed peroxide blond. I'm still not entirely sure why I adopted that look. I was just experimenting, and I had always fancied blond blokes.

---

* *On the Buses* was an early seventies British sitcom (and thus full of lewd, sexist humor) set in a London bus depot. Blakey was a middle-aged, jobsworth boss. Google him! He wasn't a great visual role model.

I was still blond, but with my hair combed into a mullet at the back, by the *Turbo* era. By then the peroxide was coming in handy. I was starting to get distinctly folically challenged, and dying my hair blond meant that my scalp didn't show through quite as much.

I had to face facts: I was losing my hair.

This is obviously a big deal for a metalhead, but I was quite stoical about it. I'd have loved to have had a sweeping, leonine mane like Sebastian Bach or David Coverdale. However, obviously that wasn't the hand, or the head, that I had been dealt.

I started receding at the front and sprouting a bald patch at the back. I had always told myself that if that started happening, I'd just shave it all off. First of all, though, I tried to fight my incipient baldness.

Rogaine is a pricey men's hair restorer which, in those days, came in a box. For months, I carefully followed their instructions and washed my hair with the shampoo, massaged a clear liquid into my scalp, then combed my hair and let it dry naturally. It made not the slightest bloody difference.

In Los Angeles, I heard about two girls who did hair weaves for all the metal bands, and I went out to their house to see them. They weaved me an insane amount of hair. I thought it looked fucking ridiculous, but they swore it would be great.

"It has to look like this at first, Rob! Just give it a few days to settle in," they said.

"Oh! OK."

I took my new false mane back to my hotel, where I was in excruciating pain. They had sewn the weave so tight to my skull that it was torture. I lay awake all night in agony and, first thing the next morning, I phoned the girls again.

"You've got to take all this shit off!" I told them.

I went back and they took the whole thing out. It took them hours to put in and five minutes to take out. And that was my sole experience of hair extensions.

Around the time of *Painkiller,* I finally took the plunge and shaved my bonce. I did it myself. It reminded me of something I had read years earlier, about Buddhism. One of its tenets is that when a man shaves his head, it helps him to remove his ego.

I felt OK about shaving my head. It took some problems away. Bands crimp themselves like crazy before they go onstage: Well, I didn't have to worry about that anymore! And it was no longer a problem to do photoshoots outside on a windy day!

I didn't feel like I'd lost my power, like Samson. I didn't feel any less heavy metal. The irony is, of course, that a shaven head is also a kind of statement and a way of separating yourself from the norm. It's just as nonconformist as having very long hair:

I'm a gay heavy metal slaphead! Deal with it!

My other recent hair development is my big fuck-off Gandalf beard. It wasn't a conscious choice: it was more that I couldn't be arsed shaving my goatee. So, I stopped, and my beard went off on its own adventure. It's fair to say the reaction on my social media has been mixed:

"Wow, Rob, that's the greatest beard I've ever seen!"

"Fucking hell, Halford, you look like shit!"

And all points in-between. I may keep it, or I may not. Who knows? Who cares? But I have to say, one good thing about it is that I inherited my grandmother's jowls, and my bushy beard helps to conceal them.

I mean, I loved my nan to bits, but the last thing that a Metal God needs is his granny's jowls . . .

TATTOOS

For a lot of metalheads, tattoos are as much a part of their uniform as their battle vest and long hair. They regard getting inked up as a further sign of their identity and an individualistic statement (even surrounded by thousands of others people making the same statement).

Tattoo culture goes back thousands of years and yet, when I was a kid, hardly anybody had them. It was really only sailors, who had often got them in the Pacific Islands, and criminals. It was just those two fringes of society. Most people thought tats were "common."

It's only been in the last thirty or forty years that tattooing has become a dominant global cultural force and tattoo shops have sprung up in all corners of the globe. Today, tattoos are a fashion statement for young people and there's a lot of peer pressure to get them.

When it comes to music, tattoos are very much the province of metal and rock fans. You don't tend to get fans of Radiohead, Coldplay, or Sir Elton John swathed in them. There again, look at Ed Sheeran! He's covered in the buggers, and good for him!

I always instinctively liked tattoos. The attraction for me, initially, was sexual. In my teens, I found and nicked a book of homoerotic photos by a famous US photographer, Bob Mizer. His male models had tattoos—real ones, not fake ones—and they looked incredibly sexy.

I thought about getting a tattoo for the longest time, but I never did it until I was nearly forty (some might say the classic midlife-crisis age—I couldn't possibly comment!). When I made up my mind to do it, I knew I wanted to go to a place that was well-known and reputable.

I wandered into a famous place in LA on Sunset Boulevard called Sunset Strip Tattoo. It used to be run by a guy named Cliff Raven. A lot of rock and metal guys used to go there. I mooched in on a quiet mid-week afternoon and Cliff Raven recognized me and greeted me: "Hey, Rob! Are you thinking of getting some work done, man?"

"I am, but I don't know where to start," I confessed.

"Well, let me help you."

Tattooists have "flashes," which are eight-by-ten-inch cards with various tattoo ideas printed on them. Cliff pulled out literally hundreds of them for me to flick through. As it happened, I did have one idea for what I wanted, and I spotted it pretty quickly.

It was an image of a little devil standing holding a pitchfork. It was—and is—an iconic tattoo in gay underground culture. Whether you were out or not, having that tattoo told other gays that you were gay. And I had long thought that if I ever got a tattoo, that would be it.

"I want *that* one," I said.

Cliff tattooed it on my bicep. It didn't take very long, it didn't hurt too much, and it looked great. "Thank you so much!" I said as I paid him at the end.

"You're welcome," said Cliff. "I'll see you again very soon."

"No, I only want this one," I replied.

"You'll be back," smiled Cliff.

He was right. I was back at Sunset Strip Tattoo within a week.

Cliff knew I would return because he knew tattooing is an addiction. If you have an addictive personality, it *gets under your skin* and you dive right in. The second time I went, I got a large tattoo of a pitchfork on my shoulder. And then, a personal tattooist fell into my lap.

While I was away from Priest doing the Fight band, Jay Jay Brown was my bassist. Jay Jay is also a skilled tattoo artist and, before long, I was at his tattoo studio nearly every day. Tattooists charge at least $100 per hour but, as a mate, Jay Jay did all of mine for nothing.

I couldn't get enough. I was totally into it. I was Jay Jay's canvas and he filled it up. He started with my biceps and arms and then spread out to my front, back, and legs. I would choose designs from his flashes and then we'd mix up the colors.

Jay Jay inked big dragons all over my back. I've always been attracted to dragon imagery. It's fascinating how these mythical creatures exist in cultures all over the world, from King Arthur and Merlin to *The Lord of the Rings* to Japanese and Chinese mythology and folklore.

I love my dragon tattoos . . . but that doesn't mean having them done wasn't bloody painful! It was a real challenge. Some days, I'd be wincing in Jay Jay's studio, thinking, *Why the bloody hell am I doing this? We've been going for hours and it's not even half finished yet! Ouch! Fuck!*

Jay Jay didn't ink all of my tattoos. I had some done when I was living in San Diego, and quite a few by a guy named Jim Watson, who was a very famous tattoo artist in Phoenix. I have no idea how many tattoos I have altogether, but it's certainly more than fifty.

Two of my favorites are PAIN across my stomach and POWER across my lower back. They're two potent, explosive words and there are good and bad definitions of both of them. To me, these two significant words sum up life, or a lot of it.

I have an amusing penis-butterfly tattooed on the back of one shoulder. It's a butterfly's wings attached to a body that is basically a penis—a shaft and a head. I call it "The Flying Cock." I was in Jay Jay's studio one day and spotted it on his wall:

"Hey, Jay Jay! I've got to get that! The Flying Cock!"

I had tattoos all over my body, but it was a psychological leap when I got one on my head. It was a totally impulsive decision. When Fight played São Paulo, Jay Jay introduced me to an incredible Brazilian tattoo artist, Junior, who tattooed a tribalistic bat on one side of my shaven head.

Later, I got a tattoo of a lightning bolt on the other side of my head. This can be infuriating. There is an American football team named the Chargers. They used to be based in San Diego but have now moved to Los Angeles—and their emblem is a lightning bolt.

This can lead to me getting embroiled in a few predictable, repetitive, and slightly tedious conversations when I'm out and about:

"Hey, dude, are you a Chargers fan?"

"No."

"But you've got the Chargers' badge on your head!"

"No, I bloody haven't!"

My parents stayed quiet about my tattoos, but my mom was mortified when I had the ones on my bonce. She never said anything to me, but I heard from my sister, Sue, that Mom had told her, "Oh, I wish our Rob hadn't had his head tattooed! I hope he doesn't get any more!"

Mom might have been right, because my head tattoos put paid to any chance of staying anonymous in public! Once I had a bat and a lightning bolt on my head, there was no mistaking me: *Look, it's Rob Halford!* If I'm out now, I always have to wear a baseball cap.

For that reason, and one or two others, I've thought of having my head tattoos removed. That used to be a horribly painful business that left a nasty scar, but the lasers are so sophisticated now that it's a relatively simple process. Well, maybe I will, maybe I won't. We'll see.

Over the years, I've met plenty of fans with Priest tattoos. I've seen the *Sad Wings of Destiny* angel, the *Screaming for Vengeance* eagle and the artwork from *Painkiller*. I've seen pitchforks, and even my fizzog inked large on chests, backs, and arms! Some of the artistry is unbelievable.

I'm always moved by gestures like that, and very appreciative of them. It's unbelievable that people should love our band and our music so much that they want to ink it on their body forever. I guess it's just a more extreme, devoted example of sewing a badge on a battle vest.

Tattoos have got much better over the years. The quality of the ink is greatly improved. You used to always have to go back to get tattoos touched up but nowadays the ink is spot on and never loses its clarity.

Some of my older tats aren't the force they were. My original little gay devil with his pitchfork is very faded now. Well, he is thirty years old! I have one on my arm and I can't for the life of me tell whether it says HARDCORE or FORBIDDEN. I had it done so long ago that I can't remember.

After a few years of intensive, enthusiastic tattooing all over my body, I haven't had any work done for twenty years or more now. I find it hard to say why that is. My life just moved on. I still love the ones I've got—but will I ever get any more done? Well, NEVER SAY NEVER . . .

Maybe I should get that tattooed somewhere.

BODY METAL

Huge numbers of heavy metal devotees don't just *listen* to metal—they also scatter the element liberally among their everyday vestments. Even more impressively, the most devout and evangelical disciples even incorporate metal into their actual bodies.

The metal world was, beyond question, the first music realm fully to embrace jewelry. It nurtured and developed the look of metal rings, chains, studs, and piercings, and then other forms of rock such as goth and emo followed in its wake.

The classic metal jewelry that everyone knows features skulls, snakes, wolves, or devil insignias. Basically anything to do with the dark side of mortality. Those symbols have a long historical place in our culture, ever since pirates flew skull-and-crossbones flags on their ships.

I think it's fascinating that rock fans and metalheads utilize the imagery of death in this way. The skeleton rings basically say that we are all just walking skeletons. Are we cheating mortality by flaunting this insignia? Is it a pushback against wanting to live forever?

As a teenage music fan, I loved all the extravagant rings that Hendrix used to sport purely because they looked so cool. I wear rings and chains in everyday life, and always if I'm having photographs taken, for exactly the same reason—because it looks more interesting.

When you take a photo, you want to engage the person who will look at it. If I didn't have my Judas Priest rings and crucifixes and spiked wristbands on, the photo would be more boring. I'm expected to look a certain way, and I'm happy to oblige because I love it.

It's the same as when I first grew a goatee beard and somebody asked me, "Why have you done that?" I said, "Because it makes my face more interesting." Likewise, why did I start wearing biker shades or leather caps? To liven things up. We're meant to be entertaining people.

Most metal jewelry concerns itself with looking powerful, potent, and masculine. It tends to use alpha male–type imagery. That doesn't mean that it can't be beautiful. Some specialists craft heavy metal jewelry from pure silver. It sells for hundreds of pounds and it's worth it.

I don't wear exclusively metal insignia. Living in Phoenix, I have some gorgeous turquoise jewelry that I bought from local Native American tribes in Arizona. I often wear it because, like the skull rings, it makes a lifestyle statement that I can embrace.

I'd love to say that I also get all of my metal jewelry from such exotic sources, but I'm afraid most of it comes from China via Amazon Prime! Some days, I have a ring on each finger and every one of them came by that route. All of modern life appears to be made in China.

Every few months I go online, search out rings I don't have, and order them. I have hundreds, in Phoenix and Walsall, because I'm always giving them away to fans. It's never a premeditated thing. We'll just be chatting and I'll hand them a ring as a memento.

I think it's fair to say that, all through my life, I've always liked to go *one step further*. Wearing rings on your fingers is one thing. Inserting metal *into* your body is a different matter entirely.

When I was out of Priest, playing in Fight and getting heavily tattooed, I also got into body piercing. It had intrigued me for a while. I felt that the connection between playing metal and putting it in your body needed to be properly investigated.

My tattooist-bassist Jay Jay was also my portal into this world. He knew friends who ran a Phoenix body-piercing company named HTC, and I went down with a couple of mates and had my nipples pierced. God, the pain was excruciating—but what a fucking power trip!

It hurts to put nipple rings in and it sure hurts to take them out! They had to be removed for my prostate cancer surgery in 2021, and they hadn't been out in three decades. The memory of three nurses, with forceps and pliers, struggling to extricate them at 6 a.m. still makes my eyes water.

This is because your body is constantly striving to push piercings out, if it can. It sees them as foreign invasions into its tissue, although it will tolerate surgical steel a little more. I had to go see my current Phoenix piercer, Marilyn, to get my nipples pierced all over again.

You're probably not surprised to learn that I indulged my penchant for going *one step further* by getting a Prince Albert in my dick. It's largely a sexual thing. Having it put in was as painful as you would expect, but probably not as bad as the nipples, because it was over so quickly.

A weird thing about body piercings is that you always want bigger jewelry. You want to go up to the next level, the next gauge, of the piercing. Marilyn has done all sorts of size adjustments and stretches to my cock piercings since I had my Prince Albert put in.

One occupational hazard of putting heavy metal in your body is going through airport X-ray body scanners. I regularly set the machines off. The security officers ask: "Have you got anything in your pockets, sir?"

"No, it's body jewelry."

"Oh, OK."

They wave their wand over me and it bleeps around my nipples and my cock. Some guards nod me through at that point, but sometimes a buff security officer will ask me: "I'm just going to put the back of my hand against your body part for a second—is that OK?"

It's fine by me, mate! Take more than a second, if you want! Cop a good feel!

Some metal fans take body piercing way further than me and become, quite literally, metalheads. I met one guy who had a flexible stainless-steel ruler inserted into his scalp. *How much must that have hurt?!* He waited for it to heal, then had three metal spikes screwed into it.

There's also a famous guy, The Enigma, who used to be in the Jim Rose Circus and has toured with various metal bands. He is covered in exotic piercings, has coral implants in his skull to look like horns, and has had his eyes tattooed so that the whites are black.

I'm not judgmental towards people like him. Why would I be? I've had enough piercings done myself. Just last year, I went to see Marilyn, my piercer in Phoenix, again, and got my septum pierced. Since then, I've been back to get the next gauge up.

It really winds up some people. I read them online, saying, *What the hell is wrong with you, Halford? You've got that stupid fucking beard, you've just had your septum pierced, and you are seventy years old! Just grow the fuck up!*

I think those (over-)reactions are hilarious! Body piercing, like tattoos, is all about personal self-identity, self-empowerment, and expression. I've had my septum pierced at seventy because it is my body, my choice, my life. And I can't think of anything more heavy metal than that.

THE BOOK OF DISCIPLES

Metal and rock are righteous faiths. We priests, and preachers, in bands strive to compose psalms, testaments, and good old fire-and-brimstone sermons. Yet without willing disciples for us to deliver our scriptures to, they are just so many empty words.

Let's put it this way: a church without a congregation is a mere shell. Everything that we do—Priest or any other band—is aimed at pleasing and satisfying our fans and enriching their lives. We practice our faith not just for ourselves, but for all of us.

We preachers have all been disciples once. That is how we know the power of what we do. We could not do it without our true believers and disciples. They sustain us and we hope that, on some deeply enjoyable but also profound level, we sustain them.

Whether we are penning sacred texts in the studio or taking to the pulpit on our worldwide pilgrimages, Priest do everything with our fans in mind. So, let's bow down and worship our disciples. Because, in so many ways, *they* are the true metal gods.

FANS

If I've learnt one thing in my fifty years in Judas Priest, it is that fans are *everything*. They commit themselves to you and it is solely through that commitment—physical, emotional, and financial—that we are able to carry on making music and living the life that we love.

You have to understand the importance of your fans. You can never be dismissive towards them. They're your bread and butter when they buy your records, come to your shows, and buy your T-shirts. That brings an important responsibility to us to treat them well. To look after them.

The crucial thing for a band to remember is that you don't just have a powerful relationship with an anonymous body called "fans" but with *each individual fan*. Each fan has their own set of beliefs, perceptions, and ideas about you, formed by your music. You have to respect that.

We understand because everybody in Priest has been a fan themselves. We still are. My first infatuation was with the Beatles. Yet as much as I love their music, I think I was mostly drawn to John Lennon—the things he said, the way he spoke, and his fervent desire for world peace.

In Priest's earliest days, we never thought of ourselves as having fans. That felt too presumptuous. We saw a few of the same faces when we went back to play pubs and working men's clubs again, but they never wanted more than a quick word at the end of the gig:

"That were a bostin' show! Ta!"

"Glad yow liked it! Cheers!"

You start getting fans, as such, when you start releasing records. That's when people can take your music home with them and play it again and again. They can scrutinize your artwork, play your album before coming to your gig, and start forming a relationship with you.

Fifty years on, of course, things are very different. When Priest turn up at shows now, there are always fans outside waiting for us. Some have been there since nine in the morning. I don't tend to stop and talk to them then, because I am fully focused and preoccupied on the gig.

After the show is easier. I'm more relaxed, and if there are fans waiting by the stage door, we'll stop and talk and do a few selfies if possible. It all depends on our schedule and where we have to be next, but we will do what we can.

It's a very different thing to have chance encounters in the street. Fans are used to seeing you on the altar of the stage, dressed up to the nines, and performing. When they bump into you out of the blue, mooching down the sidewalk in your civvies, it can blow their minds.

Particularly in America, fans sometimes clock me in the street, rush up to me, and don't know what to say. They don't know how to deal with the moment. I can see their minds whirling:

Oh, my God! I've seen your shows so many times, and I've got all your records at home and your CDs in my car, and I wear your T-shirts! You've been part of my life for all of my adult existence, and I'm such a fan, and now you're . . . here? Right in front of me? NOW?

It feels surreal to them to be suddenly in such close proximity to me. I've had fans break down in tears in front of me. They can't express how they feel and they get tongue-tied. "I don't know what to say!" they often exclaim. "I don't know where to start!"

I totally respect that process, and how they are feeling. I mean, if I'd ever bumped into John Lennon in the aisles at Asda, I'd have been gobsmacked! I can imagine myself thinking, *How do I tell this person what they mean to me? How much they've given me? The life lessons they taught me?*

Of course, I'm not remotely comparing myself to John Lennon! I'm just saying that I understand why fans feel that way, if Priest's music means a lot to them. I don't find those kinds of encounters to be embarrassing in any way. I think they're a beautiful thing.

There's still a part of me, buried deep in my consciousness, that thinks, *What are you so excited about meeting ME for? A berk from Walsall?* But I subjugate that. I appreciate the emotional moment that person is having, because I understand the nature of fandom. It's in all of us.

You can meet superfans who know every nuance of every single record you've ever made. They'll ask things like, "What did you mean by that line in the third verse of that B side that you released on seven-inch in 1980?" And I'll be going, "Er, sorry, which song was that again?"*

Other fans will say, "You saved my life when I was about to end it all! You gave me hope to carry on!" Or: "I made a big, life-changing decision

---

*One superfan is a cool American guy named Dave Hogue who has at his fingertips every nugget about Priest you could ever hope for. Dave has been a huge help when it came to checking info for both this book *and* for *Confess*, and I'd like to sincerely thank him.

thanks to your music!" How do you react to that? Well, you respect what they're telling you. Show them the courtesy that they deserve.

Inevitably, a very small minority of fans will pass a tipping point. They get so into the music and the band that their admiration topples into worship or obsession. That's when they can lose all perspective on the relationship and things start getting twisted.

It has always crossed a red line for me when fans hunt down my home address and send me things to sign. It's invading a space that I want—I *need*—to keep for myself. When I don't do it, they go online and slag me off. I read their posts and I just think:

I didn't ASK you to track down where I live and send me ten CDs to sign! And, in any case, even if I signed them, how am I supposed to get them back to you? Walk down to Walsall post office, and stand in line?

I've had fans turn up outside my home, both in Phoenix and Walsall. I see them on my security cameras. They just stand staring at the house or pose with the horns up. Or they leave notes in my mailbox: "Rob, I'm not a stalker, but I was passing and hoped that you could say 'Hi!'"

The other week in Phoenix, a teenage girl turned up at the end of my drive for three days in a row. She just sat on a curbstone by my gate with her hood up, like a brooding elf. I had to wait until she had left before I could go out for a walk.

When this happens, you have to be aware of the psychological depths of the situation you are dealing with. You have to realize that it can be very dangerous, both for you *and* the fan. From Lennon to Dimebag Darrell, we've lost people in music that we should never have lost.

Consciously or subconsciously, Priest are more aware than any other band of the tragedy that can ensue when fans' relationships to music go wrong. We witnessed it firsthand when those two young fans in Reno, James Vance and Raymond Belknap, went through with their suicide pact.

The following court case was incredibly disturbing for us, but probably the most upsetting aspect was that those two guys lived for Priest. They were in a dark place, but our music had helped to sustain them in their lives. Then we were falsely accused of telling them to *end* those lives.

There is no upside to this sort of relationship between fans and band. It went so catastrophically wrong in this case and, ultimately, we had no control over it. It was all so far out of our arena. All we can say, *still*, is RIP.

It's important to remember, though, that that tragic case, and fans who cross a line in general, are a tiny minority. For 99 percent of people, fandom is a positive, life-enhancing experience. Taking joy and inspiration from a band that you love is a wonderful process.

As an impressionable adolescent, that was how it was for me with the Beatles and Hendrix. And if millions of fans have had a comparable relationship with Judas Priest over the years, I'm humbled and grateful.

Because it is a very precious thing.

AUTOGRAPHS AND SELFIES

It's human nature for fans who meet bands to want to take away a little piece of them: a souvenir of the encounter. Back in the mists of time, the traditional way for them to do this was to ask for an autograph.

I've read about rock and pop stars who were so determined to get famous that they practiced signing their autograph before they had even got well-known. I never did anything like *that*, but starting to get asked for my autograph was an unexpectedly nice feeling.

It's a sweet request, really, isn't it? "Can I have your autograph, please?" It may make no sense logically—*Why do you want my name on a piece of paper?*—but a fan can take it home and look at, again and again: *He signed that himself! With his own hand! Right in front of me!*

I've got quite a flamboyant signature and, in the early days of Priest, I'd carefully write it as neatly as possible when requested:

To xxxx. With best wishes,

Half a century and tens of thousands of autographs later, I've curtailed my style somewhat. To speed things up, especially if there are scores of fans outside a hotel or venue wanting my signature, I just write RH.*

Priest's induction into the world of organized autograph-signing came in the eighties when we started doing in-store record-shop signing sessions. Fans would buy our albums and queue up for hours for a chance to say "Hi!" and get them autographed.

I loved doing them from the off, as it was a great chance to meet fans in different cities (plus we sold a lot of records!). My only grumble has always been that we have to sit behind a table to speed things up. I'd rather be closer to the fans and have more chance of a chinwag.

We'd get asked to sign all sorts of weird shit at those sessions. I've always been a bit squeamish about signing body parts like arms, legs, or heads, but I'll generally do it. Sometimes, the fan will go off and have the autograph turned into a tattoo then put a video of it on YouTube.

I thought we'd signed the lot: records, CDs, photos, T-shirts, arms, tits, bums, bald heads. I thought I'd seen it all. I changed my mind in 1986, at a US *Turbo* signing session, when a woman in her twenties plonked twin babies on the table. They were barely weeks old. *Days,* maybe.

"Can you sign these, please?" she asked us.

"What?"

"Can you sign my babies?"

Bloody hell!

We had a quick band conflab. "I can't sign a baby!" I muttered, aghast. That was our consensus view, so we politely demurred and signed the babs' blankets instead. Mommy seemed happy enough with that.

Priest have been lucky over the years. We haven't had any Spinal Tap–like in-stores where nobody turned up. That's just as well. If we

---

*It's not just me. When I've seen footage of Lady Gaga emerge from a gig or film premiere and pass through a mob of fans, her pen briefly touching the hundreds of pieces of paper they're holding out, I think, *Yep, she'll just be writing LG!*

ever did, and we had a hapless Artie Fufkin–style record-label rep who had organized it, I really *would* kick his ass!

We don't do as many record-store signings now (there aren't as many record stores!), but our fans still love 'em. We did a big one at the Hard Rock Cafe in New York for *Painkiller*. We had an escort of bikers on Harleys, and thousands of metalheads turned up. It was a cool day.

I said earlier that being asked for your autograph is a sweet request. Well, I would now like to qualify that statement slightly. The request is notably less charming when it comes from a member of one particular bloody tribe: eBayers.

You can always tell an eBayer. They turn up at stage doors, or outside tour hotels, with not a handful but *hundreds* of photographs for you to sign. And you know that as soon as you've done it, they'll run off home and flog the lot on eBay.

They're picky sods, as well. Some of them have been pursuing me for years and know my autograph off by heart. I'll be quickly, grudgingly, whacking off a few RH signatures for them, and they'll say, "Can you do it properly, please?"

"What?"

"Can you do the full 'Rob Halford'?"

"No, I bloody can't!"

They get everywhere and they always seem to know where we're going to be. When we started the *50 Heavy Metal Years* tour in Pennsylvania in 2021, Thomas and I flew from Phoenix to Philadelphia to meet up with the rest of Priest.

We got to Philly about eleven at night. The airport was almost deserted as we got the escalator out of baggage reclaim. And there they were, at the foot of the escalator—six eBayers, with not so much as one Covid mask between them, with their arms full of band photos.

To add insult to injury, as soon as I began signing stuff for them, one or two of them starting taking photos and videos of me on their phones. They do that to prove that I really have signed the things they're selling and they're not fakes.

I don't always sign their contraband for them. It depends on my mood. When I *do* sign, Thomas rolls his eyes and tells me I'm a fool for doing it because I'm just making the eBayer problem worse for myself. I have to admit, I think that he's probably right. Maybe I'll stop . . .

Of course, apart from the mercenary eBayers, there are far fewer fans asking for autographs nowadays than there used to be. Because they all want selfies instead.

Everybody in the world has a mobile phone today, which means that everybody in the world is a photographer. If I venture out, wherever I may be, it's a rare day that I don't get a cell phone stuck in my face a few times.

I always prefer it when people ask me first if I mind them taking a photo with me, rather than them just running up and start snapping away. But, as I said, I know some fans lose the capacity for rational thought when they bump into me unexpectedly. So, I make allowances for that.

If I'm at work on Priest business, at a gig or a TV studio, it never feels at all intrusive. If I'm out shopping, or quietly having lunch with Thomas, it can feel a little more so, but I'll generally go along with the request. It takes me a second, and it's as easy to say "Yes" as "No."

People ask for selfies in different ways in different parts of the world. In Britain, there is usually a certain polite reserve. In America, some fans are more likely to get in my face or fling their arms around me. This can obviously present problems during a pandemic.

Yet even US fans are shrinking violets next to the reaction we get in some parts of the world. If we fly into somewhere like Mexico City, the mayhem starts at the airport as the airline and passport control staff abandon their posts to get selfies with us.

We're waiting by the baggage carousel, and as the exit doors open and close as people go through them, we see—literally—thousands of fans waiting outside. *Oh, no!* And we know we have to go through them to get to where our cars are waiting, because there's simply no alternative.

Once we're in that throng, the mood can get horribly close to hysteria. The fans know that they only have a few seconds to get a selfie or an autograph, or to give you the gift they've brought for you. They can get super-aggressive and it all becomes a little bit primordial.

The situation can get dangerous. People can get trampled. I've signed something for one fan and seen another one snatch it off them straightaway, or seen fights break out between fans. I appreciate the passion for Priest, but it feels a relief to get safely in the car and away.

Japan is another story entirely. Japanese fans are incredibly polite and respectful, but they hunt us down with relentless efficiency. We end up doing nonstop selfies at every single hotel and train station. Fandom there is on a different level entirely.

Wherever in the world I'm doing selfies with fans, there is always one universal factor. As soon as they stand next to me and we start beaming for the camera, I put the devil horns up. It's automatic, almost like a reflex action.

I couldn't stop doing it if I wanted to—and I don't want to. The fan will put the horns up as well and it's a little joint bonding moment, a mutual validation of our relationship and of heavy metal, the music that brings us together. It's what it's all about, and it's why we're both there.

It's once in a blue moon that I object to doing a selfie, because I respect our fans and I'm still a fan myself. And you can bet if I ever see Paul McCartney out and about, I'll be in there for a selfie like a shot! I might even ask him for an autograph . . . and I *won't* be selling it on eBay.

HEAVY METAL PARKING LOT

In the late eighties, I began hearing about a new cultural phenomenon with Judas Priest at its core. I'd be doing a magazine or radio interview in America, and the journalist or the DJ would ask me, "Dude, have you seen *Heavy Metal Parking Lot?*"

"No!" I said, the first time I was asked. "What is it?"

I hadn't seen it, and it was quite a few weeks before I did. This was years before the internet, so you couldn't just pop onto YouTube to have a gawp. The only way to see it was to get hold of a bootleg VHS videotape, and I didn't manage to do that for yonks.

And when I finally did, and I saw it, I absolutely loved it.

Heavy Metal Parking Lot was filmed by two guys who took a portable video camera to the car park of the Capital Centre in Landover,

Maryland, on May 31, 1986. They went down a few hours before Priest were playing a headline show and they filmed the tailgate parties.

Tailgate parties are a huge thing in America. Before gigs, or big football games, fans go down to the arena parking lot with BBQs and beers, and spend hours eating, drinking, and looking forward to the event they're all gathered there to see.

It's a party and a celebration and everyone is there to support and talk about their team or their band and, largely, get wrecked along the way. Tailgate parties have a real metal-community spirit. Everyone is there for the same reason, and they're paying homage to the tribe they love.

We'd seen tailgate parties before our gigs from a distance. Our tour bus would pull into an arena parking lot and fans would wave and give us a beery chant of "Priest! Priest! Priest!" But we'd never seen one close up, so *Heavy Metal Parking Lot* was quite an eye-opener.

Like many people, my first reaction to it was to laugh—affectionately, not in any kind of condescending way. I loved the way that there were so many larger-than-life characters that just leapt off the screen, and that they were all having the times of their lives.

Heavy Metal Parking Lot wasn't even twenty minutes long, but some of the personalities in it have become legendary. A beer-swilling, shaggy-haired girl gave the camera a glazed stare when asked, "What would you say if you met Rob Halford right now?"

"Ah'd jump his bones!" she declared, clearly without the first idea of my sexual orientation. I believe that slogan actually made it on to a T-shirt. If it didn't, it certainly should have.

Fans held up bedsheets with the band name stenciled on them. A guy who could hardly stand performed a near-pitch-perfect impersonation of me singing "Living After Midnight." And Zebra Man, a heroically drunk dude in a lurid zebra-pattern catsuit, delivered a heartfelt address.

"Heavy metal rules!" he yelled. "All that punk shit sucks. It doesn't belong in this world, it belongs on fucking Mars, man! ... And Madonna can go to hell as far as I'm concerned. She's a dick ..."

A lot of fans were spectacularly trashed and playing up to the cameras. Some of the guys could have been prototypes for *Beavis and Butt-Head.* Yet my takeaway from the film wasn't remotely to mock them. It was to admire just how much they loved metal and loved our band.

A lot of people in the music industry sneered at heavy metal in those days. They felt the music was primitive and the people who listened to it were stupid and illiterate. These ill-informed, snobbish critics may have felt that *Heavy Metal Parking Lot* confirmed their prejudices.

They. Could. Not. Have. Been. More. Wrong. It was metal fans rallying around the flag and becoming even more supportive of the music they loved. I've watched it again, now and then, over the years, and I think it's a beautiful celebration of everything we believe in about metal, then *and* now.

There is an innocence about it. The world has become way too serious for my tastes now, with regards to the way that we dissect and analyze music. We have woke culture, and cancel culture, and everybody trying to pull things apart. Back in the day, gigs were just a great night out.

Not everything in *Heavy Metal Parking Lot* has aged well. At the start of the film, a twenty-year-old fan announces he is about to join the Air Force. A girl next to him explains she is thirteen years old. Then the guy has got his tongue down her neck and is snogging her face off.

Today, in these post-#MeToo days, you blanch when you see it: *What is that grown man doing, kissing that underage girl?* Back then, it just seemed like a spur-of-the-moment thing and both of them playing up to the cameras. Times, and sensibilities, change.

There is another telling moment, and sign of the attitudes around in the eighties, towards the end of *Heavy Metal Parking Lot.* A shirtless guy flashing the devil horns runs through his thoughts on the various Priest members.

"Ian Hill, I'm a former bass player, you're an inspiration of mine!" he declares. "Everybody else, you're rocking! Robert Halford, I don't know about *you,* but everybody else, you're definitely dynamite! Yeah!"

Now, I don't want to besmirch this guy, but there is a fair chance that his comment betrayed his suspicions that I might be gay. I was still firmly in the closet then, but music-industry tongues were wagging and rumors were flying.

With my short hair dyed peroxide blond, I guess I also looked quite different from the rest of the band at this point. I can imagine the guy's possible thought process: *Whoa! Halford looks like a faggot! I daren't say I like him in case these dudes think I am, too!*

I may be wrong and, even if I'm not, I don't say this to come down on that fan. But his words remind me *exactly* why I kept my homosexuality secret for so very long, terrified that if I were to come out it would ruin everything, not just for me but for everybody in Priest.

Heavy Metal Parking Lot became a cult classic. Apparently, it was a big favorite on Nirvana's tour bus. I hope it gave poor Kurt a few chuckles. He certainly needed them. Best of all, Steel Panther even named a 2019 album *Heavy Metal Rules* in tribute to Zebra Man's passionate speech! I hope the guy realized this, and that he was pleased.

I'm still very fond of *Heavy Metal Parking Lot*. It was really a microcosm of the metal world as it was turning into a major force in US society and culture. It captured how its fans looked, dressed, spoke, and thought. It's a piece of prime, loving anthropology.

The guys who did it attempted other movies in the same vein, but none of them took off. I'm not sure they chose the best subjects. I mean, *Neil Diamond Parking Lot* was never going to have the same edge. And I'm not sure *what* to say about *Harry Potter Parking Lot!**

Twenty years after *Heavy Metal Parking Lot* came out, a follow-up film tracked down some of those original fans. I'd love them to do it again now. Where is the girl who wanted to jump my bones? What is Zebra Man up to, or the fan who "didn't know about" Robert Halford?

Who knows? But I would guarantee you one thing—they would still be Priest fans and metalheads. Because those guys were not part-timers.

---

* I promise, I'm not making these up!

SOCIAL MEDIA

I try to imagine what it would have been like, more than fifty years ago, to be able to sit in my bedroom, write something to John Lennon or Jimi Hendrix, and know that they'd be able to read it instantly. The very thought blows my head off.

Yet that is what it is like for metal and rock fans nowadays. Social media has democratized everything and made every metal and rock prophet accessible to their disciples. Kids can talk directly to their music heroes in a way that was utterly impossible back in the day.

There are so many social media channels: TikTok, Snapchat, Telegram, Instagram, Twitter. Bands engage with them to varying degrees. I'm an enthusiastic user because I love being able to drop in at any time to see what Priest fans are thinking and saying.

I'm active on Instagram and Facebook and I do everything myself. Some artists have social media teams to handle that side of things, but I write every post and choose every photo. Any selfie that you see, I've always taken it.

I post fun stuff: music I love, old photos, and pictures of cats. Why cats? Because I love cats! I got into a regular ritual on both the sites of Metal Mondays, Throwback Thursdays, and cat photos every Saturday. Which I obviously call Caturday.

It's a nice routine, but it can bring its own pressures. If I am busy, or I forget to post when I'm due, the fans want to know why. In the nicest possible way, they get on my back:

"Hey, Halford! It's Caturday—where's the cat picture?"

"Oi! It's Sunday—why haven't you wished us Metal Blessings yet?

The other danger, as a bloke in his seventies, is repeating myself. I've now done more than 1,400 posts on Instagram. Before I post an old photo, I have to scroll through every single existing pic to check that I haven't used it before. It does my bloody nut in.

Some fans don't believe it's actually me running my sites. Sometimes I get people on Facebook and Instagram saying, "This isn't Rob posting. He doesn't write this. Somebody else does it for him."

"Yeah," someone else will agree. "If he's reading this, why doesn't he say something to us now?"

Good question—why don't I? I think because that way, madness lies. If I start engaging in those conversations, they will never end. What am I supposed to say? If I tell them, "No, it's really me!" they probably still won't believe me: "Nah, you're just someone who works for him . . ."

By the same token, I don't get involved in arguments on these sites. On the *50 Heavy Metal Years* tour, I've had a few fans post they're not going to come to see us because Priest are insisting on COVID-19 vaccine passports at the shows and that we're "taking our personal freedom away."

It's nonsense, firstly because Covid passports make sense to protect our fans from illness, and secondly because the rules have nothing to do with us: governments and promoters like Live Nation put them in place. But I don't want to start arguing with our fans. So, I keep schtum.

Over the years, I've had hundreds of thousands of likes and comments from my currently 660,000 (and rising) Instagram followers. The vast majority of them are overwhelmingly positive. It's a fantastic forum to show love and appreciation for each other, the band, and metal.

It's always great to log in every morning and see thousands of people liking my posts and leaving supportive messages:

"Horns up, Rob!"

"Love you, man!"

"The only Metal God!"

"Priest rule!"

At certain times, social media comes into its own. When I went public, late in 2021, about surviving prostate cancer and my successful surgery, thousands of people logged in to offer their congratulations. Some had been through the same experience themselves.

I posted advice to male fans to do what I didn't do: take preventative action and get their prostate checked before it's too late. Some fans acted on that and posted that their doctors detected cancer at an early stage and tackled it, and that they were now all clear.

That was great, and then there were thousands of people writing, "Rob, man! You beat fucking cancer! Yeah!" Or, "So glad you made it through! You rock!" I appreciated every comment. There's nothing better than the metal community coming together to support one another.

Naturally, not everything is so positive. The world isn't like that. It's well-known how poisonous social media can be, and how it can attract trolls. Like every well-known person, I sometimes attract cruel and nasty comments because that is how some people get their kicks.

Late in 2021, I posted an old photo of me sprawled across a Harley-Davidson naked except for a leather jockstrap, cap, boots, and gloves. I just wanted to see what reaction it would get. In fact, I even captioned it "clickbait."

It's fair to say that the reaction was mixed. As I write this, it has had 51,000 likes and 1,500 comments. Alongside the amused compliments—"Hot rockin'!" "Love the pic!" "Leather rebel!"—I was also regaled with the following responses:

"What are you, fucking seventy-something? Have some integrity!"

"He made good music, now nothing but politics.[*] Sad!"

"Thanks for helping me to be a man and then faking it all, sell-out!"

"Really? You're a queen, by the way. Your book sucks, boomer. Thanks for nothing."

The big test is how you react to comments like that. I'm not going to pretend that they're nice to read. Negativity can get you down. When I read about Justin Bieber closing down all of his social media

* Huh?

channels because he'd had enough, I understood and I sympathized. Even though he did return pretty quickly.

At the same time, I won't let other people have that much control over my decision-making in life. I have to accept that, as a public figure, people have ideas and opinions about me. I may not like all of them, but I can't control what people say.

To me, trolls are like water off a duck's back. I don't give their mean-spirited comments any reaction because they don't deserve it. I know some people say outrageous things just to get feedback. I'm not going to waste my time worrying about keyboard warriors.

I've reined back my social media slightly since I turned seventy. I don't always post on Caturday or Throwback Thursday. Sometimes, I wonder: *Why do I keep posting pictures of myself? Am I chasing some strange kind of validation? Should I just call it a day?*

Yet social media has so many strengths and plus points. I'm lucky in that I get so many more positive comments than negative ones, and reading them is always uplifting. It's my hotline to our fans and how they are feeling, and I love having it.

Even twenty-five years after I came out, I still get people on Instagram or Facebook telling me, "Because of you, I was able to tell my mom and dad, and my friends, I was gay. I stopped living a lie." And just one of those stories is worth a hundred toxic insults from trolls.

I suppose, in a way, band websites and social media are an infinitely more sophisticated update of the fan clubs we used to have for the Beatles or the Stones or the Temptations. They're a way to get closer to bands you love and feel like you're in contact with them.

What I love most is the sense of community. Behind the front page of my Instagram, and my daft cat pictures, there are thousands of people messaging and talking to each other about Judas Priest, and metal, and the music they love. *That* is the important stuff.

Ultimately, my social media is fun for me. I enjoy doing it and posting funny stuff and getting direct reactions from our fans. I'll carry on doing it until it stops being fun, and then I'll knock it on the head. *Delete.*

THE BOOK
OF CHRONICLES

Metal and rock bands move in mysterious ways and those ways are now chronicled in every form of media imaginable. It has never been easier for fans to keep in touch with artists and know exactly what they have been doing, are doing, or are about to do.

In addition to social media, disciples can now worship at numerous specialist TV and radio channels, access countless online magazines, or even listen to metal priests and prophets for free on (spit!) Spotify or Apple Music. But it was not always thus.

Back in the Old Testament days of the seventies, the only scriptures available for music fans to devour were the music papers—every week in Britain, monthly in America. They had some good journalists, and plenty of others who were high on their own egos and reputations.

Once they had endured this wrist-merchant hell, metal and rock bands could journey on into a wider world of photo sessions, radio, and TV appearances. Why, some of the most venerated of their number have even made it to having books written and movies made about them!

It was a media world of plenty . . . and then the internet, and streaming, came along and fucked everything up. Read that terrible tale, and many more, in this Book of Chronicles.

MUSIC PRESS

The British weekly music press documented the world of rock and (less so) metal for many decades . . . and yet, I wonder if they should belong not in Chronicles but in a separate Book of Judges? Because these self-appointed arbiters of taste truly believed they had the ability to make or break a band.

They may even have been right.

From the mid-sixties through the seventies, I devoured the weekly music press—and there is no other word for this—*religiously*. Every Wednesday, I skipped off to WH Smith on Park Street, in Walsall, to buy NME (*New Musical Express*), *Melody Maker*, and *Sounds*.

There was no alternative. For young music fans, they were the *only* source of information on your favorite band's record releases, tours, and interviews. They told you everything about British artists and also had access to big American bands, which was cool.

I bought all three papers but they all had different characters. As I got more and more into hard rock, I found myself gravitating towards *Sounds*. It was the first paper I saw use the phrase "heavy metal," and it always seemed to have the best metal coverage.

When I joined Priest and we started playing decent-sized gigs, I longed to get reviewed in the inkies.* If we heard a journalist was coming to a gig, it was exciting. It was one reason that we were so thrilled to play Reading Festival: we knew we would get written about.

This went up a notch when the papers actually started talking to us, around the time of *Sad Wings of Destiny*. When Corky told us NME wanted to interview us, we felt like we were joining the club. We'd been on the outside, looking in. Now, we were in the game.

"Wow! We're really getting somewhere now!"

Yet when we started actually doing the interviews, they weren't all that interesting. They were often a bit flat. The questions tended to be the same:

---

* NME, *Melody Maker*, and *Sounds* got called the inkies for a very good reason—the ink came off on your hands when you read them.

What inspires you?
What other bands do you like?
What are your ambitions?

The band would be interviewed together, but the journalists always seemed keenest to find out what the singer, and maybe the guitarists, thought. I've never been averse to a good chinwag, so I'd avail the lucky writer with a full range of Halford opinions.

Sometimes, after the journo had gone, Ken or Glenn would collar me: "Oi! Why did you dominate the interview?"

"What? I never! He just asked questions and I answered 'em!"

"Well, maybe give someone else the chance to answer a few as well, next time!"

"Huh! I won't say a single word next interview, if that's what you want!"

Obviously, I didn't keep to that.

Yet our honeymoon period with the British music press was pretty short. We got some decent reviews for *Sad Wings of Destiny*, with writers saying things like "A band to look out for" and "Check them out when you can!" But *those* weren't the ones we remembered.

Sounds ran a condescending, dismissive review of the album, which ended with that classic critics' remark: "Don't give up the day jobs." It was a shitty one-liner and it hurt. We felt as if all the effort we'd put into making the album had been ignored for a cheap gag.

It made us wary of the music press, and we soon realized that we were right to be. The British weeklies had a reputation for stabbing bands in the back, and they deserved that reputation. We'd do a sit-down interview with one of them and the published article would bear no resemblance to it.

It would all be the journalist's highfalutin opinions on the world, with maybe one or two quotes from us. Or they'd simply make up things we hadn't even said! It felt like a complete waste of time, but we were told by our managers we had to keep doing them anyway.

It was around this time that, between ourselves, Priest started calling music journalists "wrist merchants." I'd love to say that we made it up, but I think I just read it somewhere and nicked it. It seemed to suit the journos. They jerked their typewriters, and frothy effusions came out.

Our attitude towards press interviews soon changed from seeing them as a thrill to regarding them as a chore. As Priest got bigger, the papers started asking just to talk to me, Glenn, and Ken. Ian, and whoever our drummer was at the time, weren't insulted. They were relieved!

I enjoyed much more talking to the monthly magazine, *Beat Instrumental*, which was read by musicians. A cool journalist, Gary,* asked us all about writing songs, band dynamics, and studios, rather than flippant rubbish. It felt a classier experience all around.

Priest felt even more alienated from the mainstream music press in the punk years. The Clash, the Sex Pistols, and the Damned came along, and suddenly they were all the inkies wanted to write about. They thought that heavy metal was washed-up and dead.

The only mention we'd get in *NME*, *Melody Maker*, or *Sounds* would be if our record label or tour promoter bought the back page for an ad, which cost an arm and a leg. I remember getting agitated once because I got a copy of *Sounds* and saw that our sold-out tour only had a quarter-page ad.

I phoned our management: "Bloody hell, why has our tour only got a quarter-page ad and not a full page?"

"Er, we don't need a full page, Rob? It's sold out."

Priest were so used to being pilloried, ridiculed, or, usually, ignored by the weekly press that we were amazed at the end of the seventies when the New Wave of British Heavy Metal came along. It was the last thing that we expected.

The New Wave of British Heavy Metal, or NWOBHM, was coined by a *Sounds* journalist, Geoff Barton, and picked up by others on the same paper. It was an attempt to create and celebrate a scene around the new breed of metal bands emerging at the time.

---

*I got quite matey with Gary and his girlfriend at the time, who was a white witch. She had long black hair and always wore a cloak. Once she engraved for me a wooden talisman as a good-luck charm. I wore it onstage so much that it went green from my sweat. I wish I still had it.

Sounds began running loads of interviews and reviews praising bands like Motörhead, Iron Maiden, Def Leppard, Saxon . . . and Priest. Geoff Barton, who became a mate, was a big figure in chronicling the scene, and so was a guy named Neal Kay.

I could tell from the start that Neal was one of us. He was a DJ and a total metalhead who ran a rock club, The Bandwagon, in the back room of a pub named the Prince of Wales in an obscure part of northwest London called Kingsbury. Neal's club nights were legendary.

I went down a few times and it was just a sea of headbanging blokes in battle vests. The place would go mental when Neal played Motörhead's "Ace of Spades." Neal used to compile a "heavy metal chart" for *Sounds* every week. I'd always check anxiously to see if we were in it.

Priest were gratified and grateful for the NWOBHM, and it was nice to be praised in the music papers for a change. We weren't exactly part of it, though. Most of the bands coming through were brand new, and we were already five albums to the good.*

We felt more *vindicated* by the movement. It seemed a validation of what we were doing, and proof that heavy metal *wasn't* dying out: in fact, the exact opposite was happening. Maybe we'd been among the building blocks, helping to create the desire for the scene that was growing.

One upshot to the explosion in heavy metal after NWOBHM was the creation of exclusively metal magazines such as *Kerrang!* and *Metal Hammer*. It was great reading them and talking to them because there was no snark. They were metalheads. They were our people.

There was also no snark when we started talking to American mags. They were notably more enthusiastic and positive than their British counterparts and they took Priest seriously. Getting in *Creem, Circus, Hit Parader*, or, later, *Metal Edge* or *Metal Maniacs* was a big deal.

Nowadays, of course, virtually none of these magazines still exist. Even those weekly British goliaths *NME, Melody Maker*, and *Sounds* are

---

* In fact, I remember Ken being worried that NWOBHM would lift those new bands onto our level without them putting in all the graft that we already had. But that's Ken for you!

no longer dishing out insults and making and breaking bands. The world went online and music journalism went with it.

Online, I look at *Kerrang!* and *Metal Hammer* but mostly read *Loudwire*. It's good at getting the news across, even if it sometimes gets a bit too *TMZ* for my liking. I mean, a recent headline said: YOU CAN BUY ONE OF KURT COBAIN'S CHILDHOOD HOMES! Do I *really* want to read that?!

On the very rare occasions that we talk to a print mag now, it will be something like *Classic Rock*. Now that we're a long-standing, venerable band they treat us with respect. Magazines know, as do bands, that the old rules have changed. These days, they need us more than we need them.

Music journalists used to rule the roost, in the UK at least, and now they don't. I can't pretend I'm sorry. The problem was, music writers don't know what it's like to be in a band: the hopes, the dreams, the setbacks. They don't know what being a musician *feels like*.

I always found the idea that music writers were tastemakers, leading fans by the hand to *this* band or *that* band, to be condescending. They can decide for themselves, ta very much! The internet has done a lot of crap things, but one good one is it has put the fans back in control.

Why? Because they can listen to *what* they want, *when* they want, with the flick of a dial or button. They don't need no education from wrist merchants! Metal, rock, and music as a whole belong to the masses.

For all of my fond youthful memories of them, I don't mourn the passing of *NME*, *Melody Maker*, or even *Sounds*—and yet they gave me a sweet, touching moment a few years ago. A clue that, maybe, I wasn't the only Halford heading down to WH Smith in Walsall on Wednesdays.

After my mom passed in 2016, my sister, Sue, was sorting through her things and she came across some old scrapbooks. Sue opened them up and found that they were full of neatly cut-out and glued-down newspaper and magazine pieces about Priest and about me.

I had no idea Mom was doing that: she never said a word to me about it. The thought of her privately chronicling my progress is so poignant it can move me to tears. But I guess it shows that, all through my long life and career, Mom was proud of me and believed in what I was doing. And who can ask for any more than that?

PHOTO SHOOTS

Let me hit you with two clichés in one go. Two for the price of one!

1. Every picture tells a story.
2. A picture is worth a thousand words.

They're two pretty commonplace statements, right? Yet both of them are true, and significant, when we come to consider the mystical and mysterious art of the band photo shoot.

Photo shoots are *so* important for metal and rock bands. You're trying to do something very difficult. You're trying to capture the essence of the band in an image: to establish a visual connection with the music. It's a statement of your mission, your purpose, your very existence: *This is what we are! This is us!*

For a while, at least, this can be a very hard thing to do. And Priest were certainly a long way from doing it when we did our debut photo shoot, taken by our first manager, Corky, with his trusty Kodak Instamatic in a local Black Country beauty spot in 1974.

I look at that photo now, nearly fifty years on, and I boggle. We're in a snowy wood, a gaggle of bad sweaters, awkward poses, and gormless facial expressions, looking like we've been caught doing something we shouldn't. We look utterly clueless, and so we were.

I mean, does that photo say "Heavy metal!"? *No!*

When Priest first started getting a small modicum of success, we began doing photo sessions for album releases or music-press interviews. It was the first time we posed together for a professional photographer—and it felt *weird*. We just weren't used to it.

When you're a working-class boy from the Midlands, you don't get photographed. Not *properly*. The only times you get your picture taken are with a fixed grin in school photos, or gurning away on the beach on holiday with your family or your mates.

In the same way, a group of young lads in a band are basically having a laugh. You don't talk about what the band *means*, or what you all signify to each other. So, when you're all suddenly lined up in front of a professional photographer doing a shoot, it can feel uncomfortable.

You're glancing at one another awkwardly, and dealing with emotions and observations about each other, and about the band, that have never crossed your mind before. *This is a bit weird, ay it? What are we supposed to do?*

You're trying to process what's going on, and all the time you're doing it, the photographer is giving you instructions: "Don't put your hands in your pockets!" "Don't cross your arms!" "Lift your chin up!" "Look *this* way!" "You, at the back—move to the left a bit . . ."

It's such a strange process. You want to represent the band, and what you sound like, and what you're about, but you have no idea how to do it. You haven't got a mic, or guitars, or drums to pose with. You're just a load of blokes staring at a camera, your arms hanging by your sides.

In those early sessions, I felt a disconnect. They just didn't work for me. I knew we had to *project* something and we weren't doing it. Of course, it didn't help that not only did we not have a band image; we all seemed to have a different image within the same band.

As I said earlier, there are some visual atrocities in early Priest photo sessions. We knew we had to tart ourselves up a bit, but we all went in different directions. I'd turn up in flared denims, white clogs, and a pout—and don't start me on Les Binks and his bloody cowboy shirts!

Our photo shoots never made much sense until we had our epiphany, donned our leather vestments, and invented the classic heavy metal look. Then they all fell into place. Suddenly, we knew *exactly* how we wanted to portray the band, and we knew how to do it.

By the time we signed our major-label deal, we knew what we were doing. Our timing was good. The photo budgets had grown, we were getting shot by big-name photographers, and we were arriving in the studios to find hair and makeup girls waiting for us.

The great big-name photographers are always chasing the unbeliev-able picture. They're after an instant iconic image; nirvana in a snap. In my experience, the trick they have, the *magic* if you like, is knowing exactly when to click the shutter. They just know: *This is it! Click!*

Some photographers have a prima donna attitude. Their basic approach—whether they say it to you or not—is, *I am the very best at what I do, so stand there and do what I say!* You might humor them in the shoot, but the pictures had better be bloody good!

Priest have worked with some of the best rock photographers in the world. One of them is Ross Halfin, a London lensman who started out on *Sounds* back in the late seventies and has shot every big name in metal from Zeppelin and Sabbath onward.

Ross works very quickly and he is extremely temperamental. If a band don't know him, they could easily be rubbed up the wrong way by him. If somebody is inadvertently doing something he doesn't like during a shoot, he doesn't hold back from telling them:

"Oi! Don't fucking stand like that, it looks shit!"

Some rock prophets might bridle at that: "Excuse me, do you know who I am?" But Ross doesn't do it because he's blasé or rude or cynical. It's because he knows exactly what he wants, knows the job he has to do, and knows how to get that perfect shot. *Nirvana in a snap.*

Fin Costello is a very different kind of photographer. Fin is very simple and undramatic in the way he works, and very respectful. He's worked a lot with Priest over the years and always got amazing results—he even managed to get Les Binks into leather!

One of my best shoots with Fin was when I was with the Halford band. He wanted an industrial background, so he told me to meet him in some old dockyards near the O2 in Greenwich in south London. It was a night shoot, in the middle of winter, it was raining, and it was fucking freezing.

Fin got held up and turned up an hour late in his Volkswagen camper van, by which time I was so upset and agitated that I'd started smoking again—after having quit for ten years! It could not have been more miserable and yet the photos turned out brilliantly. *That's* a great photographer.

After fifty years of posing and pouting, I'm good at being photographed now. I have a reputation for being able to give photographers what they want. I know that the slightest nuance of the way I tilt my head, or move my body, can make the world of difference to a shot. *Click!*

And we always have ideas for our shoots now. We always know what to do. I remember when we came to do promo pictures with Travis Shinn for the *Redeemer of Souls* tour, I phoned everybody in the band and told them to show up in black leather to reinforce our image.

I didn't mean our pleather stage gear, but leather coats and jackets. Everyone turned up in long black leather coats: I wore the one that I'm in on the front of this book. When we looked back at the hundreds of shots Travis took during the session, one jumped out at all of us.

It was just a fantastic, moody picture with so much atmosphere and attitude. It said: *We are Judas Priest, we are heavy metal, and we will always be heavy metal!* So, you see what I mean? It told a story, and it was worth a thousand words . . .

RADIO

When I was a little kid, I was fascinated by radio. My grandparents had a radiogram, one of those hefty old wooden combined radios and record players. It was so big that it was a piece of furniture. And when I went to their house, the wireless (as we used to call it) was always on.

They would usually be listening to the Light Programme. This was the BBC's entertainment channel, which hadn't moved on from the postwar years. It was all variety shows, big bands, comics like Arthur Askey and Tommy Trinder, and newsreaders with ridiculously posh voices.

I wasn't so bothered about *them*, but what really transfixed me, at the age of six or seven, was the dial on the radio. I would sit on the floor by the radiogram for hours, twiddling that dial, and the world would come out.

There would be every kind of music you can imagine. Every language: French, German, Swedish, Russian, Serbo-Croat. Snatches would blast out as I turned the dial. I didn't have a clue what each language was, but they all sounded so exotic and exciting.

I could just about read by now so I would avidly scrutinize the names on the screen: BERLIN. PARIS. VIENNA. LIMOGES. SOTTENS. I'd wonder: *Where are they? WHAT are they?* They might as well have said NARNIA or MARS. Radio felt like a world of fantasy and adventure.

As I grew into my teens, got into music, and got bored of the stuffy Light Programme, I got into offshore pirate radio stations like Radio Caroline, as well as Radio Luxembourg 208. They played the pop that I loved but, sadly, Walsall is a long way from either the coast or Luxembourg.

This meant the reception for those stations was annoyingly patchy. I'd sit in my bedroom listening to Luxembourg, but the Beatles or the Move would always fade in and out under waves of crackly interference. I'd be swearing under my breath: *Bloody hell! Bollocks!*

So, when the BBC launched Radio 1 in 1967, when I had just turned sixteen, it was a huge deal. It was their first station aimed at young people like me and I loved it from the off.

Their young DJs like Simon Dee, Tony Blackburn, and Kenny Everett, nearly all defectors from the pirate ships, were a breath of fresh air. I felt properly connected to them: *You're like me! You're a hip, cool young person! You know what the scene is all about, man!*

I quickly selected my favorite DJs. Alan "Fluff" Freeman played a lot of the artists I loved, and he talked about them as if he knew what he was on about. Some of the DJs seemed to like to go on about themselves more than the music, but Fluff wasn't like that.

I also liked John Peel's downbeat presenting manner on his show *Top Gear.* He clearly loved the prog rock and blues he played and I liked his cut-the-crap anti-showbiz style.* When he talked to musicians, I could tell they felt relaxed and comfortable with him.

---

* In fact, the first time I saw John Peel on *Top of the Pops*, it pissed me off: *What are you doing? You shouldn't be on that show!* I thought he'd "sold out." How daft.

My love for radio meant that when Priest slowly started taking off and got our first airplay, it was a real thrill. I loved hearing us on the rock shows on the local commercial stations, BRMB and Beacon 303. It was our home turf and I knew our mates would be listening.

Even this paled next to the excitement of our first few plays on Radio 1. *Bloody hell! Judas Priest! On Radio 1!* Our management or record label would always tip us off in advance what show we were likely to be played on, and I would listen in avidly. Every. Single. Time.

Yet for many years, being a metal fan, or in a metal band, meant that you listened to one DJ on Radio 1 over all others: Tommy Vance.

Tommy, who had a great voice for radio, hosted the *Friday Rock Show* from 10 p.m. till midnight on Friday nights for fifteen years. It was the sole oasis of hard rock and heavy metal on Radio 1 for nearly all of that time and was a must-listen show.

All the metalheads listened to Tommy Vance's show and all the bands wanted to be on it. If you were at home, you never missed it, and you talked about it for days afterward. Tommy was supportive of Priest and played us a lot. Over the years, we had a good friendship with him.

Another DJ I liked a lot in the early years of Radio 1 was Stuart Henry. He was a cool Scottish hippie, he had great intro music, and he always seemed to ignore the station's playlist and spin whatever he wanted. I discovered so many new records and bands through him.

Stuart left Radio 1 and moved over to Radio Luxembourg in the mid-seventies. He remained a bit of a hero for me, so when I heard from Priest's management that he wanted to talk to me about *Screaming for Vengeance* in 1982, I was delighted: "Yes, please! I'm *there!*"

It entailed a flight from London to Luxembourg on a tiny twin-prop light aircraft. I had occasionally got in planes like that before with the band, but this was to be one of the most terrifying experiences of my life. My life which I thought was about to end.

We hadn't long taken off when we hit an apocalyptic thunderstorm. We were shaken about like peas in a colander. The plane was going any which way but forward. There were twenty businessmen on the flight, and half of them were crying. I was near to tears myself.

When I was a lad, my dad, who absolutely loved airplanes, explained to me that nearly all planes that crash come down in turbulence.* I felt certain we were about to be one of them. When we finally landed in Luxembourg, I wanted to kiss the tarmac.

It was all worth it to meet Stuart Henry. He had just announced he had multiple sclerosis, but he was as charming, charismatic, and cool as I could have hoped for. Stuart went on for years before MS finally got him. He was an amazing bloke.

When Priest first started touring the States, I fell in love with American rock radio. I adored the DJs' full-on raucous enthusiasm and energy. I mean, as much as I loved dear old John Peel, you could never exactly have called his monotone exciting or uplifting!

American rock DJs virtually smashed you over the head to get your attention, and it really worked. They were big, brash, and larger-than-life and they talked as if they were talking to *you and you alone*. It's a very engaging way to broadcast, and I like it as much now as I did then.

From our very first US tour on, Priest did a lot of radio interviews. I mean, *a lot*. Every city and town we went to, we called in on the local rock station. We did a huge amount of legwork and it helped establish us. It meant that metalheads all over the States knew who we were.

We'd do a program with the mad name *King Biscuit Flower Hour*. It broadcast live gigs and was aired by more than three hundred stations across the US. We also regularly talked to a guy named Bob Coburn on a syndicated show named *Rockline*. We reached a lot of people that way.

I still do a lot of US radio interviews, even today. I get requests from local stations all the time and, if I can, I talk to them. It's such an important thing: those stations helped to put Priest where we are, and if I can repay them in a little way, even now, I will.

---

* Years later, I learned Dad was talking rubbish and virtually no planes have ever been brought down by turbulence. But when you're a little kid, you believe everything your dad says.

Radio remains an important medium today, wherever you may be in the world. It's crucial for new bands that are trying to break through and, whatever stage you are at in your career, being played on the radio will always be a big deal. It's just a fact of rock and metal life.

Yet radio is not what it was. Like everything in music, it has been hit by the internet. There are far fewer big commercial rock stations now, because who wants to listen to five minutes of ads when you can just switch to Spotify and hear nonstop music of your own choice?

Radio has fragmented and, in some ways, it is a good thing. In Britain, metalheads no longer have to wait all week for Tommy Vance to play metal for two hours on a Friday night. Now, you can tune in to an internet rock station like Planet Rock and listen 24/7.

Internet radio is a game changer. It's amazing. You can be anywhere in the world and listen to your favorite radio station! The rise of podcasts is also crucial. Nowadays, I reckon I do as many promo interviews with podcasts as with actual radio stations.

California used to have a great rock radio station called KNAC. The internet torpedoed them and they nearly went under, but then they came back as an internet station: KNAC.COM. After that change, I went along to Long Beach to be interviewed by them.

It was just one DJ with headphones and no engineers, working out of a poky little office. We jabbered away for an hour then, as we went to a commercial break, I couldn't help noticing that all the wires under his desk were tangled up in a horrible mess.

As a Virgo, I can't stand clutter, so as the ads played, I told the guy, "I'll sort that out for you!" and vanished under the table. I could hear him saying, "No, you don't need to do that, Rob!" as I was faffing around with the wires. When I came back up, he looked horrified.

"You've knocked us off the air!" he said.

"What?"

"You pulled a plug out! We've gone off the air!"

I looked around and noticed that all the computer screens had gone blank. *Oops!* The cell phones were still working, though, because thirty seconds later the DJ's phone rang. It was the station boss.

"What the fuck's going on?" he asked.

"I'm sorry, it's Halford, he was tidying up and he accidentally pulled the plug out . . ." said the DJ. His phone wasn't on speakerphone, but I still heard what his boss yelled at him next:

"GET MY GODDAMN RADIO STATION BACK ON THE FUCKING AIR! AND TELL HALFORD TO KEEP HIS HANDS OFF MY STUFF!"

When I listen to the radio today, I have a couple of go-to stations. In Phoenix, there's a decent rock network called 98KUPD Arizona. If I'm in Walsall, I listen to Planet Rock—or, occasionally, stick Classic FM on.* It's a nice background noise as I potter around the house.

Yet most likely I'll be scanning across Radio Garden. It's an amazing app and website that allows you to listen to radio stations around the world. I discovered it a year or so ago and now I can't get enough of it. If you've never heard of it before, really, check it out!

When you go to the Radio Garden site, you see the world revolving, covered in thousands of green dots. Each dot is a radio station. Click on it and you hear that station's output live, whether it is in Nebraska, Nice, Norwich, or Novosibirsk.

It absolutely blows my mind. I sit, click from dot to dot, and every kind of music and language in the world spills out. Flamenco, opera, metal; Spanish, Mandarin, Urdu. And, for an hour or two, I turn back into that kid sitting by his grandparents' radiogram, sixty-five years ago.

TELEVISION

Radio was my passion as a kid, but it wasn't the main entertainment medium that I interacted with day to day. Growing up in a working-class family in the fifties and sixties, every evening was spent sitting around the television.

Britain had two channels—three, after BBC 2 came along in 1964—and, every night, we watched whatever was on *because it was on*. And as for the thought of ever going on television yourself? You might as well dream of going to the moon! It seemed about as likely.

---

* And there go my fifty years of heavy metal cred, right there!

I watched music programs avidly from a very early age. My first memories are of grainy black-and-white shows like *Juke Box Jury* hosted by a very clipped bloke called David Jacobs, who sounded like a wing commander just returned from a bombing mission over Dresden.

Two shows were essential viewing. At 7:30 p.m. on BBC 1 every Thursday, right after a dull science show called *Tomorrow's World* that I couldn't wait to end, *Top of the Pops* counted down the week's chart. The whole family crowded round the TV for this national institution.

Over on BBC 2, *Old Grey Whistle Test* played more leftfield music. As I got older and snobbier, I preferred it to *TOTP* because I thought it was more sophisticated, and it gave me a chance to see acts like New York Dolls, the Tubes, and Dr. John, which I'd read about in the music papers.

Years later, with Priest, I got to go on those shows. Both of them were nothing like I expected. I wanted to record *Whistle Test* in London so I could meet its legendary host, "Whispering" Bob Harris, so I was pissed off to be told we were recording our slot in Birmingham.

It was a soulless, joyless experience. I hoped the production staff would all be hippies or rock fans, but instead they were uptight BBC lifers and trades union jobsworths. They had no interest whatsoever in us or our music and we went home afterward feeling quite deflated.

Despite that, our 1975 *Whistle Test* appearance, singing "Rocka Rolla" and "Dreamer Deceiver" while I wore my sister Sue's frilly pink blouse, has gone into Priest folklore. Our fans love it. And even though the day was a bit flat, one thought echoed around my head as I sang:

Bloody hell! I'm on the telly!

If there was little celebratory about our appearance on *Whistle Test*, at least doing *Top of the Pops* was fun. It was exciting to drive down to the famous BBC TV Centre in London, get shown to our poky little dressing room, and see the other acts milling around.

There was a weird rigmarole about *Top of the Pops*, driven by the then very powerful Musicians Union. You mimed, but you weren't allowed to mime to the single you'd released. You had to go to a studio the day before the show and record a fresh version of the track.

It made no fucking sense at all—how were you supposed to reproduce in an hour what might have taken you days in the studio? In practice, no bands actually rerecorded their song. Your manager would slip the union man a backhander and they'd pretend that you'd done it.

From seeing it on telly, I thought *Top of the Pops* was recorded in front of a gig-size crowd, but there were only about thirty teenagers gathered in a small studio. The floor managers rudely barked instructions at them and shepherded them around like collies herding sheep.

Years later, it came out that some of those kids were sexually exploited by people like the serial pedophile Jimmy Savile, but we never saw any of that. We were more focused on getting into the BBC bar after the show, where all the bands would drink until they couldn't stand up.

In America, television and pop music have a very important, symbiotic relationship. In the fifties and sixties, *The Ed Sullivan Show* attracted fifty million viewers a week. It helped to make Elvis, and the Beatles broke in the States after their appearance on that show.

Not even Priest are quite old enough to have been on *The Ed Sullivan Show*, but when we were making inroads in the US in the early eighties, another televisual phenomenon put a lot of wind in our sails: Music Television, better known as MTV.

MTV was such a simple idea that it was brilliant. They took the radio format of playing nonstop hits and put it on TV, with videos. I was addicted to it as soon as it launched. When I moved to Phoenix, there were some days I would watch nothing else all day long.

I thought that MTV would be humungous, and it was. It was certainly massive for Priest. They played tracks like "Turbo Lover" and "You've Got Another Thing Coming" to death. Like every band, we started making videos for songs with MTV specifically in mind.

We got even more closely interwoven with MTV after they launched *Headbangers Ball* in 1987. Their suits realized there was a huge metal market out there, and suddenly we had our own forum. Metal fans would all pile round their mates' houses every week to watch the show.

They took *Headbangers Ball* off after grunge came along and MTV had a bit of a personality change. After Kurt Cobain died, in 1994, they played nothing but wall-to-wall Nirvana for days. It felt like the whole channel had gone into mourning.

Nowadays, MTV is a very strange beast. It has no music programs whatsoever and has basically transformed into a reality-TV channel. I sometimes wonder why it is still called Music Television, but its shift is just part of a wider trend.

There are very few music shows on television nowadays. I don't think music enthusiasts even watch TV anymore: they access music via the internet on their phone, laptop, or iPad. The gap where dedicated music programs used to be is filled by TV talent shows.

These are a weird phenomenon. They're broadcast on television, often on Saturday nights, on both sides of the Atlantic, and millions of people tune in and vote for their favorite contestant every week. Then the winner puts out an album and, more often than not, it sinks without trace.

It's hard to say why. Partly it's just the fickleness of the record-buying public, but I think it's more than that. Most successful artists have spent years grafting, paying their dues, and slowly accumulating fans. Talent shows try to take a huge shortcut, and it doesn't work like that.

Priest made one very high-profile talent show appearance. In 2011, we were approached by the producers of *American Idol*. They said one of the contestants, James Durbin, was a metalhead and a total Priest nut—would we go on and perform with him?

Despite my reservations about those shows in general, I had no doubt about our response: "Oh, we've *got* to do it!" In those days, *American Idol* was watched by between twenty and thirty million people a week. Who the fuck would want to pass up exposure like that?

Richie had just joined the band to replace Ken and we figured it would be a great way to debut him to the world. In fact, it was such an attractive offer for us that we actually flew all the way from the UK to Los Angeles to be on television for three minutes.

When we got there, it was great fun. Priest wailed away as James and I strutted around the stage at the Nokia Theatre, duetting on "Living After Midnight" and "Breaking the Law." James didn't win but he was a lovely, genuine bloke. We're still in touch: he emails me occasionally.

When it became known that Priest were going on *American Idol*, we got some pushback. Some of our horrified fans took to the internet to bollock us for doing it: *That's sacrilege! You can't go on a shit show like that! You're selling out metal!*

I have no time for that argument. I believe we should reach out to as many people as possible to convert them to Priest and to metal. In any case, we'd had the same issue when a few fans complained about us going on *Top of the Pops* in 1979! Some things never change.

I occasionally wonder, if shows like *American Idol* or *The X Factor* had been around in 1973, might Priest have entered them? Part of me thinks, *why not?* But, then again, we had *Opportunity Knocks* back then, and it never occurred to us to write to Hughie Green!*

You never get blasé about going on television but you do get used to it. We knew thirty million people were watching us on *American Idol* yet we took it in our stride. I still enjoy our occasional TV appearances, and I'm over feeling like I did on *Old Grey Whistle Test*, nearly fifty years ago: *Bloody hell! I'm on the telly!*

VIDEOS

When MTV happened along at the start of the eighties, we knew that it was to our advantage to supply them with quality Judas Priest content. And we threw ourselves into the task with relish.

Making videos is a funny thing, really. When you start a band, you do it because you want to play music and go on tour. You certainly

---

* *Opportunity Knocks* was seventies British telly's equivalent of *The X Factor*. The host was a fast-talking shyster called Hughie Green. His catchphrase was "I mean that most sincerely, folks!" despite the fact he appeared to be the least sincere bloke on the planet.

don't do it because you are dying to do bits of acting, or film a pile of little three-minute mini-movies.

Having said that, we knew that MTV was giving us the potential to make visual commercials for the band and get them shown all over the world, again and again. And the first person we turned to, to help us to do this, was Julien Temple.

It was our record label's suggestion for us to work with Julien, but we were very open to the idea. He'd already filmed the Sex Pistols' iconic video for "God Save the Queen" and their full-length movie, *The Great Rock 'n' Roll Swindle*, so we knew there was a real buzz about his name.

Julien was a very well-spoken Cambridge graduate and an extremely confident individual. He was a real pioneer of music videos; he always knew exactly what he wanted to do—and the first video he made with us, straight off the bat in 1980, is still one of our most famous.

For "Breaking the Law," Julien came to us with a storyboard about us robbing a bank. He booked some actors and a disused former Barclays bank in Soho and we shot the whole thing in one working day. It was fucking fantastic fun.

Ken, Glenn, Ian, and Dave Holland had never acted, and my only proper experience was amateur dramatics in Walsall ten years earlier, but as soon as Julien barked "ACTION!" we all went for it. Terrorizing the bank staff and customers with the power of heavy metal was a right laugh.

Julien wanted to film a getaway sequence in a gold convertible Cadillac he'd hired. He knew we wouldn't be able to do it along Oxford Street and in central London because we'd have to keep stopping at traffic lights, so he told the driver to speed along the Westway.

It was dusk by then and Julien didn't have any lights with him, so he was panicking about losing the light and missing the shot. He was squeezed in the Caddy's front passenger seat together with the cameraman, barking instructions as I mimed in the back.

We got it wrapped up in that one day and we were all really pleased with how it turned out. It's quite a contrast to later days, when some videos got so complex that they'd take days to make. It was credit to Julien's organization and efficiency that we pulled it off.

Priest have made a lot of live videos over the years. It's partly because being live is where we are strongest, but also because fans love them. They've all seen us live, so they can watch a concert video back and imagine that they are there.

Julien filmed the live vid for "Living After Midnight" at a gig at Sheffield City Hall. The fans were waiting outside for the doors to open, and he asked them all to cheer and shout when I pulled up in the middle of them on my motorbike. They were going nuts so it looked great.

I love that video. It may seem like a straightforward live vid, but it was so skillfully filmed that it is like a microscopic analysis of heavy metal and how it works. You could watch it in slow motion, frame by frame, and get the definitive idea of what Priest were all about then.

Julien's next offering for us remains one of the more . . . *unusual* items in the Priest video canon. For the promo for "Hot Rockin'," he had the novel idea of shooting us playing live, as if at a gig, but starting off the vid with us in a gym and then in a sauna.

I don't think any of us were all that enthusiastic about the idea, but we went along with it. So, the video opened with the five of us, shirtless for some reason, pumping iron and lifting weights, before all showering as I yowled and threw water on the coals in the sauna.

We had advertised in *Melody Maker* for fans to come and be extras in the video. I hoped loads of people would turn up and it would be like playing an actual gig, but hardly anybody saw the ad and only about ten people showed up. It was really disappointing.

If I am honest, I cringe slightly now when I see that vid again and us all half-naked and working out, but it was the eighties and it made sense at the time. I guess it worked because our fans still talk about it now. A lot of them have a pet theory:

"Ah, that was Rob in a gay sauna, sending out a secret message!"

To which I can only say: "No it bloody wasn't! It wasn't a gay sauna, and it wasn't my idea in the first place . . ."

Even this early into Priest's promo-making career, our attitude towards filming videos was changing slightly. Initially, it was a right laugh and, in its own way, quite exciting, but there were times the process could get so boring that the sense of adventure wore off.

Professional musicians have a phrase: "Hurry up and wait!" It describes the many times when managers or tour managers will chivvy you to get to a place—a studio, a gig venue, a TV station, whatever—for a certain time, and you then sit around for hours waiting for anything to happen.

There was a lot of "Hurry up and wait!" going on when we filmed "Hot Rockin'." Luckily, there was a pub, bang next door to the shoot in London. "How long will this take to set up?" we'd ask Julien, as his team fiddled with cameras, lights, and sound equipment.

"About twenty minutes."

"Sound, we'll go and have a pint, then!" By the end of the video, as we were setting fire to the drums and, God knows why, to my shoes, I was completely out of my tree.

I used to go and stand by Julien and watch through the monitor when he was filming the other guys and I wasn't in the shot, but otherwise we never saw the work in progress until he sent us his first cut a few days later. We'd watch it, then give him our feedback.

This might be Ken or Glenn complaining that the other one had more screen time, or us all saying "We need a bit more of Ian," or me asking Julien to cut a few seconds because I didn't like how I looked. It might sound petty but we had to all be happy with it. That mattered.

Julien's next vid with us was filmed at Kempton Park Waterworks in Surrey for "You've Got Another Thing Coming." It showed an official in a bowler hat conducting a noise pollution test at the site as Priest rocked out and gave the track both barrels.

The bureaucrat was horrified at our racket so we upped the volume even more and blew his head (and bowler hat) clean off his shoulders. Say what you like about Julien, he never lacked ideas! It worked, and MTV put the vid on heavy rotation as the song broke in America.*

Julien hit on another bright concept when he dropped a kid playing an arcade video game into the promo for "Freewheel Burning." I liked

---

* Those early promos for "Breaking the Law," "Living After Midnight," and "You've Got Another Thing Coming" are still my fave Priest vids of all time. They really helped to establish and define us in people's minds.

the idea from the off, because gaming was just getting big and I hoped it might introduce us to a new demographic. And I think it did.

It was around this time, in the mid-eighties, that we began shooting vids with Wayne Isham. Wayne was an intense character with long, blond hair, a scruffy beard, and shitloads of energy, and he was very much the go-to guy for metal bands making videos in America.

Wayne's first Priest promo was skeletons and robots riding Harleys down a desert highway for "Turbo Lover." He wanted to continue that concept and storyline with our next video, for "Locked In," and he came up with an absolute fucking doozy.

Wayne hired the disused zoo in Griffith Park, Los Angeles—and he hired a whole lot more besides. The concept was that I had been captured by a tribe of Amazonian women, plus the robots and skeletons from the "Turbo Lover" vid, and the rest of the band would come to save me.

To say the least, it was a major fucking production. I was tied to a metal rack and swung like a pendulum over a pit of fire. Glenn and Ken crept through subterranean tunnels to rescue me. The style, hair, makeup, imagery, and huge cast of extras were pure OTT eighties excess.

This meant it also cost a fortune to shoot. I've got no idea how much—I didn't even ask at the time. That was the whole ethos back then, when bands used to boast about spending a million dollars on a video. Which was pretty daft, when ultimately it all came out of our money!

I could have been vulnerable filming "Locked In" because I'd just come out of rehab and was newly sober. I couldn't get wasted or even have a sneaky beer to take the edge off things. Being at the center of a high-pressure shoot like that could have been nerve-racking.

Instead, I was relieved to find I felt relaxed, and I actually enjoyed making the vid. I was delighted to be back with the band, to not be trashed all the time, and to be finally on the mend after years of alcohol and drug abuse and mental torture. I was in a good place.

In fact, I enjoyed the preposterousness of the "Locked In" video so much that I had a smirk on my face through most of it. I used to do that a lot. I look back now at old videos and gig footage and, yep, *there I am*, every time, grinning away. I dunno why—it's not very heavy metal!

Wayne filmed a few live promos for us. One was "Parental Guidance" at an arena show in Dallas. That was the one where Ken had to wear dark glasses in the vid, after I accidentally smacked the end of a guitar string into his eye and left him with a bleeding eyeball.

Yet the other iconic, memorable video that Wayne filmed for us was for "Painkiller" in 1990. We went into a power station at Huntington Beach, just south of Los Angeles International Airport, and shot a promo that was entirely in line with our agenda as a band at the time.

Metal was getting heavier via bands like Megadeth and Pantera and we wanted to reestablish Priest as a strong, aggressive heavy metal force. Wayne shot in black-and-white and made one of the fastest, edgiest, most brutal metal vids ever. It was a masterpiece. I didn't even grin.

Nowadays, videos are not remotely the force they were. MTV no longer exists in the form it was, and vids aren't even that important as a force for selling your records. I don't think that there is any way today that an artist would consider spending a million dollars on one, unless they're nuts or it's for a tax write-off!

To show how much things have changed, when Priest heard our label was going to put out "No Surrender" as a single in 2018, we shot our own vid! We were rehearsing for the *Firepower* tour in Andy Sneap's studio in Derbyshire and decided to get it done *right here, right now*.

We all got our mobile phones out and set them up at different points around the studio. Everybody pressed their "Record" buttons, we ran through the track, and then we sent all the footage off to someone to be edited. *Simples!* And our fans seem to really like that vid.

Priest have been making videos for more than forty years now, and do you know what I think is cool? When MTV first came along and really popularized the art form, a lot of people sneered at music vids. They said they were just bits of fluff, with no artistic worth or real value.

But it hasn't worked out like that. If I go to YouTube now, I see from the number of views that people are still discovering the "Breaking the Law" video in 2022. *Forty-two years* after Priest robbed that disused bank in Soho! And that has got to be a bloody good thing.

BOOKS

It's strange, because I used to be a voracious reader, of science fiction especially, but I have read hardly any rock scriptures. I am told there are scores of brilliant metal and rock memoirs and autobiographies out there, and I haven't opened any of them.

Hunter Davies's Beatles books. *The Dirt* by Mötley Crüe. Lemmy's *White Line Fever*. Keith Richards's *Life*. The famous Doors book: *No One Here Gets Out Alive*. Slash's autobiography. They're all apparently rock-and-roll classics. I've never picked up one of them.

It's hard to say exactly why that is. Maybe, because I live the metal and rock life myself, I'm just not that curious to know more about musicians outside of their work. I feel like I know Lemmy, or Slash, through their music, and that's good enough for me.

It always surprises people that I haven't even read Ken's book about Priest, *Heavy Duty*. It's not through spite: I've just never felt the urge to get hold of it. Plus, wrist merchants would only ask me what I thought of it. If I haven't read it, I can't have an opinion, positive *or* negative!

Another drawback is that a lot of rock bios tend to be similar. They all follow the same trajectory: teenage dreams, years of struggle, sudden breakthrough, success, fame, excess, addiction, crash, rehab, recovery. You can skim them and think that you know this story already.

Given all that, it's a fair question to ask why I decided to write my own autobiography, *Confess*, two years ago. I never thought that I would. I'd had publishers coming to me for years asking me to write my life story, and I'd always turned them down flat.

It just didn't appeal. I was still living my life to the full, there were lots of things I didn't want to talk about, and I'm quite a private person. It all seemed like too much hassle. The idea didn't make any sense to me whatsoever . . . until, suddenly, *it did.*

As I neared seventy, I realized that I *did* want to tell my story, and I'd reached the right age to do it. Barring surprises, I have now done most of the things I'm going to do in my life. So, why *not* tell the world about them, the good *and* bad? I realized that I wanted to *Confess.*

I also wanted to counterbalance all the unofficial Priest biographies out there. I see them in bookstores, or on Amazon: *The True Story of Judas Priest!* How can they be the true story, when we haven't had anything to do with them?!

The authors have never spoken to any of us, so those books are no more than reheated old interviews and information that everybody already knows about us, rounded up and fleshed out with speculation and waffle. What's the point? They're mere cut-and-paste jobs; money for old rope.

I love writing lyrics, but I'm not a professional author, so I knew I'd need to work with a cowriter. I was wary of this prospect. I mean, your life story is the most intimate, personal subject imaginable. How could anyone else help to capture and convey *what it is to be me?*

There were a few cowriters in the running, but when I heard about Ian Gittins, I knew it had to be him. Ian had cowritten bestselling memoirs with people as various as Nikki Sixx and Billy Connolly, but that wasn't what drew me to him. No, what appealed to me was this:

Ian is from Walsall.

It was *such* a big factor! How could an outsider know what it was like to grow up in the industrial Black Country, in the sixties and seventies? Well, Ian knew because he was there, too. He knew the estate I grew up on, the places I went, the way I talk. He knew . . . *what I came from.*

After all my reservations about sharing my gospel truth with the world, when I came to start talking about my life, and getting it all down on paper, I absolutely loved it. As a heavy metal minstrel and lyricist, I'm a communicator, and spilling out my soul was totally cathartic.

I held nothing back. Everything I've done, good *and* bad, went in there, from teenage sexual abuse to hunting glory-hole trysts in Texas truck stops; from arrests for DUI and cruising to the suicide of my first true love, Brad. I mean, if you're going to tell your story, *tell your bloody story!*

When we'd finished writing it, I read *Confess* aloud for the audio book edition. This was a testing process. I think I found it more challenging and difficult than actually writing the book.

At the time, I was weak and vulnerable from having my treatment for prostate cancer, and sitting in a studio reading aloud about my lowest points, and Brad's death, made me very emotional. I had to stop a few times to compose myself. It took two weeks. There were tears.

It was all worth it. I knew that I was proud of *Confess* when I held it in my hand, and that it was a truthful portrayal of my life, but that didn't mean people would like it. Priest have made albums we've loved only to see them torn to pieces!

But the reaction was great. Critics and wrist merchants loved it. Even papers like the *Times* and *Daily Telegraph*, who wouldn't normally bother with Judas Priest, were kind about it. It even made a few book-of-the-year lists. It was surprising, and humbling.

That was nice, but it was even more important that fans liked it. Quite a lot praised it in reviews on sites like Amazon, but a few had a caveat: "I don't *mind* Rob being gay, but he doesn't have to ram it down our throats!" (which is quite a funny phrase when you think about it!).

It made me lol. Rock-and-roll biographies are usually full of rock stars shagging hundreds of chicks and nobody bats an eyelid! Don't those readers *see* that hiding my sexuality, and the angst it caused me, dominated my life for nearly forty years? Without those memories, it wouldn't have been my life story. It wouldn't have been *Confess*.

Strangers told me what they thought of my autobiography but most of my nearest and dearest never said a word. Thomas read it and offered encouragement as I wrote it, but I still have no idea whether my family have read it, nor Ian or Glenn.*

I expected that. It's just that classic yam-yam thing of not giving out too much praise, and avoiding emotional or awkward conversations. I've been like that my entire life, so I'm not surprised my kin are the same. In fact, I wouldn't have them any other way.

One big surprise around *Confess* was that the audiobook made it onto the long list for the Grammy Awards for best spoken word album! *Bloody hell!* It blew my mind even to be *considered* alongside the likes of Barack Obama and the eventual winner, Don Cheadle.

---

*I guess I can't complain about the rest of Priest not reading my book—I mean, I never read Ken's!

I always said I'd never write my memoir, but I'm so glad that I did. And did I enjoy writing a book? Well, I'm writing this second one right now, so it can't have been too bad, can it?

MOVIES

The first band that I ever loved was also the very first band that I went to see in their own movie.

When the Beatles began making films, I think they were probably taking their cue from Elvis. He made loads of movies after telling Colonel Tom Parker he wanted to do something "more substantial" than just sing. He was certainly the reason that Cliff Richard made *Summer Holiday!*

As a teen, I could take or leave Elvis or Cliff movies but the Beatles were a different matter. When they put out *A Hard Day's Night* in 1964, I was straight down the flicks to see it, not least because the poster promised it would have six new songs.

It was a mad story about the Beatles trying to look after Paul's bonkers grandad, played by Wilfrid Brambell, the "dirty old man" from *Steptoe and Son*. The plot didn't really make much sense, but I didn't care. I just loved seeing the Beatles in a new context.

I carried that enthusiasm through to *Help!* and then *Yellow Submarine*. That was a very bizarre film, but I found it fascinating. I went to see it three or four times at the Walsall Gaumont, searching hard for deep meanings that may or may not have been there.

Those Beatles films were a bit hit-and-miss and, if I am honest, I think that's true of a lot of music-movie crossovers. In 1967, I went to see a film called *Privilege*, set in Birmingham, just because the star was Paul Jones from Manfred Mann. It was eccentric, but I enjoyed it.

Rock movies haven't always got the best reputation because they can be very ambitious and they can come a cropper. I enjoyed seeing The Who in *Quadrophenia*, which was partly masterminded by our manager, Bill Curbishley, but, before that, I thought *Tommy* was very bizarre.

In more recent years, I haven't sought out so many rock films. It may be for the same reason that I don't read loads of music memoirs. Because I'm steeped in the metal and rock life 24/7, maybe I subconsciously look elsewhere for my recreational entertainment.

I'm also more likely to get irked by stupid mistakes in rock movies and films that misrepresent what it is really like to be in a band: *Huh! My life is NOTHING like that!* So, perhaps it's fitting that my very favorite music film is a spoof.

I've said it many times, but I still think *This Is Spinal Tap* is the greatest music movie ever made. It's a satire, yes, but one steeped not in cruelty or meanness but in affection. Every single band that I've ever spoken to about it can totally relate to it.

You watch the indignities that befall Tap—playing support to a puppet show; accidentally ordering miniature stage sets; getting lost on the way to the stage—and you both laugh and wince. You think: *Shit, there but by the grace of God go we!* Or I do, anyway.

The nearest British equivalent to Spinal Tap was Bad News, a fictional metal band put together in the eighties by The Comic Strip team of Rik Mayall, Adrian Edmondson, and Nigel Planer. They did a couple of TV mini-movies and they had me in fucking stitches.

Bad News made some god-awful singles and then got drenched in bottles of piss chucked by the crowd at Monsters of Rock. Priest still sometimes play their best song, "Warriors of Genghis Khan," in the warm-up music for our gigs. I think it's what they would have wanted.

I'm skeptical about metal and rock movies simply because there haven't been many great ones, but I was an aspiring teen actor myself and I've never quite lost the bug. That was why it was such a thrill to do my sole cameo role in a film (so far, anyway!) back in 2003.

A director, Jonas Åkerlund, invited me to do a bit part in *Spun*, a black comedy about drug dealing that he was shooting in Oregon. Despite having the shits on the day, I loved doing it . . . and how many people can boast they've been thrown against the wall of a porn shop by Mickey Rourke?

Recently, for the first time, I watched a rock movie that was made in 1975, but which somehow totally passed me by when it first came out. And it totally fucking blew me away.

How the hell did I miss *Slade in Flame* first time around?! It was about a struggling young Black Country band, driving to gigs in their knackered old Transit van. When it first came out, I was . . . in a struggling young Black Country band, driving to gigs in their knackered old Transit van! Plus, I've always loved Slade!

Seeing it for the first time in 2022, it was a time warp for me. My life flashed before my eyes. So much was familiar from those early Priest years. It made me both feel nostalgic and thankful, thinking, *Thank God we haven't got to go through all that anymore!*

There were the shitty clubs, with mirrored walls, we played for ten quid a night. The Corky-style wide boys. The rip-off agents. The mates who became roadies. The casual sexism: Noddy sniffing a pair of Dave Hill's girlfriend's knickers onstage, and saying, "Hmm, still warm . . ."

It wasn't just the music. The seventies West Midlands landscape looked Victorian and yet felt like yesterday. The tiny terraced houses, crammed together. Don Powell on a drop forge in a factory, then walking with his dad along a filthy cut* full of litter. *Wow!* It was all my yesterdays . . .

Slade in Flame ended (spoiler alert—but the film is nearly fifty years old!) with the band falling out and breaking up as they stood on the brink of fame. *That* never happened to Priest, but it did happen to so many bands and, to me, the whole movie rang true from the first frame to the last. What a bloody great film!

I'm sure there have been plenty of great rock biopics over the years—it's just a shame that I've rarely seen them! Now and then, there has been talk of a dramatization of Priest's career, which always leads to me getting asked in interviews which actor should play me.

I haven't got a clue. I instinctively feel it should be a British actor, but the only bloke I can think of with a persona like mine is Frank

---

*Black Country–speak for canal.

Skinner.* And, I mean, bless dear old Frank, but I'm not sure he's got the *Wow!* factor that puts bums on seats in New York or LA multiplexes.

But when it comes to rock movies, I'm going to end where I began. One band in particular first drew me to the cinema screen and, virtually sixty years on, their appeal hasn't waned for me.

I saw the Beatles movie *Let It Be*, chronicling their final weeks together, when it first came out in 1970. And when I heard last year there was to be a new eight-hour documentary-movie version of it by *The Hobbit* director, Peter Jackson, I was a pig in shit.

I sat transfixed through the full eight hours. There is such amazing footage—and when they got to the bit where Paul McCartney, sitting in a studio strumming on a bass, casually produces the genius tune that is "Get Back" from thin air, I had my heart in my mouth.

There is great songwriting, *there* is great music—and *there* is a great movie moment, right there. It may even be better than Spinal Tap . . .

STREAMING

The Book of Chronicles is not a tablet of stone. The media world is constantly altering and has changed many times in Priest's lifetime. And the most disgusting, pernicious, and properly evil development of all for artists was the invention of streaming services like Spotify.

When the internet emerged, my first thought was that it was a classic double-edged sword. I loved the accessibility aspect. It was a great place to discover new bands and I liked that the latest news about Priest was just a click away for anybody, 24/7.

The downside, for metal and rock bands and all artists, of course, was the proliferation of piracy and illegal downloading. It was always going to happen, and for a while it was like the Wild West out there. Like the movie industry, the record industry got hit hard.

When Lars Ulrich and Metallica went after Napster in the late nineties, they got painted as the bad guys: *Boo! Fucking greedy millionaire rock*

---

*Frank Skinner is a British stand-up comedian. Like me, he grew up on a Black Country council estate and is a lugubrious sod.

stars, taking their music from the kids! But it wasn't really like that. I could see *exactly* where Lars was coming from.

From those years of anarchy has emerged a world where artists no longer sell millions of records, and Spotify is king. Well, *I fucking hate Spotify.* To me, they are no better than Napster and those other original chancers that created a world of copyright piracy.

Spotify make millions from artists' music, divvy up their pie chart of earnings, and pay bands like Priest what we used to call, back in our Gull Records days, "four-fifths of five-eighths of fuck-all!" The artists make the music and they get the smallest piece of the pie.

Spotify pay artists derisory amounts: peanuts. When we first saw the breakdown of how much we get for an album stream on the site, compared with a physical CD or even single sale, we were horrified. It is just fucking criminal. How did they get away with it?

They got away with it because record labels had been badly burned by the Napster experience, and hard negotiations with Apple Music, and wanted to get something rather than nothing. I suspect, at the time, they didn't understand the new tech, the same as the artists didn't.

The problem is the streaming world is unregulated. In a way, it's *still* the Wild West. Spotify make up the rules as they go along. They used to say they couldn't pay artists much as they were "still developing." They're now worth trillions of dollars—and they're *still* paying shit!

Spotify are so entrenched and wealthy that they are hard to go up against. Money is power, and their basic argument seems to be: "You need us! What we are paying you is better than nothing!" To which the only answer is, "Not *much* fucking better!"

The only way to combat the power of Spotify and their ilk would be for artists to come together and remove their music from the platform. I'd love Priest to be able to do so but, ultimately, it's out of our control. Our record label holds the rights to—ugly phrase—exploit our music.

Record labels have got a lot of history when it comes to *exploiting* artists. I've always hated how they put out "budget," cut-price versions of albums without asking us: *Who the bloody hell are they to say our music is worth so little?* But the Spotify fiasco is their worst fuckup yet.

Spotify's business model has robbed Priest of a lot of money, but we're OK. We have a well-paid recording contract, and fans who love buying physical albums. It's the new bands starting out now that are struggling to make any sort of living even when their music is reaching healthy-sized audiences, and that is immoral and unforgivable.

If Priest were starting out in 2022, would we still be able to make it, and earn enough to survive? I don't think we would, and that's because of the impact of streaming services. I'll say it as clearly as I can: Spotify and their like should be banned. And *that* fact is worth chronicling.

THE BOOK OF
RITUALS AND SERVICES

All great faiths have their rites and ceremonies. Islam has its prayers to Mecca and its hajj. Roman Catholicism has its masses, confessions, and communions; its amices, albs, thuribles, girdles, maniples, and stoles.

Rock and metal are no different. They are just as much of a religion to their most devout disciples, and they are delineated by countless rituals and services that may appear confusingly arcane to outsiders but which, to their adherents, are utterly sacred.

What are these sacrosanct rites of passage? Why do metalheads raise devil horns, and why do they headbang? Why do metal and rock attract congregations of bikers? And what is the purpose of that odd, unique strain of rock-idol worship that is the tribute band?

It's time for these heavy metal scriptures to hail some divine rituals and services . . .

HEADBANGING

Anybody who assumes that headbanging began with Zeppelin and Sabbath may be surprised to learn that, to say the least, its roots run a little bit deeper than that.

History records that in countries like Iran and India, followers of Islamic devotional Sufi music were passing into trancelike states and banging their heads to drumbeats at religious services *six hundred years ago*. It does my head in to think about that (whether I'm banging it or not).

When did headbanging cross over to metal? Wikipedia (so get a pinch of salt out!) claims it was first seen during a Zep tour of the US in 1969. Not to be outdone, good old Lemmy once said that Motörhead fans invented it, and named it after themselves: *Motörheadbangers*.

What's the point of it? Why do metal fans headbang? At its most basic, it's a show of unity. It's a primitive, uncluttered form of expression that is attached to the hard beat of the music, and it says: *We are metalheads. We are all here together and we belong together. We love heavy metal and this is what we do!*

Headbanging gets seen as crazy and extreme, but it's not the first dance style to be attached to music. You can go right back to the twist (I was good at that, in my youth!) or the locomotion. In fact, if you think about it, headbanging isn't so different from doing the hokey cokey (or the hokey pokey, as Americans oddly prefer to call it).

I'm being serious. Anybody can put their left leg in, their left leg out, and shake it all about, and anybody can headbang. You don't need any skill or practice. It's a great leveler, and that's something I love about it.

I first became aware of headbanging when I was going to see bands like Sabbath and Deep Purple in the early seventies. I joined in, but I wasn't a mental headbanger. There are different degrees, from gentle, subtle nodding to full-on, insane banging.*

Some metal bands totally embraced extreme headbanging, but Priest were never like that. We did it, but it didn't *define* us. Ken was

---

* A lot of people back then also did that Status Quo thing of putting their thumbs in the belt loops of their jeans and bending from the waist. I always saw that as more of a rocker dance than as actual headbanging, though.

normally banging away, as was Glenn to an extent. I joined in now and then, but it was never my main focus.

The three of us would stand in line, with crossed legs, during the middle eight at the back end of "Breaking the Law" and headbang together. It became a Priest ritual, a party piece, and now fans love it and expect it. We've kept it going with Richie in more recent years.

Like most metalheads, Priest fans like a good headbang. It's always the ones down the front. The fans at the back take everything in and have a broader perspective on the gig, but the guys down in the mosh pit are more frenzied in their appreciation.

When I look out from a festival stage and see twenty thousand or thirty thousand people banging their heads, and jumping up and down, it's extraordinary. It's powerful, primordial, and moving. I find it hard to describe the emotions it excites. You have to be there.

When we get a mosh pit, or circle pit, in front of the stage, there's a lot of testosterone flying around with the hair. There's a sense of solidarity like you get in sports fans supporting their team, but it can also kick off at any minute. Our mosh pits in South America get very wild.

I can't sense when a mosh pit is going to erupt—often just one or two people can send it crazy—but I know when during the set it's most likely to go off. It's nearly always during "Painkiller," or sometimes during our encore for "Breaking the Law." It can happen as soon as the first riff kicks in.

Headbanging is a sacred metal ritual, but it's not without its risks. Tom Araya from Slayer did so much damage to his back that he needed surgery. Dave Mustaine from Megadeth says it's left him with a spinal condition. Craig Jones from Slipknot headbanged so hard that he gave himself whiplash.

I never tire of telling this story: when I went to Buckingham Palace in 2005 and met the Queen, she asked me why heavy metal is so loud. I was a bit thrown, and I said, "So we can bang our heads, Ma'am!" Her Maj gave me a regal smile and wandered off.

Ah, well. At least I didn't try to teach her how to do it . . .

DEVIL HORNS

I start every Priest gig in the same way. I come out and, during the first number, I go right to the front of the stage and I throw the devil horns at the crowd. And they go absolutely nuts. Every. Single. Fucking. Time.

Every metal maniac puts the horns up. It's a sign of identity and unity. It doesn't matter if you're a doctor, a bus driver, a binman, or a female judge in the European Court of Human Rights in Brussels (one of them is apparently a big Priest fan). You flash the horns and you're all together, as one.

Like headbanging, the sign of the horns has a long, fascinating history. In Buddhism, it's a gesture to exorcise demons and ward off evil. There is a statue in India of Padmasambhava, founder of Tibetan Buddhism, throwing the horns like a total metal nut.

It was the Beatles' time in India that led to a cartoon of John Lennon putting the horns up behind Paul McCartney's bonce on the sleeve of *Yellow Submarine*. The first metal musician seen doing it was Geezer Butler, in a 1969 photo in an old Sabbath compilation album.

Yet the metalhead who gets the most credit for popularizing the horns in the metal world is Ronnie James Dio. Ronnie always said his granny in Italy used to do it to ward off evil spirits and see off the devil, so he started doing the same thing onstage.

Ronnie was a lovely, sweet bloke and he always denied he deserved any credit for getting metal fans throwing horns.* He said he knew that Ozzy used to flash the peace sign, so when he replaced him in Sabbath, he started doing the horns just to differentiate himself from Ozzy.

I started doing the horns in Priest from the off. This helped to put us in the firing line in America in the eighties, with a load of other bands, when right-wing nutters and evangelical Christians began calling heavy metal the Devil's music and saying it encouraged Satanism.

---

* Ronnie was far too modest to claim he invented devil horns, but Gene Simmons isn't! In 2017, Gene tried to trademark putting the horns up, saying he'd pioneered it in 1974. He abandoned his trademark bid five days later . . .

It was so stupid that it was hilarious and some bands had fun with it. A lot of metal bands use demonic imagery and "666—the Number of the Beast" visuals, and I think that all started with them taking the piss and pushing back against the daft shit we were getting accused of:

"Huh? You really think we're devil worshippers? OK—what do you think of THIS, then?!"

Devil horns are meant to expel the Devil, not praise him! I can safely say the vast majority of metal bands throwing the horns onstage are not practicing Satanists . . . although, admittedly, there are a few exceptions.

A handful of Scandinavian death metal bands are devil worshippers. I know that a Swedish group called Watain are Luciferians. They come onstage and perform a ritual satanic service before their set. Which is quite a long way from Ronnie James Dio's granny warding off evil spirits!

You'd think it would be hard to get throwing the horns wrong but Glenn manages it. He doesn't put his index finger out so it always looks like he's doing the Hawaiian "hang loose" sign. It's a tiny thing in the scheme of things but, I must be honest, it's always infuriated me:

"Fucking hell, Glenn! That's not metal! Do the metal sign!"

And Glenn just grins, and carries on doing it wrong. Well, I suppose he's only had fifty years to learn it! Maybe he'll get it right, one day . . .

BIKERS

If we were to draw a Venn diagram with metalheads and rock fans in one circle, and bikers in the other, there would be a serious degree of overlap. There are a lot of similarities between those two tribes and lifestyles.

Rock and metal fans and bikers are both seen—and see themselves—as rebels and outsiders. They wear the same leather jackets and metal jewelry. They share a potent, masculine, alpha male image. And they only need to look at one another to know they're in the same gang.

Motorbikes have a powerful allure and it started for me when I was a little kid. My dad was bike-mad and would ride his Norton to work every day. When he came home at night, I'd hear him *vroom!* down our street then he'd push it down our entry and park it in the kitchen.*

Dad took me up and down our road on the back of his bike a few times and I was hooked. Then, when I was barely a teenager, I'd go with my mates after school to a bit of wasteland where an older lad would let us take turns on his Triumph. Zooming along with no helmet was dead thrilling.

Walsall is the leather center of Britain and when I got taken on a school trip to the town's leather museum, I loved it. I was getting into music, and the bands, the bikes, and the leather jackets felt part of the same thing. They all made sense together.

Getting my first bike in my late teens was brill. It was a putt-putt Yamaha moped that I rode to my job at Wolverhampton Grand Theatre. One day, I slipped on some mud where they were building what is now the M6, came arse-over-tit off it, and cracked my helmet (as it were).

As soon as I could afford it, I upgraded my moped to my first proper motorbike: a BSA. I felt so cool speeding around on that, especially after I'd painted those flames on it in honor of my first, short-lived metal band, Lord Lucifer.

A car gives you independence but a motorbike gives you *freedom*. It feels primal to be powering along exposed to the elements. There is also that frisson of edge and danger about riding a bike that you just don't get behind the wheel of a Vauxhall Viva.

Priest always had a few biker fans but that ratcheted up after I started riding a Harley-Davidson onstage. I did it on a whim at a gig in Derby, on the *Hell Bent for Leather* tour in 1979, and the rest is history. It's been the best-known and best-loved moment of our set ever since.

It made our biker following go through the roof, particularly in America. At Californian gigs, we'd get chapters of Hells Angels and other gangs turning up at the stage door before the show. There'd be all these big burly guys with long hair and beards wanting to meet me.

---

*Dad said the bike would get nicked if he left it outside, but Mom used to bollock him for keeping it in the house. She moaned even more when my sister, Sue, climbed on it when she was a toddler, the bike fell over, and Sue broke her arm!

I usually went out to say hello because (a) it was easier than saying no, and (b) *who wants to say "No" to a gang of Hells Angels?* They generally just wanted a handshake and a chinwag and they were always friendly and respectful.

Bikers have a ferocious image, but you can't tar everyone with the same brush. They're not all trouble. Some of them raise thousands of dollars for charity. I've got a mate who is a cop who belongs to a chapter of older bikers and they're always doing fund-raising charity runs.

Motorbikes get into your blood when you're young and they stay there. I've got mates in their seventies who are still bikers. I'd love to still have a bike and go riding myself, and I would do it if my bloody back didn't give me so much gip.

One little thing has changed. I used to ride my Harley onstage then get off to sing "Hell Bent for Leather." Now I do the whole song from on the bike. Singing on a motorbike looks strong and totally heavy metal, and it also yields an extra bonus:

I get to have a bloody rest and a nice sit-down for three minutes.

MERCHANDISE

If Elvis Presley invented rock and roll, his manager may well have been the man who dreamt up rock merchandising.

Colonel Tom Parker was very good at plastering Elvis's face on anything and everything, and he was a frugal businessman. After every show he'd send a lackey out into the auditorium. If any fans had dropped their 25 cent program, he'd pick them up, dust them down, and flog them again.

Merchandise is a big thing for metal and rock bands *and* for fans. For the bands, it's an increasingly important income stream. For the fans, it's a way of affirming their identity and showing their commitment to an artist: *I love this band so much that I wear them on my chest.*

It's a multimillion-dollar industry, unrecognizable from when I was a kid. I used to gawp at Zeppelin or Deep Purple T-shirts but never buy them. They always seemed too expensive and, in any case, I was saving my hard-earned cash to buy their albums.

It felt like a big thing when Priest took our first nervous baby steps into merchandising around *Sad Wings of Destiny*. Our opening items were pretty primitive: band T-shirts, patches for battle vests, and little enamel button badges.

We'd flog them from a trestle table at the back of gigs or, later, via mail order. There were a couple of pages at the back of the music papers for selling stuff like that. For some reason, the ads always said that delivery would take between four and six weeks. *Huh? Why?*

Fast-forward to today, when overnight delivery is a given and metal and rock fans can buy pretty much anything with a band's name on it. Beer mugs, bottle openers, necklaces, rings, scarves, wallets, baseball caps, tote bags, key rings: you name it and it's a click of an iPad away.

Priest have two online stores now, one for the UK and Europe and one for North America. They're run by fiercely efficient merch companies who monitor our sales digitally. If we're on the road and sell five hundred shirts at a gig, they FedEx five hundred replacements to our next show.

Our merchandise is vast and varied nowadays but one thing doesn't change. Classic items like T-shirts from our *British Steel*, *Screaming for Vengeance*, or *Defenders of the Faith* eras always sell. Often, it is fans replacing the moth-eaten original shirts they bought forty years ago.

The merch companies will present our management with ideas to show us, but I also like thinking up items myself. I was proud of our *British Steel*–logo necklace, shaped like the razor blade on the album cover. It's been a steady seller for many years now.

If you have a gander at our site, we've got everything under the sun. Priest aprons and branding irons for barbeques. Socks and pants, in a neat little box. Metal Gods pendants and *British Steel* tankards. Well, who could resist *those* winning items?

You can get Priest hoodies, bobble hats, or coloring books: the latter have become a big thing in recent years. Or you can buy a 500-piece *Painkiller* jigsaw puzzle. I must admit, I've never sat down and tried to do it. I haven't got the bloody patience.

As soon as Richie Faulkner joined us, I started calling him the Falcon and he totally ran with it. Now he sells his own merchandise, stuff like "The Falcon" T-shirts. Well, good for him, even if I'm quietly thinking: *Oi, Falcon! Where's my 10 percent?*

Some bands sell limited-edition luxury items because they know they have a few wealthy fans who don't want a $40 T-shirt but a $400 leather jacket. The Rolling Stones do that. We did a £70 battle vest, which I think was good value (well, I would say that, wouldn't I?).

You never know what's going to sell. Over the years, we've introduced one or two things I've thought will fly out and nobody has bought them. Or we've tried to get too clever with a T-shirt design, or tried out a new color scheme, and they've died on their arse.

We're also always battling against bootleg merchandise. There are a lot of sharp, quick operators out there. In fact, one of the most famous Judas Priest merchandise items of all time was a bootleg product and we never saw a penny from it.

When I started cracking a bullwhip onstage, black button badges soon sprang up saying "I'VE BEEN WHIPPED BY ROB HALFORD!"* They were a great idea, and I've still got a couple myself, but they were all flogged by dodgy bootleggers outside venues and via mail order.

We could try to go after those guys, but what's the point? For a while, in the States, bands were hiring private security to see off the bootleggers. Even the police got involved sometimes—but ultimately, bootleg merchandise is just pure capitalism. You can't stop it.

I have to grudgingly admit, some of the bootleg merch is brilliant. When we go to Mexico City, we will be driving to the venue, and we'll see stall after stall after stall of vendors selling knock-off Priest stuff all along the side of the road.

Once or twice, we've stopped to have a look and been amazed by the quality of the shirts: "Fucking hell, that design is better than ours! It's brilliant!" They'll be selling them for $1, compared to the $40 we have to charge. We don't even bother taking merch to South America now.

Priest have never gone as far down the merchandise route as a band like Kiss. They used to sell everything from condoms to caskets (oops,

---

*For some reason, that slogan always reminded me of that famous old headline in *The Sun*: FREDDIE STARR ATE MY HAMSTER! I suppose there are similarities.

sorry: kondoms to kaskets). Have a look around the room you're sitting in now. Whatever you see, you can probably buy Kiss-branded versions of it.

Kiss toasters, Kiss kettles, Kiss microwaves, Kiss air fresheners, Kiss lamps, Kiss doormats, Kiss pajamas, Kiss Swarovski coffee tumblers (a steal at $500!) . . . they've put their logo on everything, and good luck to them, I guess. They're the kings of rock merchandising.

Merchandise is a bigger deal than ever for bands nowadays. As companies like Spotify take away our income from record and CD sales, merch is an important income stream even before the Covid pandemic killed the touring industry stone dead for nearly two years.

When you can't sell CDs or gig tickets, T-shirt sales matter. It's been a tough time for every band recently and merchandise income has paid a lot of bills for a lot of musicians. We can't afford not to take it very seriously.

I wanted us to have some special merch for our *50 Heavy Metal Years* tour and came up with the brainwave of medallions. They're big, gold-colored aluminum commemorative coins that come in a case, and I don't think any band has done anything like them before.

I got so carried away when I had the idea that I suggested we make some from plastic to throw into the crowd at the end of our shows. Our management gently pointed out that hurling medallions into thousands of fans would most likely end up taking someone's eye out: *"We're not sure our insurers will be too keen on this idea, Rob . . ."*

So that was the end of that. Fair enough, really. I mean, I wanted to give our fans something special for our golden anniversary, but I didn't want to blind them.

AWARDS

Ever since I got clapped for chirruping "Speed, bonnie boat . . ." in primary school, I've always loved being told: "Well done!" *Everyone* does. It's just human nature. And in the rock and metal world, the primary ritual and service for giving out prizes is the awarding of sales discs. That is, silver, gold, and platinum records.

I'm not going to lie: when Priest first started being given silver and gold discs, in the early eighties, it was a great feeling. They obviously proved that we were selling a ton of records and also established a connectivity to our fan base and showed how we were growing together.

Because when you get a silver or gold disc, it's not just for you. It's for your bandmates, for your fans, and for metal as a whole. It reinforces your belief in the very concept of heavy metal: *Wow! Just look how many fucking people are into it now! This is big league!*

Sales discs are great but they also make you greedy. Once you've got a silver disc, you want a gold one. Once you've got a gold disc, you can't wait to get a platinum one. And then you want a double-platinum disc. It definitely gives you a *more-more-more!* buzz.

The industry gives you a disc for each member of the band. In the old days, there'd often be a little ceremony, with a photographer from *Music Week* or *Billboard*. Nowadays, they generally just get posted to our management office, and they send them on to us.

Everybody has a different approach to sales discs. Glenn has every one we've ever been given up on his studio walls. Ian is the same. He's just moved house and I know it'll be no time before he hangs them all around the place.

I'm a bit different. It's a big deal for me that we get these discs, and I appreciate the gesture, but I never hang them out on display. I have a closet full of silver, gold, and platinum discs in my house in Phoenix and I never even look at them (not the first things I've hidden in a closet . . .).

Most are still in their boxes and envelopes, unopened. I find it hard to say exactly why I *don't* hang them on the wall, except that I don't like shining a spotlight on them: *Ta-da! Everyone, look what I've won!* It's not very yam-yam. I'm just content to know they're there.

In Priest's imperial eighties period, we got a shitload of sales discs. In the States, *British Steel*, *Defenders of the Faith*, and *Turbo* all went platinum. *Screaming for Vengeance* went double-platinum. It wasn't unknown for name bands to sell half a million albums a week.

Now, in these Spotify* days, if an album sells fifteen thousand units in its week of release, it's seen as a decent accomplishment. The music biz has adapted accordingly and now awards silver and gold discs based on not just physical sales but also downloads and streams.

There is (or was) a purity to sales discs as a measure of success: they simply reflect how many records you've flogged. The other prizes that bands get given are discretionary awards. These come from magazines or bodies that run votes or decide for themselves that you are worth rewarding.

Some artists are very dismissive of these awards, but I'm not. I think they're a nice gesture. They show that people are thinking about us. When Priest are put in *Kerrang!*'s Hall of Fame or I'm given *Loudwire*'s Lemmy Lifetime Achievement Award, it means a lot.

The biggest bauble for music acts is the Grammy Awards. They're almost like an equivalent of the Oscars; they don't dish Grammys out willy-nilly. Even being nominated is a huge deal and gives you a certain cachet, whether you win or not.

Priest got nominated four times between 1991, for "Painkiller," and 2009, for "Visions" and "Nostradamus." When you are nominated, you get given a medal on a ribbon and a certificate, which is a nice enough token. But we didn't win any of them.

All nominees are automatically invited to the Grammys ceremony. But then you have to buy a ticket, which is bloody expensive. I didn't go to any of those first shows. I didn't know if we'd win or not, but that wasn't the issue: I was just busy elsewhere on the big nights.

My Fight producer, Attie Bauw, went to one of those ceremonies with his wife, Mary. I asked Mary to phone me in Walsall when they got to our nomination, at midnight UK time, and to hold her phone up so I could hear what was going on. I can't remember who won, but it wasn't us.

"You didn't win, Rob," she told me.

"Yeah, I know," I sighed. "Cheers, Mary."

---

*I can't remember—have I told you what I think of Spotify?

When Priest *did* win in 2010, for Best Metal Performance for "Dissident Aggressor," I went to the ceremony. I didn't know in advance we'd won, but I just had a gut feeling that we might. I flew in to LA from Phoenix, Scott Travis came along, and Jayne Andrews flew all the way from London.

The Grammy Awards ceremony is hideously long. It seems to go on for days. To try to expedite it a little, they announce some of the winners of the non-showpiece awards in a pre-ceremony, in a separate building by the main venue, which was then still called the Staples Center.

After we'd done the red carpet, Scott, Jayne, and I were taken there and sat at the back. Even this mini-ceremony went on for yonks, and the metal award was the very last one. They read the nominations—Priest, Lamb of God, Megadeth, Ministry, Slayer—then announced the winner:

"Judas Priest, for 'Dissident Aggressor'!"

Whoosh! And Scott was out of his seat and off down the aisle like an Olympic athlete! He was almost sprinting as I followed him towards the stage. In my tuxedo and bowtie, I made a short speech: "Fifth time is a charm! This is our fifth nomination . . ."

Scott and I just had time to grab some grub and then it was over to the Staples Center for the main show. They gave us good seats near to the front and I loved star-spotting the A-listers: Elton John and Lady Gaga opened the show, and Ringo was onstage. I found it all very exciting.

My Grammy is in my bedroom in Phoenix now. When it was given to me, it was all sparkly, but now it looks tarnished. If you send it to them, the Grammy people will clean and polish it for you, but I actually like it more the way it is. It feels a bit more authentic.

Our Grammy was a massive deal, but sometimes it is the less famous, more left-field awards that move me the most. In December 2020, I was truly honored to be given a Cultural Icon Award at the Tom of Finland Foundation Awards in LA.

The Scandinavian designer Tom of Finland died more than thirty years ago, but he is still a bit of a god in the gay world. In fact, Tom's style and influence, his very *essence*, permeate throughout gay art, culture, and erotica.

Although I was still firmly in the closet at the time, I was wearing a Tom of Finland T-shirt—all cocks and blow jobs—when I handcuffed myself to Andy Warhol in 1979. Now, here was my first award that was linked not to music but to me being gay, and it meant the world to me.

The Tom of Finland Awards were low-key, but I met Larry Flynt, the legendary publisher of *Hustler* who was paralyzed in a murder attempt in 1978. In his gold wheelchair, Larry got a lifetime achievement award for fighting censorship. I have such fond memories of the whole night.

In 2022, Judas Priest got nominated for inclusion in the Rock and Roll Hall of Fame. It wasn't the first time this had happened. We also got nominated in 2018 and 2020 but didn't get in on either occasion. We got the bum's rush both times.

This time was different. At the start of May, it was announced that we were to be inducted into the Hall alongside Eminem, Dolly Parton, and Duran Duran (the green room should be fun!). They were to give us what they call their Award for Musical Excellence.

My thoughts on this are straightforward: *bloody great!* Some people slag off the Hall of Fame and call it meaningless, but I don't agree. *So, awards mean nothing?* Well, you could say the same about the Oscars, the Grammys, the Emmys, whatever! And it's simply not true.

For me, the Hall of Fame is an acknowledgment of our work; our career; our contribution to music. It's decided by a voting system that includes past winners, so, really, it's an approval of Priest by our predecessors and our peers. It feels a bit like passing on the baton.

Third time is the charm. For some reason, when this nomination came in, I thought we'd get it. I don't know whether it was just gut instinct—or the fact that my mum's mum was a clairvoyant! It just felt to me like our time had come.

Well, our time *has* come and I'm chuffed: chuffed for us, chuffed for the fans—because it means a lot to them—and, most of all, chuffed for heavy metal. Look at the list of Hall of Fame members. There are only three metal bands: Black Sabbath, Metallica, and now Priest!

I know some people will point to Led Zeppelin or Deep Purple, but I don't think they're heavy metal. They're great hard rock bands. And even if we *do* include them, it's still not remotely enough for a genre of music that is loved and bought by millions and millions of people.

After the result got announced, *Loudwire*, the metal website, ran an opinion piece asking why Priest were nominated in the "musical excellence" category and not just as performers. They called it a "backhanded compliment" and, um, a "feckless cop-out."

Are they right? I've lain awake one or two nights pondering that question but, ultimately, who knows? *Who cares?* The musical excellence category is for "artists, musicians, songwriters and producers whose originality and influence have had a dramatic impact on music," and, well, *I'll take that*. Frankly, I'm just happy to be in there. At last.

Because, as I say, I've always loved and valued being given awards. And I'd much rather get them while we're still going strong than when I'm long gone and pushing up the daisies . . .

SUPERGROUPS

Not all metal and rock rituals and services last forever. Back in the late sixties and early seventies, famous musicians had a tendency to form themselves into what used to be known as supergroups. It's a practice that has now largely fallen out of favor.

Those supergroups were often known simply by the names of their rock-celeb members: Emerson, Lake & Palmer. Crosby, Stills, Nash & Young. Beck, Bogert & Appice. Paice Ashton Lord. Or, they'd get named after their most famous member, like Ginger Baker's Air Force.

None of them really meant much to me. The only supergroup that I can remember impacting me at all were Blind Faith, who were made up of Eric Clapton, Steve Winwood, Ric Grech, and Ginger Baker. And for all the hype around them, they only ever made one album.

It's possible that supergroups are a bit of a flawed concept. When normal bands form, they're gangs of mates, starting from scratch and taking on the world. Supergroup members are already rich, famous, and successful, with rock-star egos most likely firmly in place.

One sort-of supergroup were Humble Pie, who included Steve Marriott from the Small Faces, Peter Frampton, and Greg Ridley from Spooky Tooth. In 1981, Priest played some dates in America with a later version of the band, by then without Frampton and Ridley.

We were in a lift with them when Steve Marriott made a homophobic comment that was obviously aimed at me. Glenn heard it, and pinned Marriott against the wall by his throat: "Don't *ever* fucking say that again!" I was still in the closet then, but I was chuffed that Glenn stood up for me.

The closest I've ever come to being in a supergroup was the Three Tremors concept back in 2000. It was my partner Thomas's idea. We were talking about opera's Three Tenors—Pavarotti, Plácido Domingo, and José Carreras—and a light bulb came on over Thomas's head:

"Hey! Wouldn't it be great to have three metal singers called the Three Tremors?"

We tried to make it happen, firstly with me, Bruce Dickinson, and Ronnie James Dio (how cool would *that* have been?!) and then me, Bruce, and Geoff Tate from Queensrÿche. Everyone was dead up for it, but sadly we wouldn't make our schedules match up and make it work.

As it happens, there *is* a Three Tremors trio of metal singers now, with my temporary Priest replacement, Tim "Ripper" Owens, in it. When I first heard, I was pissed off they had nicked our name without asking us—but we never trademarked it. Well, it is what it is.

Supergroups work if they are just a bunch of musicians getting together to play for the love of the music, with no egos attached. An example is Bad Penny, a group made up of guitarist Mike Holzman, former Queen + Paul Rodgers bassist Danny Miranda, and Blue Öyster Cult drummer Jules Radino.

They've made collaborative singles with ex-Journey singer Steve Augeri and current Queensrÿche front man Todd La Torre. Mike recently asked me to guest on a song called "Push Comes to Shove." I loved the track so I went into a studio and laid the vocal down. No messing! Job done!

I've always loved playing a game I call Fantasy Supergroup: idly speculating in my head about what would be the greatest ever band line-up. Where do you start? Ian Gillan, Hendrix, Paul McCartney, and Buddy Rich? Robert Plant, Lennon, Lemmy, and Gene Krupa? The possibilities are endless!

I decided to play a little game and pick the best supergroup I would love to be in. In fact, I have picked two: the best metal and the best rock supergroups. I've set myself the ground rules that members can be alive or dead, but I can't choose any Priest members, past or present.

My best metal supergroup would have Dimebag Darrell from Pantera on guitar, Cliff Burton from Metallica on bass, and Joey Jordison from Slipknot on drums. I'd be co-vocalist with Ronnie James Dio. It means it would be me and four dead guys, but what a fucking band!

For the rock supergroup, I'd have Hendrix on guitar, Jack Bruce from Cream on bass, Ringo on drums, Jon Lord from Deep Purple on keyboards, and I'd share vocals with Janis Joplin. *Wow!* If that band is going to play any festivals in the afterlife, we'll definitely be headlining . . .

TRIBUTE BANDS

In all the world of metal and rock, there is no more arcane or singular ritual of worship than the tribute band.

Tribute bands are musicians paying heartfelt homages to artists that they love, and they are frequently much maligned. In fact, the term is often used to condemn groups that are seen as mere copyists, without any originality of their own: "Ah, they're no more than a tribute band!"

I think this is unkind and unfair. Tribute bands are simply fans showing how much they love the music you make, and the songs you've written, by playing the songs themselves. It's an act of love and it should be a humbling phenomenon for the original artist to witness.

It's strange that I feel this way, because, when Priest started out, we were determined only to play our own material and not cover other bands' songs. We stuck to this at our early working men's club gigs, even if the promoter dangled a financial incentive in front of us:

"Lads, I'll pay you an extra fiver if you'll do some tunes from the charts!"

"Sorry, no, we're Judas Priest and we only play our own songs."

"But nobody *knows* any of your bloody songs!"

"They soon will!"

But I don't mind tribute acts at all and some of them are enormous. The Abba tribute band, Björn Again, have filled theaters for more than thirty years and headlined the Royal Albert Hall. The Australian Pink Floyd pack out arenas all over the world in their own right.

Priest also have tribute bands dotted around the world. I wish them all well. I've never been to one of the gigs, but I've seen a few of the groups on YouTube. Metalachi play mariachi versions of songs like "Breaking the Law" and are . . . quite something.

When I did "Push Comes to Shove" with Bad Penny, a metal singer called Militia Vox duetted with me. Militia also sings in an all-female New York tribute band, Judas Priestess,* who are brilliant. They've headlined biker festivals and toured with Twisted Sister and Pentagram.

Interestingly, of course, Priest turned to the tribute band world when I accidentally defenestrated myself from the group in the nineties. The replacement for me that the group chose was Tim "Ripper" Owens, who was then the singer in a US Priest tribute band named British Steel.

I guess they got some flak for this, with some wrist merchants sneering they'd hired a tribute to Rob Halford, but I think this was a bit unfair. Tim also sang in a band playing original songs and he had his own vocal chops. He certainly wasn't just a copycat of me.

Plus—how on earth could they begin to replace a vocalist as unique and iconic as me?! (Sorry, I just couldn't resist that!)

The whole question of replacement musicians is a thorny one for metal and rock bands. There are some old-school fans who will simply

---

*We're not the only metal band to have our own all-female tribute act. Also out there are Lez Zeppelin, The Iron Maidens, and Black Sabbitch.

never accept any line-up changes. If groups make too many, they can end up being accused of being their own tribute band.

Priest get that sometimes, since Ken left and now Glenn can't play with us as much. Some Queen fans will never accept Adam Lambert, cool as he is. And what about The Who without the Ox and Keith Moon? The Rolling Stones without Brian Jones or Charlie Watts? Are they still viable?

Well, of course they bloody are! If a member leaves or, in a worst-case scenario, dies, a band have to either find a replacement or call it a day. *Do fans really want the band to split?!* You can get groups with only one original member left: Dave Hill's Slade or, dare I say it, yeah, let's say it, KK's Priest.

For me, the test is: *Are those bands still writing and playing new songs?* If they are, good luck to them. If not, and they are merely churning out the old hits, they may have to face the possibility that they've become their own tribute band. At least they should be pretty accurate.

THE BOOK
OF TEMPTATIONS

That other Bible is full of tales of temptation. The serpent tempted Adam and Eve to eat the apple from the forbidden tree, after which they got booted out of the Garden of Eden. Samson's lust for Delilah made him careless, he allowed his hair to be cut, and he lost his divinely given strength.

Even that book's star turn, Jesus, was almost tempted by Satan to turn stones into bread while he was in the wilderness. There again, I'm not surprised JC nearly cracked: he hadn't eaten for forty days and forty nights! I'm the same: I'm a right mardy sod until I've had me dinner.

The metal and rock world's temptations may be different but they're just as powerful. Many a metal god has turned out to have feet of clay. And the temptations facing us can be just as diabolic: not for nothing is alcohol known as the demon drink.

Rock prophets can be just as venal as anybody else, or more, and their falls from grace always happen in the harsh spotlight of public scrutiny. Weakness of spirit and hedonistic abandon lead us sinners to drink and drugs, and who *hasn't* succumbed to the siren voices of sins of the flesh?

When the world of music leads its stars into temptation, how can they deliver themselves from evil—and is there a cure for the dreaded rock curse of Lead Singer Disease? Take my hand, my children, it's time for these heavy metal scriptures to wallow in the world of sin . . .

ALCOHOL

I would have been an alcoholic whether I was in a metal band or not. But being in a band certainly helped me on my way.

I was a fiend for booze from my very first sip. Like most working-class British lads, I started drinking when I was about sixteen. I absolutely loved it. As soon as I had left school, started work, and had a bit of dosh in my pocket, getting wankered every night was my priority.

As I explained in *Confess*, I could never just go out and have a pint or two. It was barley wine with Mogadon chasers all night long, until I puked or passed out, or both. *Drinking was my social life, but I wasn't a social drinker.* I was on a quest for oblivion.

Looking back, it was the first clue that I was an alcoholic. Obviously, I didn't think that way at the time. Alkies were tramps on park benches! If anyone had suggested that *I* was one, I'd have thought that they were mad: *"Fuck off! I'm not a bloody alkie! I just like a drink!"*

Alcoholics will do anything to get a drink. If they work in an office, they will sneak booze in and hide it in their desk. Well, I never needed to do anything like *that* because I started doing a job where drinking isn't just tolerated and encouraged, it is virtually compulsory.

I joined a heavy metal band.

Alcohol is totally part of the lifestyle of being in a metal or rock band. If you're in the studio: you drink. If you're in rehearsals: you drink. And if you go out on tour, promoters buy you gallons of beer and wine and leave it on a table in your dressing room for you! *Wahey! Jackpot!*

In the studio, in the early days, I'd drink to take the edge off my nerves. Singing is such a personal thing and you can feel so vulnerable when you do it. When we were in the studio making our first albums, and I knew my vocal tracks were coming up, I would get *so* anxious.

The other Priest members would know, and they'd often suggest I had a snifter to calm my nerves. I didn't need telling twice! By the time I got behind the mic, I'd always have a few bevvies inside me. Tom Allom, our producer, positively recommended this solution.

"Robbo!" he'd say, in his plummy, patrician tones. "Have a glass of wine, old boy! It'll help you to relax and get into the song a little more!" So, I would. I even started believing—or, at least, telling myself—that it was making me sing better.

Live shows were different. Priest would always—and I mean *always*—get hammered after gigs, but initially we had an unspoken rule that we didn't drink before a show. We'd heard horror stories about bands going onstage pissed, and we didn't want it to happen to us.

It was a wise policy, but it went right out the window for me as we got bigger and my already-heavy drinking got totally out of control. By the time we were playing US arenas in the early eighties, I was taking to the stage in a horrible state. I was basically a heavy metal pisshead with a microphone.

The routine would start with me arriving at the venue still feeling shit from the night before and having a quick vodka tonic before I went on. Except it was never *one* vodka tonic. You know what they say: one drink is too many, and one hundred is not enough . . .

Soon, I was lurching to the stage with a pint of neat vodka in my hand. I'd swig from it through the show, after each song. Every time I put it down, one of the roadies would top it up. If I was sweating like a pig under the lights, I'd get through a full bottle of Smirnoff by the end.

I'd hold it together, *just about*. My vocals didn't go *totally* to shit. But if I listen back to any of those gigs now, I wince at how substandard they were, and I was, compared to how I should have been. I was pissed and just hanging in there.

The drinking made me put on weight. I look at photos of myself from the *Metal Conqueror* tour in 1984 and I was Fat Rob. My face was fatter and so was my waist. It meant that, during gigs, I wasn't just pissed: I was knackered from running around the stage.

In fact, I'd sometimes wake up the next morning, or more likely early afternoon, with no memory of the show at all: *Fuck! Did we even play last night?* And my hangover would be killing me. *I know! Time for a vodka tonic . . .*

I was falling to bits but nobody from the band or management had a word with me. That's not how bands worked back then. We were five guys, getting pissed every night—and, anyway, that was the cool rock-and-roll lifestyle! Shit, it was almost expected of us!

Glenn drank. Ken drank. Ian drank. Dave drank. They either didn't drink as much as me or they handled it better. Plus . . . don't forget the macho factor! Blokes back then simply didn't tell each other to drink less. Had one of them even tried, I'm sure I'd have told them to fuck off.*

There were a few reasons I was drinking so much. I had the pressure and headfuck of hiding my sexuality and living a lie in the spotlight. And I was in a volatile, passionate, and dysfunctional relationship that was to end in tragedy. No bloody wonder I took refuge in a bottle!

It couldn't go on and it didn't. By the time we came to make *Turbo* in the Bahamas in 1985, I was scarcely functioning. I'd drink from when I woke up until I passed out that night. Alcohol was my reflex, my prop, and my only way to get through the day.

The music? Fuck that! That was just my accessory to the drinking!

Everything was wrong with my life, but it was alcohol that drove me to my suicide attempt at the end of '85. I'd been drinking for hours, but it was the culmination of twenty years of alcoholism when I sat on my bed, downed a bottle of JD, and swallowed sleeping pills like Smarties.

Nobody loves me, I told myself. *There's no point in anything. If I die, no one will miss me. Why bother being alive? Nobody loves me . . .*

I could, and would, have died that night had there not been a friend in my house who drove me to ER to have my stomach pumped. And I had one last week of binge drinking, blackouts, and self-loathing before my mind told me the message that I should have absorbed years earlier:

I. Need. To. Go. To. Rehab.

Some people are dragged kicking and screaming to a facility. I wasn't like that. I remember feeling very calm and relaxed as I was checked into an alcohol recovery unit. *This is the right thing to do. I have to do this.* In a weird way, I felt at peace.

---

*The world has changed a little today. Nowadays, somebody in a band might tell another member: "I care about you and it upsets me that you're drinking so much." But that stuff never happened in the big bad eighties!

Wherever they may be—even fronting a hugely successful heavy metal band—alcoholics will always feel lonely. You think, *Nobody else is like me. Nobody else knows what I'm going through.* So, suddenly being in rehab, with people in precisely the same boat, is a revelation.

I'd sit in a circle with people suffering from exactly the same illness as me, and we would talk about it. We'd discuss our disease. That group therapy gave me reassurance. I enjoyed the calm and peacefulness of the place. And I enjoyed being off the booze.

I didn't even miss it. I think my body and mind knew drink had almost destroyed me, and now I was done with it. If I carried on, I wouldn't be able to go on with Priest . . . and I wouldn't be able to go on with my life. Because I would die. It was that simple.

I left rehab, after thirty days, having made a life affirmation and commitment to staying clean and sober. I wanted to feel physically and mentally well and to do a better job as a singer. And I wanted to connect to Priest's music again. Because, for a while, I had lost that.

That didn't mean I wasn't nervous. I went back to finish *Turbo* not knowing if I could sing sober in the studio—because I had never done it before. It was wonderful to learn not only that I *could* do it but that I loved doing it. And that I was singing so much better.

Pissed, I always had to be cajoled or coaxed by the producer to give my best vocal performance. I'd never really know if I'd done a good take. Now, suddenly, I felt that I was where I needed to be to get the best result. I was connected to my voice, to *myself*, again.

Even so, I was still returning to a world where booze reigned supreme: life in a band. I distinctly remember going out on tour sober for the first time and thinking, *Well, that's it! I can't even come offstage and celebrate with a drink anymore! The fun is over!*

Priest tried to help. They knew I might be struggling and they asked me: "Shall we ban booze in the dressing room? Knock it on the head?" I appreciated that, but I said, "No. Why should *you* have to change your lives for *me*?" And I'd just leave the room when they drank.

It's a mindfuck for recovering musicians. Alcohol counselors tell you to remove yourself from all temptations. Well, when you're in a rock or metal band, that's not an option, because booze is embedded in the lifestyle. All that you can do is stay strong.

When I came out of rehab, they gave me helpline numbers and told me I'd need to go to AA meetings for the rest of my life. I've never been to one. Most counselors would have told me that I was kidding myself if I thought I could do that. How've I done it? Fuck knows! But I have.

I'm lucky that I have that stubborn personality because I have a lot of close friends in bands who have gone through rehab, come out, and lapsed. They've done it again and again, three or four times. And, you know what? I know exactly why they can't stay away from the booze:

Because drinking is fucking great fun!

I mean, that's why people become alcoholics! They equate drinking with a good time, and they're right. When I look back on my early- and mid-period drinking years, I had an absolute blast, right up until I lost control, it took over, and everything went to shit.

In fact, because booze can be so great, I still sometimes wonder: *Could I go back to it? Could I do it again, and get the great kick and the laughs of drinking, and not get addicted this time? Why not try it and find out? Why not have a little drink? Just a sip?*

That temptation is still there after thirty-six years sober, but I just have to stop and tell myself: *No. I can't. Some people can drink, even drink heavily, and still function coherently, but I can't. I can't because I'm an alcoholic, and I will be until the day I die.*

Luckily, there are so many great aspects to sobriety. I've found I can still function as a singer, and live the metal life, while not drinking. I have a lot more self-respect than I did. And I enjoy myself, in the studio *and* onstage, far more than I did when I was wankered all the time.

It's a big *Biblical* fact: alcohol is a massive part of life in a metal or rock band, especially in the early days. It's not a career path that any rehab counselor would recommend. I'm proud that I've proved you can still fly the metal flag on the straight and narrow. But let me tell you this:

It's not been bloody easy.

DRUGS

Once a metal or rock musician is well acquainted with alcohol, there is every chance they will soon meet its close friend, drugs. In fact, it's very likely that it is alcohol who will introduce them: "You like me? Then meet my best mate, cocaine! You'll *love* him!"

I was only in my late teens when I took my first drugs. If I was out on the piss, which I always was, I'd supplement the booze with the Mogadon tablets I'd buy from dodgy blokes down my local. They were strong antidepressant pills that gave me a nice chilled-out buzz.

I didn't see them as *drugs*, as I didn't the Valium and other painkillers me and my mates used to neck. My thinking was: *Well, these are just medicines that doctors prescribe to people like my mom! And if doctors give them out, they must be OK! Sound! Let's have another one!*

It's strange in a way that I used to take those because, in my youth, I was virulently anti-drugs. I associated cocaine or heroin with rock stars whom I loved that had died of overdoses, which made me hate those drugs. I thought they were a horrible, destructive force on music and on life.

I extended this dislike to cannabis and marijuana, which I thought just as bad as smack and coke, or at least a gateway to them. In my early twenties, I lived in a shared house with a massive stoner—Nick, who, as I've mentioned, used to roadie for Priest—but I was never tempted to join in.

Nick would come home from his shift as a nurse at the local hospital and roll a spliff or fire up a massive bong. I'd sit next to him and I'd sometimes even get high from passive smoking. *Hmm, this is a nice feeling!* I'd muse. But I stuck to my puritanical guns. *No, thank you!*

I was still on the moral high ground when Priest played Reading Festival in 1975 and I took it upon myself to lecture the crowd: "You might enjoy this one, if you can be bothered to take the needles out of your arms!" The irony that I was pissed out of my head when I said it escaped me.

It wasn't until I moved to Phoenix in 1981 that I dropped my anti-drug agenda—and I didn't mess about. I just decided one day: *Fuck it, let's try it!* One of the guys I was hanging out with would buy industrial-strength marijuana and I began to demolish it.

He would get hold of a "lid": about an ounce of grass, so named because that's how much can fit in the lid of a Mason jar or in a tobacco tin. I'd smoke a massive bong, drink a few shots, get in my Corvette, and somehow get from my home in Paradise Valley to Rocker's Bar right on the other side of Phoenix.

I'd still be high from the bong as I glugged pitcher after pitcher of beer at Rocker's. Then I'd drive home. It was shitty behavior because I'd be in a hideous state. I'd pull up outside my house and realize I couldn't remember where I'd just been, or why:

I know I've been out somewhere and done something. I think I went out at nine o'clock and now it's two in the morning. So, what have I been doing? Fuck, let's go inside and have a hit on the bong . . . *

Once I'd embraced marijuana, I didn't know when to stop. I got through *so* many lids. I'd have a ziplock bag full of hundreds of dollars' worth of grass and work my way through the lot. It reached the point it didn't hit the spot on its own anymore, so I'd neck Schnapps with it.

Like so many people in metal and rock bands, though, I could handle my dependence on cannabis and marijuana (or, rather, I *thought* that I could). My real downfall came when I met cocaine.

There is often coke knocking around bands, especially in LA, and that was where I first tried it. It was the same process as grass: there had always been people asking me if I wanted some. "No, thanks," I'd tell them primly. "I don't do cocaine." And then, one day, I decided to say yes instead.

Big. Fucking. Mistake.

I loved coke from my first snort. I could feel it firing into my brain and it gave me an instant euphoric high. Suddenly, I had loads of things to say, I was the sharpest and wittiest person in the room . . . and the only thing that mattered was getting more coke. A *lot* more.

---

* It took my arrest for DUI to stop me being a drunk-driving wanker. It didn't seem like it at the time, but it was the best thing that could have happened to me.

The coke buzz would last about twenty minutes, then I'd need to top it up. It also helped me drink more (as if in those days I needed any fucking help in that department!). The Charlie was never hard to get hold of. Some hangers-on around the band saw to that.

There's no point in doing coke on your own, or with people who aren't taking it. You have to all be on it together. Then, you can gather in a great big huddle, show off, and jabber nonstop bullshit to one another, all the time grinding your teeth, feeling paranoid, and fiending for more.

When I was with the first love of my life, Brad, who was tragically to kill himself, we did mental amounts of coke together. At times, it felt like that was *all* we did. We were both totally addicted by now, and we'd finish up nearly every night twitchy, agitating . . . and fighting.

It came to an end the horrible night in LA when we went to watch *The Tonight Show Starring Johnny Carson* being recorded. I had always liked the show, and Carson's quick wit. I remember that Bob Hope appeared at the end and I was starstruck: *Oh my God! That's Bob Hope!*

After the show, Brad and I got totally hammered and finished up in a Mexican restaurant. A mariachi band were wandering from table to table, playing for tips. When they got to our table, a pissed Brad turned on the charm. *Sort of.*

"Huh! I can play the guitar better than that!" he announced.

One of the mariachi guys stopped playing straightaway and handed Brad his guitar. Brad obviously *couldn't* play it better, and he felt put on the spot, which he hated. It sent him into a filthy mood for the rest of the night.

This filthy mood only got worse when we got back to our hotel room and dug out the coke. *Mountains* of coke. The night ended with a full-on row, the LAPD being called, then Brad and I having a fist fight that left both of us blooded and bruised. We could have killed each other.

And we would have, if we'd both carried on taking coke. But I was only a week or so away from the bottom of the shitpit, my suicide attempt, and me finally agreeing to go into rehab. Sadly, Brad was not so lucky and he never stopped. I've never touched a drug since.

It's the weirdest thing. Unlike alcohol, I don't look back on my drug-taking days with any fondness or nostalgia whatsoever. I don't have any happy memories of drugs. I just remember them damaging my health, my relationships, my self-esteem, my self-control, *my life*.

I have mates in rock and metal bands who are casual, recreational drug users. They can just have the occasional joint or the odd line when they feel like it. They party and indulge now and then . . . but I reckon they are the exception that proves the rule.

I still think my first, teenage instinct was correct. Drugs fuck with metal and rock musicians' minds and careers. They can *end* those careers, and, as we tragically know, they can end their lives. Rock-and-roll history is littered with stars who lived too fast and died too young.

I've been in a band for nearly fifty years and I've partied fucking hard in my time. But when it comes to drugs, my advice is as safe, conservative, and old-fashioned as it comes: *Just say no, kids.* Does that make me a hypocrite? No. I think it just means that I grew up.

SEX

I said earlier that most guys join metal or rock bands because they want to play music and go on tour. That's true, but we need to add another motivation to that list: because they want to get as many leg overs as is humanly possible.

Blokes have always formed bands to try to get women. They long to do a show every night, then do a groupie afterward. That's a total rush for them and there's no point in denying it: *it is what it is.* That's men for you, and male sexuality.

It was very bloody different for me, of course! As a gay man, I certainly didn't join a metal band thinking it would be a good way to score some action with fans. It was the furthest thing from my mind. In fact, I knew from the off I'd have to hide my sexuality for a very, very long time.

Priest started getting groupies surprisingly early in our career. We'd do a pub or working men's club gig and there'd be a few girls hanging around afterward. Sometimes they were schoolgirls, or "jailbait" as the charming phrase used to be. Happily, nobody did anything dumb there.

If a band member and a girl did the dirty deed after a show, it was very much *wham-bam-thank-you-ma'am*! They might do it in a cubicle in the dressing-room toilet, in the back of the van, or up against the wall in an alleyway. Sometimes it was discreet and sometimes it wasn't.

When we got big and started breaking America, the band members' sexual attractiveness miraculously escalated. Let's face it, there are women who see sleeping with a rock star as a trophy, a *scalp*, and it's fair to say that most of Priest were very willing to get scalped.

We found groupies in many parts of the world, but it was primarily an American phenomenon. Certain cities had reputations. There was a major groupie scene in LA and San Francisco, but it was also big in New York, Chicago, Dallas, and down in Miami.

Sometimes women would be waiting outside venues in the morning when the road crew rolled up to start setting up the show. They'd do a roadie as a way to get to the band. Other groupies were choosier and would only do the band. They thought the road crew were beneath them.

Some groupies became famous, like Pamela Des Barres. They'd have hit lists and only go with A-lister musicians for the bragging rights. Or there was Cynthia Plaster Caster in Chicago, who died this year. She used to make plaster casts of rock stars' erect dicks. I suppose it's good to have a hobby.

By now, if a band member copped off with a groupie, they did it in nicer locations than a loo cubicle—a posh hotel room, or a luxury tour bus—but the same principle applied. They weren't about to start dating, or to promise to keep in touch. It was just sex. Everyone knew the deal.

I got to know a few of the groupies who hung around Priest, and they were lovely women. I'd see them every tour. They just loved fucking musicians. I guess today you'd even call them sex workers . . . but their recompense wasn't money. It was simply hanging out with bands.

Straight society saw groupies as immoral and wrong, but I was never judgmental towards them. I saw it as all part of the rock-and-roll lifestyle. If everybody involved was a consenting adult, I figured it was just a bit of fun, with no harm or damage in it.

I watched it all going on around me and, of course, I was jealous. The band were copping off and I wanted to cop off as well. I'd see a guy in the crowd, or at an after-show party, and think, *Yeah, he's buff! I wish I could do him!* But the rules were very different for me.

The percentage of fans at a heavy metal gig who would be gay *and out* in the eighties was miniscule. I was the lead singer, but if I strolled up to a guy and started flirting and chatting him up, I'd knew I'd probably get a smack in the mouth. Plus, I feared me being found out as gay would kill the band.

So, I got virtually no action on the road. Diddly-squat. I told the story in *Confess* of accidentally wanking off a Priest fan through a truck-stop toilet glory hole. *Oops!* Plus, I met one partner, Josh, at a gig. But nearly every night ended with Lonely Rob and his right hand in a hotel room.

Although we never talked about it, the rest of Priest knew that I was gay from day one. The road crew sussed it as well, so they never asked why I didn't pursue groupies. A lot of female fans also twigged: women have way better gaydar than straight men.

But a band's singer is always the biggest scalp, and some less sussed girls would hit on me. I'd try to be kind and dissuade them nicely: "Now, now, you don't want to do anything to upset your mum!" Once they realized they weren't going to get to, ahem, jump my bones, they'd get bored and wander off.

It's funny: even now, as a gay bloke in his seventies who's been out for twenty-five years, I still get female fans giving it a go with me! I walk out of a stage door and they paw my arse and start trying it on. I guess they must think they can "turn" me. I admire their optimism.

It must be said, especially in the wake of the #MeToo movement, that not all sexual interactions between musicians and female fans are free and innocent fun. Over the years, I've been around other bands, at gigs or festivals, and I've seen things that have really upset me.

It wasn't underage girls, but grown women who were so wrecked on drugs or alcohol that they were all over the place. They just got used:

legs wide open and come one, come all. The band and the crew would all pile in and it was horrible to see.

As a gay man I've always had massive respect for women, and when I saw them behaving like that, it really disturbed me. I don't know why it should, because they were adults and entitled to do whatever they wanted to. But I just couldn't bear being around it.

Post-#MeToo, I hope and pray that sort of thing doesn't happen today. In fact, I wonder if the groupie phenomenon has largely fizzled out. Ultimately, I'm all for that hoary old metal and rock cliché, Excess All Areas, as long as nobody ends up hating themselves in the morning.

MONEY

If you listen to the Bible, the love of money is the root of all evil. I'm not sure about *that* but wealth is a huge temptation that can easily lead metal and rock bands away from focusing on their music. In fact, that love of money has been known to create the kind of awful greed that can even break up bands.

When I was a kid, growing up in a working-class household in Walsall, money and wealth were something that other people had. We weren't exactly poor as a family but every penny counted, and I had absolutely no reason to imagine that my life as an adult would ever be any different.

I certainly didn't get into music to be wealthy! I started off singing in bands as a hobby while holding down day jobs. I imagined jacking those jobs in to do a band full time would probably lead to a life of penury where I could barely afford a pint.

I was right for a long time! Priest struggled in the early years and we had to sign on or get cash-in-hand jobs both when we were starting out and when we had our miserly deal with Gull Records. It wasn't until the eighties that we started making any kind of proper money.

The real change came when *British Steel* took off. I had never had a thousand pounds, barely even a hundred pounds, in my bank account, yet suddenly I was getting cheques for tens of thousands of quid. It may sound daft but initially I found it a bit shocking.

When I first started getting those cheques, I was living in a tiny box room in a shared house with three mates on a council estate. They all worked in a local hospital, and the disparity between what they earned and what I did was suddenly glaring.

I could have felt guilty but, oddly, I didn't. I was already getting an understanding of how the music industry worked. I knew how fickle it was, and that the dosh could dry up as quickly as it had appeared. I'd read about bands who'd gone from *Top of the Pops* back to the dole.

If you work in a factory for thirty years, and get a gold watch at the end of it, there's a safety and security to your income. I knew we had none of that. If people stopped buying our records, we were done. So I didn't feel guilty about suddenly being flush. I just figured:

This can go tits up anytime! So, if we're getting well paid for our effort and our work right now, that's brill! We've been skint in this band for years, so we've earned the money we're getting now—and who knows how long it will last?

I don't remember being elated at suddenly having money. What I felt was *relief*, that the day-to-day worry of whether I could afford a bus fare, or a pint of milk, had been taken away. I'd lived under that mental strain for years and it was nice to lose it.

How you react to sudden wealth depends entirely on your character. Some bands spunk it away. I was practical with my pounds: I'd grown up seeing my mom count out my dad's pay packet and make it last for a week. I wasn't about to spend, spend, spend like Viv Nicholson!*

I was never going to go mad like that. The first thing I wanted was to move out of the tiny box room, so I bought a modest house in Walsall for cash. Then a few years later, I got a place in Phoenix, Arizona. Forty years on, those two houses are still my homes.

I'm not saying I had no indulgences. I couldn't drive but I went out and bought an Aston Martin. I guess my subconscious thought process

---

*Viv Nicholson was a working-class British woman who won £150,000 (£3.3 million today) on the football pools in 1961 and told the tabloids she would "spend, spend, spend!" She was true to her word: she splashed out on a mansion, sports cars, fur coats, and exotic holidays and was bankrupt four years later.

was: *I'm a rock star now, so I'd better buy an expensive sports car!* It was so stupid, especially as I hardly ever drove it.

My clothes also got a bit high-end fashion designer for a while, and I became more blingy in terms of gold and diamond jewelry. I never went totally over the top, though, and in my defense, well, *it was the eighties!* Everybody was doing that shit back then!

I didn't pick up any rock-star hobbies, though. I never started collecting Ferraris or buying racehorses. Material possessions aren't important to me, so I didn't stockpile Rembrandts or curate a spectacular fine-wine cellar. That behavior just never appealed to me.

I reckon more bands break up over money than anything else. The way songwriting royalties are split is a regular grievance. Priest avoided that by crediting every song equally between our three songwriters: Glenn, Ken, and me. We carried that system over when Richie replaced Ken.

After fifty years in the game, I'm financially comfortable now and at peace with that. I don't feel guilty about it. Spotify has eaten into our album sales but we still make money from touring. I think it's worth saying, though, that it's not nearly as much as people might think.

Fans might sometimes go to our arena shows, have a look around and think, *Bloody hell! There are twenty thousand people here! The tickets are £75 each! This band are making a fucking fortune!* But the reality is the mathematics are not nearly as simple as that.

When we take a gigantic Priest production out on tour, the expenses are colossal. The stage production costs alone are in excess of half a million dollars. The trucking costs, even on a relatively short tour of Europe, say, will be the same again or even more.

Crew wages will write off another half a million dollars, and that's all before we even get into the commissions for management, agents, and promoters. You chop up the pie of a tour's earnings, and the band—the people everyone is paying to see—get the smallest slice.

I've had to accept this for a long time now. When you're in a band, you make a lot of money for other people and you get what's left over. I'm not mithering about it, just pointing out that getting bigger and bigger as a band doesn't necessarily always mean that you make more money.

I get that a lot of fans don't understand that, and I don't blame them. I imagine they read that Priest fly between tour dates on a private jet and think, *Wow, they must be making hundreds of millions of dollars!* But the truth is, using the jet actually increases our workload.

As I said earlier, if we fly on a private plane, rather than sitting on our arses on a tour bus from A to B for eight hours every day, it's easier on both our minds and bodies. We're less likely to keel over, at our huge ages, and we can add more dates to the tour.

When I fly between my homes, from Phoenix to the UK, I never fly first class. I go in business. I want to fly in comfort, and I can afford not to be stuck by the toilets at the back of the plane. But I'm not stumping up silly money for a first-class seat. I still know the price and the value of things.

Nor do I splurge on fancy holidays. A lot of people work all of their lives then travel when they retire, but Thomas and I are different. We travel nonstop with Priest, so when we're off we just stay home. We've been everywhere,* so we like to hunker down in Phoenix and Walsall.

I have my sins, but a temptation for ostentatious wealth isn't one of them. I don't need twenty cars or a house with twenty bedrooms. I've got music mates who spend thousands of dollars a month on clothes, fine wine, jewelry, or cars. But that's not for me and it never will be.

I've got enough dosh for the occasional side-project. Last year, with my brother, Nigel, I launched a beer: Hails & Horns Halfords Ale. I like doing it, but I know it's never going to sell a million pints. Certainly not to a bloke like me, who's been teetotal since 1986!

Money can destroy bands if they get too much too soon. It goes to their heads and they lose all perspective. That temptation never seduced me or Priest because *we've kept it yam-yam.* We've prioritized stability and security over everything else.

---

* Except Iceland. I still want to go there.

I've never had to say, "Get thee behind me, Satan!" to money. I just like knowing that I've got enough to live the rest of my days at my current level, modest as it is. And the best thing of all is knowing that I've made my money by doing something that I love for nearly my whole life.

Because that is a wonderful feeling.

FAME AND CELEBRITY

They say that every kid, and certainly every teenager who joins a metal or rock band, longs to be famous. It's probably true, and I've just got a little word of warning about this particular temptation:

Be careful what you wish for—it might come true!

Getting famous can fuck up a young band even more than suddenly earning shitloads of money. Celebrity can easily go to the head. It may be all that a tyro singer or guitarist has dreamt of, but, when it comes along, it can bring its own special problems.

Kids today certainly want to be famous. I think they feel it's their right! I saw a thing on telly recently where a reporter went into a school and asked ten-year-olds what they wanted to be when they grew up. They all answered:

"I want to be a social media influencer!"
"I want to be a TikTok star!"

Well, that's the digital generation for you! When I was young, it never even occurred to me that I might one day get famous. I worshipped some rock stars and singers, but I never dared dream that I might become one myself. The whole idea seemed ridiculous.

Perhaps that's why, sixty years on, I still don't really think of myself as "famous." I certainly don't think of myself as a *celebrity*. What does that word, that concept, even *mean*? In my head, it's a nebulous idea. It doesn't have any real substance.

I live in dread of ever hearing myself say, "Don't you know who I am?" It's a terrible temptation and a trap that it's all too easy to fall into.

Once you start saying that, and thinking like that, you can find yourself hurtling down into . . . *a bottomless pit of shallowness.*

Psychologically, I reckon not thinking of myself as famous is linked to the fact that I can't stand listening to my own voice, whether I'm talking or singing. I wish I could get past that, but I can't. Subconsciously, I must figure, *If I don't like that, why should anyone else?*

I suppose it's super ironic that I don't feel famous when thousands and thousands of people know me as the Metal God. Yet whenever I say *that*, my tongue is wedged so firmly in my cheek that I must look like a hamster. Let's face it, yam-yams don't think of themselves as deities!

I accept that I'm a bit famous because, when I'm out and about, people recognize me and come up to me. As I said earlier, I know that's all part of my job and I accept it. The only way to avoid it is to be a recluse, and who wants to live like that?

I'm relieved that I don't have the mega-fame of someone like Ozzy or Taylor Swift, with paparazzi outside their door who trail them every time they go out. I couldn't function like that. It makes me wonder, *How the fuck do they live their lives?*

I can't deny there are good things about even my level of fame. I can get a nice table in a restaurant even if it's packed! Or I go to check in to business class on a flight, and get upgraded: *"Oh my God, it's you! I'll bump you up to first!"* I'll admit I like that! I mean, who wouldn't?!

Once you get seen as a celebrity, even if you hate the word like I do, you get offered weird things. Last year, I got asked to make a TV advert in the US for an insurance firm. When I got asked, I wondered, *Do I want to do this?*

I realized that I did. The money was good, loads of my mates had done TV ads, and the script was funny: a couple buying home insurance on a laptop as I yowled away in a corner of their living room. I just figured, *Yeah, why not? It's no different from Johnny Depp selling perfume!**

The other big TV thing that we semi-famous people get offered today is reality shows. I believe you have to think very hard about

---

*Well, maybe it's a *little* bit different from that.

taking on shows like that because, if you're not careful, they can tarnish and spoil your hard-earned reputation.

The first big music reality show, twenty years ago, was *The Osbournes*. I hated it because I thought it turned Ozzy into a cartoon character: a bumbling, falling-down idiot. But everybody loved him and it made him an even bigger star than he already was, so what the hell did I know?

Soon after, I got asked to be in *The Surreal Life*, the US reality show that had famous people living together in a mansion. Rock and rap stars like Vince Neil and MC Hammer did it, but it seemed a bit too exploitative to me, so I turned it down. It just didn't feel right.

In Britain, I got asked to do *I'm A Celebrity . . . Get Me Out of Here!* when it was still being filmed in Australia. I was tempted, because the money was ridiculously good, but we couldn't make the schedules work, and I suspect now that was probably a blessing.

I'm not sure that I fancy having cockroaches dropped on me or eating kangaroo's testicles and, without wanting to be unkind, some of the "celebrities" are a bit D-list. I mean, can you imagine Elton John going on that show? Madonna? Lady Gaga? Billie Eilish?

I'm not saying I'm anywhere near *their* level of fame, because I'm not, but I know my value and I know what I represent. I think you have to guard your reputation and not just run after the money. You need to consider what each show represents and how you'll be viewed.

By the same token, would I want to be a telly talent-show judge, just because I'm a bit famous? Some big music names have done that, and I can enjoy those shows, but they all feel too manufactured. Who the hell would want to be a judge on *The Masked Singer*? Ugh!

The funny thing about fame is that the longer you stay in the game, the more your fame increases. Now Priest, as a band, have survived for fifty years, we get regarded in a completely different way from how we were many years ago.

We get called icons, living legends, metal superstars, rock royalty—you name it! I don't think we're doing anything that different from what we were doing thirty years ago, and no one called us that stuff then! But, like most things to do with fame and celebrity, it's out of our hands.

When I get praised to the skies like that, the most important thing for me, as the front man, is not to succumb to the deadliest ailment in the metal and rock world. It can be fatal! It's LSD—Lead Singer Disease.

Lead Singer Disease is the condition that has singers believing the sun shines out of their arse and the other band members are lucky to be sharing a stage with them. It has them believing *it's all about them*. It's a nasty virus and some rock doctors believe there's no cure.

I've heard about nasty cases of LSD over the years. There was the front man who insisted that nobody looked at him as he walked to the stage pre-gig. The singer who sometimes wouldn't leave for his band's shows, by helicopter, until one hour after they were due to start. True stories!

My Black Country stoicism mostly protects me from a life-threatening case of LSD. I'm no saint, though, and even I've had my moments. There was the tour back in the day when I declared that I needed a separate dressing room from the rest of the band.

My thinking was that I'd be able to focus and get ready better before the shows if I was free of the noise and kerfuffle of the rest of the band faffing about. It didn't last: I missed the camaraderie and our pre-gig banter, and after a few shows we were all back in together.*

Fame and celebrity are such weird concepts. They are classic double-edged swords. *I don't want to be famous, but . . . I DO want to be famous!* I've been well known for so many years now that if, by some miracle, I were suddenly anonymous again, I think I'd miss it.

So, when it comes to being stopped in the street, I try to accept it in a grateful manner. I've never forgotten that it's the fans who've given me the life in metal that I love. Fame is a part of that life, and to hide away from it would be disrespectful.

In any case, if I'm having a Greta Garbo day and *vant to be alone*, I can stick my street disguise on. With my baseball cap on and my hoodie up, not many people recognize me. When the Covid pandemic came along, masks made me even harder to spot.

---

* And if I'm honest, the main reason I wanted my own room was to get a break from Ken and Glenn pecking at each other.

Or so I thought. I have one distinguishing factor that is a giveaway: my sticky-out ears. My whole family has them: *the Halford ears.* Last year, I was walking down a road in San Diego. I heard a screech of brakes as a car pulled over behind me. I glanced over.

A metalhead was jumping out of the driving seat and scrambling for his phone to take a selfie. "Hey, Rob!" he greeted me. "Awesome! I just saw those ears, and I knew it *had* to be you!"

There you go! The best way to avoid being seduced by the temptation of celebrity is to keep your feet on the ground. And if the most famous thing about you is your sticky-out ears, you *really* can't take yourself too seriously.

THE BOOK
OF LAMENTATIONS

As we near the end of my heavy metal scriptures, dear pilgrim, we have reached one that possibly contains more gospel truth than any other. And this sacred sermon is:

There is nothing better than being in a band when everything is going well. Writing and recording your metal psalms and testaments, then setting off on pilgrimages to be lauded by hundreds of thousands of disciples all around the world . . . truly, you are in heaven!

When things start going wrong, though . . . it can so easily turn to hell.

So we turn, with a heavy heart, to our Book of Lamentations—a sad but necessary examination of what happens when everything goes, as the technical term has it, tits up. No matter how closely knit and long-standing, can a band survive when everything goes to shit?

We are bands of brothers, but what happens when those brothers turn against each other and the band becomes toxic? And after decades on the road, how do groups cope when sudden illness strikes and they can no longer rely on their bodies to perform—or even their minds?

Metal never rusts, and, with willpower, you can survive anything: but it can be an infernal, diabolical struggle. So, let's raise our voices for these songs of woe in our scriptures' Book of Lamentations . . .

BAND TENSIONS

We marveled, early in *Biblical*, that metal and rock groups are bands of brothers who grow so close that they become like families. Yet not all families are happy, healthy units. What happens when those close ties become sundered and suddenly that family is at war?

Every family has its squabbles, but you always hope they are no more than that. Sometimes the jokey piss-taking that is the norm whenever young blokes get together to form a band can get out of hand. Feelings get hurt and it can take days for the fallout to be sorted out.

I have a great example of a time when harmless banter in Priest turned into a major incident. We played a handful of Scottish dates, very early in our career. The morning after one of the gigs, we were heading in our van through beautiful mountains in the Lowlands.

Our first drummer, John Hinch, was driving, and Glenn was sitting next to him. Some idle chitchat broke out about the size of the mountains.

"Look at that one!" said Glenn, pointing out one nearby mountain, its peak lost in the Scotch mist. "That's proper high, that is!"

"That's not that big!" countered John. "That's a hill, not a mountain!"

"Oh, yeah?" Glenn disagreed. "Well, I bet *you* couldn't get up it!"

"I bet you I bloody *could!*" said John. Suddenly, somehow, small talk had turned into a macho challenge.

We were due a piss stop and a short break, so John pulled up in a lay-by at the foot of the mountain. We all climbed out of the van . . . and Hinchy took off up the start of the slope like a rocket.

We stood and watched him go. It was a difficult, steep ascent but John kept going and going until he was out of sight, lost in the thick mist. We squinted, but couldn't see him. *Oh, well.* We sat at a picnic table, got out our Thermos flasks, and had a brew and a chunter.

Thirty minutes went by.

"John's tekkin' his time, ay he?" Ian noted.

He was. We carried on talking, and waiting. An hour passed. Ninety minutes. I started to wonder—should we be worried about him? Had he fallen down a crevice and broken his neck?

Two hours had gone by. We were all looking at our watches, and, by now, we really *were* worried about him. And then, suddenly, Hinchy lurched back into view.

He nearly fell over as he staggered down the last few yards of the slope. He looked bedraggled and exhausted, his trousers were torn, his shirt was ripped, and he had mud all over his face and his hands.

Oh, yeah, and there was one more notable feature. John was carrying a huge pair of deer antlers. He slammed them down on the picnic table and stared at us triumphantly.

"I did it!" he declared.

"Did what?" asked Glenn.

"I've been right to the top!" he said, pointing up at the mountain. We followed his finger. By now the mist had cleared, and the peak was towering hundreds of feet above us.

"Well, *we* never saw you," said Glenn.

"I've been to the top!" repeated John. He picked up the antlers again, and waved them at us. "Where do you think I got these from, then?"

"You could have got them from twenty feet up, for all we know," said Glenn. "We couldn't see! It was misty."

It was a deadpan wind-up. Hinchy was always highly strung and now he lost it. He went red in the face. "None of you fuckers believe me!" he yelled. "But I am the strongest bloke in this band, and I just proved it by going *right to the top* of that fucking mountain!"

There was an awkward pause, and then Glenn shrugged, as if nothing could be less important. "Whatever, mate," he said, his voice dripping with skepticism. "If you say you did it, maybe you did. Who cares?" I thought John would explode—or deck him.

It took a couple of days for that one to blow over. But it was small fry next to a personality clash in Priest that formed a major fault line in the band and was to bedevil and blight us for nearly forty years. This was the many, many tensions and fallouts between Ken and Glenn.

For decades, those two guitar titans were the propulsion, the driving force, the very *essence* of the Judas Priest sound. But that doesn't mean that they always got on. Offstage, that pair were far from harmonious: at times, they were out-and-out at war.

It's ironic that so much conflict festered between them because it was Ken who coaxed Glenn into the band! When we first decided to try having twin guitarists, Ken liked Glenn's playing in his then-group, the Flying Hat Band, and invited him to join us.

The tensions between them began early, I'd say around the time of *Sad Wings of Destiny*. I've always thought one of the causes was rooted in their backgrounds. They had very different childhoods, and we all know how much childhood experiences shape our later personalities.

Glenn came from a very comfortable upper-middle-class background in Birmingham. His mom and dad were hardworking and the family was well-established financially. It meant that Glenn had the easy manner and the confidence that kind of background can engender.

Ken was a different story. His family were more working class and not without their issues. Without going into details, it's fair to say Ken didn't have an easy upbringing. I think the resentment and insecurity he took out of that childhood are entirely understandable.

That resentment and insecurity came into play soon after Glenn joined. Glenn didn't try to take control of the band, exactly, but as a confident, forceful person, he wasn't shy to tell us what he thought Priest should be doing, musically or in terms of career strategy.

Glenn was always open to argument and discussion, but he had a vision for the band and was good at articulating it. Words didn't come so easy to Ken, and I think he thought Glenn, as our new boy, was being a bit presumptuous. Sometimes, I'd see Ken brooding:

Bloody hell! I've been here from the start, I brought you in, and now you're trying to take over? You're out of order! You need to wind your neck in, mate!

They were totally different characters and personalities and that was reflected in their guitar styles. Glenn was a very methodical, measured guitarist. He was a very *deep* player, and would practice and practice for hours to get his lead breaks just right.

Ken was a Hendrix freak, like me, and thus much more improvisational with his wah-wah pedal and his whammy bar. There was a lot more chaos and freedom in Ken's playing. They were both amazing guitarists but in totally different ways.

From Priest's perspective, this was brilliant. We didn't want two guitar players doing exactly the same thing and duplicating each other, and Ken and Glenn sounded unbelievable together. Sadly, they didn't make such sweet music when they put their guitars down.

He didn't say so much about it while he was in the band, but it's since become clear that Ken thought Glenn was getting too many lead solos. He resented having to do the rhythm guitar work while Glenn took the lead breaks in a lot of our songs.

If this happened, it wasn't a deliberate policy. Ken and Glenn would both bring riffs and guitar lines to our songwriting sessions. They had to speak up, stand up for themselves, and decide who played the leads. They had to fight hard for what they wanted.

The three of us were a songwriting triumvirate for so many years and it was an exciting process. We'd come up with a constant stream of ideas. I'd have the casting vote sometimes but I never favored Glenn over Ken, or vice versa. I would divorce myself from who'd written the riff.

That was crucial. It wouldn't work to think, *Oh, we've used Glenn's riffs in the last two songs: better choose Ken's for this one!* It was *always* all about the music and what sounded best in each song. And I was always honest and straightforward in saying what I thought.

As I said in *Confess*, I detected a definite pattern to their fallouts. Glenn might make some flippant, wind-up comment to Ken, then forget he'd said it a second later. Ken would take it to heart, brood and go mardy, and might not snap back for hours. But snap back he *would*, eventually.

It meant there would be loads of tensions and angry silences where you could have cut the air with a knife. The pair of them would simmer like a pot of milk heating up on a stove. Somebody only had to nudge the knob a fraction to the right and *whoosh!* The pot would boil over.

If they *did* have a stand-up fight, it would be in the studio, on the tour bus, or right after we came offstage. The rows were intense but never physical. I actually preferred them letting off steam by yelling at each other over the days that we had to tiptoe around them on eggshells.

I understood from very early on that was just the way it was going to be between Glenn and Ken, and I never picked sides. I was neutral: Switzerland! There were so many great things happening in the band musically that we had to just live with the flak.

That doesn't mean the tension wasn't incredibly stressful for the rest of us in the band. Ian, Dave, and I—or later, Ian, Scott, and I—would raise our eyebrows and sigh. Or we'd have a conflab between ourselves:

"Christ, Glenn and Ken aren't talking *again*! Being in this band is like constantly waiting for a volcano to erupt! Can't they just talk it out and get rid of all this bloody anger?"

If only. *If only.*

We never intervened or tried to weigh in. There were enough tensions going on in the band without us adding to them, and the easiest thing was to do nothing. We felt powerless, anyway: it was out of our hands and all rooted between Glenn and Ken.

I've seen the wonderful Metallica documentary, *Some Kind of Monster*, where they're doing group therapy and all opening up and screaming at each other, and part of me wishes we'd done that. But we just weren't those sorts of blokes. That wasn't us. It wouldn't be very yam-yam.

Occasionally, I'd be the Metal God mediator. Ken is a very emotional bloke and he'd sometimes come to me to unburden how he felt. I'd be a bit of a shoulder for him to cry on (not literally). Glenn never did. He had that masculine thing that blokes don't talk about feelings.

The sole saving grace was that they never took their tensions onstage. As soon as we got out there, it was just all about the performance, and everyone firing on all cylinders and *delivering the goods*. We were a band of brothers again. Until we got back in the dressing room.

There's no doubt that the grief between Ken and Glenn shaped some of my work decisions. As I said, I passed on being a coproducer on *Nostradamus* so that I wouldn't be stuck between their bickering at the control desk. It was also the main reason I briefly took to having my own dressing room.

In their own ways, Ken and Glenn sometimes tried working their issues out. They would go for meals, or even play golf together on days off. At times the tour banter would flow and they would rub along fine. But the toxic tensions were never far away, waiting to resurface.

For decades, it was our private dysfunction within the band. Our dirty secret. Our management obviously knew but the record label didn't, and the fans and the outside world in general didn't have a clue. We got very skilled at putting on a good face.

I don't want to exaggerate things too much. I'm not saying that Priest were always miserable at the height of our fame! We had thousands of cool times and adventures as a band of brothers. Yet the angst was always there: the scab being picked and picked, time and again.

For all the friction and turmoil, I didn't remotely see it coming when Ken walked out of the band. I thought the strife would go on forever: it was our normal. So, I could not have been more gobsmacked when he wrote to us just before the *Epitaph* tour in 2011 to say he'd quit.

I didn't want Ken to go. I'd always wanted Priest to stay together for as long as we could with the original line-up.* We all, Glenn included, made multiple attempts to reach out and get him to change his mind. But in my heart, I knew he wasn't going to do a U-turn.

Ken wrote two resignation emails. One was just a short notice that he had left the band. The second, weeks later, was a full-on attack in which he said he hated Glenn and Jayne Andrews. I've never even seen that email. I was told what was in it and it made me not want to read it.

It was a painful process, but we didn't have time to wallow and lick our wounds because we had a tour coming up. We had a major hole to fill in our band of brothers, and it was the quest that led us rapidly to our new guitar hero: Richie Faulkner.

---

* Except for our drummers, obviously. In the early years, our drum kit had a revolving door next to the stool!

When the Falcon joined, we had a sense of excitement and of making a fresh start. I also knew the tension that dominated the band for so long would dissipate, and it did. At our first gig, the metal felt as strong and potent as ever with Richie now on my right and Glenn on my left.

Glenn and Richie got on like a house on fire from day one. Where Glenn and Ken could be rivals, or even nemeses, Glenn and Richie were more like master and pupil. Glenn and Ken were the same age, but the Falcon was thirty years younger. The whole dynamic was so different.

As a huge Priest buff, Richie was a massive fan of Glenn *and* Ken. He's so passionate about the guitar, and when Glenn talked to him about sounds and techniques, he lapped it up. He saw Glenn as a well of musical knowledge and he drank from it thirstily.

Richie also slotted into Ken's place in our songwriting triumvirate. He was understandably quite nervous and intimidated at first. He would suggest ideas a little gingerly: "I've got this riff, but I'm not sure . . ."

"Just play it, Richie!" we'd say.

"OK, as long as you don't mind . . ."

"Of course we don't mind, Falcon! You're not a hired hand: you're a full member of Judas Priest!" Richie grew into the role so quickly and gave us a fresh, very positive feeling about the band. We still have it today.

Having left the band, Ken has now and again, over the years, intimated that he'd like to return. He weighs in on Priest matters in the media. He initially said he thought we'd hired Richie as a "clone" of him, which was a bit silly and a low blow. To his credit, Richie took it stoically.

When Glenn had to largely retire from playing live because of his Parkinson's, we got some fans online saying we should get Ken back.* I understand that. Fans always want "classic" line-ups of bands to get back together. Everybody wants Ace Frehley back in Kiss.

---

*Ken certainly agreed: he told the press he was "shocked and stunned" when we asked Andy Sneap to step in rather than him!

But it's not that simple. I once read David Byrne saying that people are always telling him he should reform Talking Heads. David said: "It's like being told, 'You should get back with your first wife—you guys were good together!' And I think most people would pass on that offer!"

He is right. Bands, like marriages, are complex relationships and nobody else really knows what goes on behind closed doors. The band and Ken have been a bit estranged since he left the group. It's a pity because we went through so much together, but *it is what it is.*

At the time of writing, we're due to see Ken again in November, just as this book is coming out, when Priest are inducted into the Rock and Roll Hall of Fame. It is going to be great and I just can't wait.

Of course K. K. Downing should be at our induction! Ken was there right at the start of Judas Priest. He cowrote so many of our classic songs, he stood on my right onstage for nearly forty years, and he is a huge part of our history. And all the bad stuff can't extinguish that.

When it comes down to it, all that counts is the music. That's all that matters, and that will be still be there long after all the fallouts and the dirt and the tensions are forgotten. So, Ken and Glenn had a load of tiffs: *So what?* It's all about the music. And that will go on forever.

You know what? We always say that bands are like families . . . but maybe that's wrong. The members aren't cut from the same cloth as each other, and don't have the shared heritage and background that real families do. They may be thick water—but they're not blood.

No, I prefer to go back to our original description: the tightest metal and rock groups are bands of brothers. And let's not forget: *everyone knows just how bad sibling rivalries can get . . .*

SICKNESS

When you're the young Metal God, you don't give your health a second thought. You are in your prime, your body can do whatever you want it to, and you assume that it will always be that way. You feel invincible. No, you feel *immortal.*

If I look at my younger performances with Priest, I was running around like a possessed drag queen. My moves were like heavy metal disco-dolly dancing. I suspect some might well have got a thumbs-down on *Strictly*, but who cared? I loved bombing about and putting on a show.

As a younger bloke, you don't get aches and pains, but that changes with advancing years. The aging process combines with the sheer wear and tear of being in a band to drag you down, and you get more suscep-tible to illnesses that can stop you in your tracks.

My first professional concession to growing older came when I was out of Priest. I began using a teleprompter in the Halford band for the very good reason that I'd started forgetting my lyrics. And I continued that new habit when I rejoined Priest.

My memory syntax just wasn't working like it once did. It was partly an age thing, but it's also a long-term effect of alcoholism. In any case, I'd seen other, far younger vocalists such as Jonathan Davis from Korn do the same thing, and I felt fine about it.*

Yet the first part of my body to start falling to bits was my back. Priest has taken its toll on my lumbar regions. The throwing myself around stage, the heavy stage clothes I wear, the sleeping in different hotel beds every night . . . it all combines to give your back a right kicking.

The trouble started in 2013. I went to Las Vegas to record a guest vocal on a Five Finger Death Punch track. I was in a vocal booth away from the main studio, but it had a monitor screen so that the producer, Kevin Churko, could see me.

I had a mic on a stand rather than a handheld one, and as I leaned into it to let rip on my vocal . . . *it happened.*

Argh! My fucking back!

The pain was excruciating! I reeled backward and didn't so much sit as *fall* onto a chair. I thought I would faint. *That wasn't a spasm,* I thought to myself. *That was my actual spine!*

"Rob? Are you OK?!" Kevin's concerned voice came over the monitor.

"It's my back!" I gasped. "Just give me a minute!"

---

*The irony is that now I can't always read the teleprompter properly! Eyesight is another victim of aging, and nowadays I have to wear glasses offstage.

I'd had back issues over the years. Once, in Japan, a tiny woman who looked three hundred years old had walked all over my spine and seemingly cured me. That had been OK, but I'd never experienced anything like *this* torture.

Kevin brought me a glass of water and I managed to do the vocal ... but I knew my problems were just beginning. *This felt serious.* When I left the studio, I could hardly walk. Every step was agony.

A worried Thomas got used to me having to sit down and breathe heavily after every few steps. I saw various chiropractors, who pulled me this way and that. It made bugger-all difference. I felt like my lower back was on fire.

When I had to go to New York to do a load of press interviews, I don't know how I survived the flight from San Diego to JFK. Even in first class, my seat felt like a bed of nails. When a driver met me to take me to my hotel, he had to push me to his car in a wheelchair.

Richie and I were doing interviews to promote our live DVD of the *Epitaph* tour. Except I could hardly talk through the pain. My nights in bed were spent groaning, in the fetal position. Richie pushed me across Times Square in a wheelchair to our various interviews.

He was doing that the day we left our hotel with Jayne Andrews ... and bumped into Roger Daltrey.

"Hello, Rob!" he said, looking down at me. "What's up?"

"It's me bloody back, Rog!" I moaned.

"Right! Are you doing anything now?" he asked.

"I've got to—*ouch! Fuck!*—do some promo in an hour."

"Come to my back doctor right now!" said Roger. He looked at Jayne. "Am I OK to take him?"

"Please do!" said Jayne. I think she and Richie were glad to be rid of my whining.

Roger pushed me across Central Park at a fair old lick. New Yorkers are blasé, but Roger Daltrey pushing Rob Halford in a speeding wheelchair certainly attracted a few double takes. Rog hailed a taxi and helped me into it.

"This guy has been sorting my back ever since I've been in The Who!" he said as we pulled up at a brownstone building. The elderly specialist put me in traction and used a few of his new age gadgets. It gave me a bit of relief. *A bit.*

It helped me to endure a transatlantic flight . . . but as soon as I got to London, then Walsall, I was in agony again. On the day we were to begin work on *Redeemer of Souls*, I called Glenn from home.

"Hey, Rob! How's your back?" he asked, breezily.

"I can't do it, Glenn," I said. "There's no way I can get to the studio today and sing."

"Eh? But we're set up! Everybody's on their way!"

"You don't understand. *I can't!*"

"Oh, you'll be fine when you get here. I've got you a chair!"

I was in so much pain, and so frustrated, that I burst into tears on the phone. At which point, Glenn realized how serious it was. "OK, sorry, mate," he said. "Call me when you're OK."

I felt like I'd never be OK again . . . until I went to see Spencer Harland, a neurosurgeon, in Solihull. He gave me an MRI scan that showed I had a damaged sciatic nerve at the base of my spine. Spencer operated and fixed it. *Wow!* I had never enjoyed *the absence of pain* so much!

I was lucky that a surgeon could work his magic and make the problem go away. When the next big health crisis struck Priest, it was a lot more permanent. It was when Glenn got diagnosed with Parkinson's disease.

We didn't see it coming even though we'd been aware of Glenn's hand shaking for a while. He was making occasional errors onstage and he'd apologize after the shows. I'd tell him, "Don't worry, mate, we all make mistakes! I was singing like a strangled cat tonight!"

A tipping point came when it was clear Glenn wasn't playing with his usual fluidity. He took diagnostic tests that suggested it could be down to him playing the guitar for so many years. It's a lot of work for the body, and the medics were saying it could be muscle tremors.

So, the definitive diagnosis of Parkinson's disease, in 2013, was a bolt from the blue. It was a horrible shock for all of us but, obviously, mainly for Glenn. He was very, very down when he first heard the news . . . but Glenn Tipton is an extremely resilient individual.

His medication helped to control the worst effects of the condition; he learned to live with it and he was back on top form on the *Redeemer of Souls* tour. But Parkinson's is an insidious disease; it gets worse, and by the time of *Firepower*, Glenn had no choice but to step back from playing live.

So what? He doesn't play live with us now, apart from the encores, but Glenn remains a full-time, fully contributing member of Priest. He has a big say in our decision-making and he remains just as much a part of the songwriting process as he ever was.

Glenn can still articulate his musical ideas and show them to us, and he has engineers in his studio who can help him with that. When we get together to write songs, he can still pick up a guitar and dream up riffs that blow our bloody heads off. His inventiveness hasn't dimmed.

Glenn has said to me, "When I start to sound bad, just tell me, because I will know when to stop. Don't do anything for me out of sympathy." He loves this band as much as we all do and doesn't want to do anything that is detrimental to it. I think that is fucking great.

As I've said before, I wrote the lyrics to "No Surrender" for Glenn Tipton: *"Living my life, ain't no pretender / Ready to fight with no surrender."* Glenn is no quitter, he's still valid as a musician, and he's still connected to the heart and soul of Judas Priest. Long may it continue.

Aging brings with it the increased risk of many life-threatening diseases, and the most prolific and pernicious of them is cancer. A specific strain that can afflict us older guys is prostate cancer, and that is exactly what I was diagnosed with during the Covid pandemic lockdown in the summer of 2020.

I don't want to go into too much detail on this, partly because I went into chapter and verse in a special edition of the paperback of *Confess*,* but also because I don't want to be That Old Geezer boring you to death about his ailments. But let's just say that it was a fucking shock.

I took the news in the same way that Glenn handled hearing about his Parkinson's. The first stage was shock: *"Oh, shit! I've got cancer! Why*

---

*The one with the black-edged pages, appropriately!

me? Fuck!" But as I absorbed the news over the days that followed, I resolved that I was going to fight it—and I was going to beat it.

I asked the cancer surgeon treating me, Dr. Ali, the all-important, all-consuming question: "Am I going to die?" When he assured me that I wasn't, I knew I would come through it to the other side and get back to work. Get back to Priest. I knew I wasn't finished.

It wasn't easy. There were intrusive tests, a four-hour surgery, and then two months of radiation therapy after Dr. Ali found more cancer on my prostate bed. I then had polyps removed from my colon and a tumor taken off my appendix. I survived and I count my blessings every day.

Once I had come through that, the Covid restrictions had finally lifted, and in late 2021 Priest started our *50 Heavy Metal Years* tour. We imagined that was full steam ahead. But it never rains but it pours. Which has to bring us to Richie Faulkner's major heart incident.

It was September 26, 2021, and we were playing with Metallica at the Louder Than Life festival in Kentucky. We were doing a shorter set than usual that night but it had gone down an absolute storm and the crowd were going wild as we all went off at the end of "Painkiller."

I was last off the stage and as I went into the wings, I saw the Falcon sitting on a stool holding his left knee. I thought he must have twisted his knee or pulled a ligament because his face was in anguish. There was no doubt that he was in serious pain.

I couldn't speak to him because his guitar tech, Addie, was standing over him and the crowd were chanting for us to go back out. As usual, Thomas gave me a load of picks to throw out to the fans as Priest took our final bow. Richie didn't come out to join us.

I didn't see Richie for the next thirty minutes. Wilf, our tour manager, said to stay in the dressing room and told us paramedics were looking at Richie. He might need some check-ups. We were all wondering what was going on . . . and then the Falcon walked into the dressing room.

He didn't look too bad, all things considered. Richie said the paramedics thought he had had a heart flutter and wanted to take him to hospital to do tests. *OK!* We had to get the jet to Denver, where we had two days off before our next show. We told Falcon we'd see him there.

We were in the air when Wilf started getting texts from the crew who were still on the ground in Kentucky and from Richie's partner, Maria. Richie hadn't just had a heart flutter. He had a serious heart condition and they were going to have to do immediate surgery.

It wasn't until we got to our hotel in Denver at two in the morning that we learned that Richie had a torn aorta and was in full-on emergency heart surgery. His aorta had ruptured—he had had what is called an aortic aneurysm—and it was spilling blood into his chest cavity.

Shit! I couldn't sleep all night. I told Wilf to text me immediately when he got any news. But it wasn't until the next day we found out that the Falcon had been in surgery for ten and a half hours. The doctors had told Maria beforehand there was no guarantee he would survive it.

That was understating the situation severely! When Richie came to after the surgery, the medics told him that 90 percent of patients who undergo that type of extensive heart surgery do not survive. They had had to replace five parts of his chest with mechanical components.

It's true: the Falcon is now literally *made of metal.*

I'm not sure I'd recommend it, because it's grisly, but if you watch the gig on YouTube, you can see the exact moment when Richie's aorta burst. A torn aorta feels like being stabbed in the heart. Richie carried on playing but you can see from his face that he is in utter agony.

He carried on playing "Painkiller." Talk about fucking irony!

The surgeons said it was the show that had saved him. He had been so pumped up with adrenaline that it had increased his blood flow and helped his heart to cope with what was happening to it. If he had not had that adrenaline, the outcome would have been very different.

It sounds daft but Falcon was *lucky.* He was lucky he had the adrenaline and he was lucky Priest were on before Metallica. If we'd been on last, and our fans had been leaving the venue, the traffic would have been too heavy for the ambulance to get to hospital in time to save him.

That sequence of events is extraordinary and, me being me, it makes me think that there was some spiritual intervention that helped the Falcon to survive. It's just uncanny. I think someone, or something, was telling him: *Not yet, mate! It's not your time to get called up now!*

When Richie woke up in the hospital the next day, the first thing he said was, "I've got to go. I need to get back on the road."

"You can't, Mr. Faulkner," the doctors told him. "You've had a major operation."

"But we're playing Denver! Where are my clothes?"

No chance. The remaining tour dates were obviously postponed. Richie was in the hospital for a week before he was discharged. A medical team supervised his trip home to Nashville and set him up in bed there so he could begin to recuperate.

Richie and Maria were under strict instructions from the doctors that he should have zero contact with anybody apart from immediate family as he recovered. Falcon sent me occasional texts to say he was on the mend. They were great but that was all he was allowed.

It was a few weeks later that my phone started ringing. It was a number that I didn't recognize, so I kept canceling the call. When I finally picked up, on about the fifth time, a voice said to me, "Hello Rob?"

"Yes?"

"It's Richie."

I nearly burst into tears on the spot. To suddenly, unexpectedly, hear the voice of someone I loved so much, and who had just been so close to death, was overwhelming.

So, obviously, I made it all about me.

"Falcon!" I said. "I can't believe I'm hearing your voice! It's the best thing I have ever heard in my life! Oh my God! How are you?"

Richie was laughing, which was great, and we had a bit of chitchat. At this stage, he still wasn't able even to hold a guitar, because the weight of it could wrench his chest and delay his recovery. Even so, all that he wanted to talk about was when we could pick up the tour again.

I could tell he was on the mend, and I knew that for sure a few weeks later. Because a mate texted me.

"Hey, do you know Richie is live on Instagram right now?" they asked.

"What?" I texted back. "You are fucking joking!"

"He is! He's playing guitar and he's sounding great. Have a look!"

I did, and his playing sounded as sharp as ever. He was back on top of his game—and just six months after Richie survived one of the most complex medical procedures a human can endure, Priest picked up the North American leg of the *50 Heavy Metal Years* tour in March 2022.

Richie's surgeons were delighted with his progress and his prognosis was to make a full recovery. *Which he has.* His doctors worried for a bit that flying could be an issue, as air travel expands and contracts internal organs, but they've given him the green light and he's back on the jet.

Richie came back as good as new and raring to go, and it's like his heart thing never happened! He never mentions it: all he wants to talk about is Priest's plans for the future. He's the same old Falcon he always was and it's fucking brilliant.

When you get to our huge ages, the health ailments keep on coming. While we were off the road as Richie recuperated, Ian took advantage of the downtime to have a double hernia operation. Which was also due to the wear and tear of life on the road.

Bass guitars are heavy contraptions and Ian Hill has been wielding one in studios and on stages around the world for fifty years. It may not be hard labor like our dads used to do every day in the foundries of the Black Country, but it still takes its toll!

With my cancer, Glenn's Parkinson's, Richie's heart, and Ian's hernia, Priest are a right bunch of old fogies nowadays! We sit around in the dressing room comparing our ailments, and, like typical blokes who refuse to take anything seriously, we take the piss out of each other.

We all moan about our bad backs and make groaning, granddad noises when we have to get up from a chair. We have to keep going for a wee. I sometimes wonder if we've turned into a heavy metal version of *Last of the Summer Wine.**

---

* *Last of the Summer Wine* was an inexplicably long-running BBC sitcom about three Yorkshire pensioners getting up to mischief. For some reason, it always seemed to end with them whizzing down a country lane in a tin bathtub. That's *one* thing Priest have never done. Yet.

The other day, we had a band video conference call. I began it by asking the others: "Have you all moved your bowels today?" Because, as you move into your autumn years, you realize you need at least one good bowel movement a day. Otherwise, you feel tired and irritable.

When I'm writing our contract riders now, I put on some prunes or prune juice to keep us regular. We always ask for laxative pills and paracetamol, too. We're all on so many pills that there's a corner of the rider table that looks like a medicine cabinet.

There's no doubt that having so many major health issues among us has made Priest feel even more precious to us. We realize how quickly this band could get whipped away from us. But until we get so poorly that we can't totter onto the stage, we'll carry on doing what yam-yams do:

We'll get on with it.

MENTAL HEALTH ISSUES

There are so many diseases and ailments that can stymie a rock or metal band. Yet another kind of illness that is far less visible can be just as insidious and dangerous. I'm talking about mental health issues.

It must seem inconceivable to outsiders that any rock star should want to kill themselves. *Shit, they lead lives of creativity, success, fame, wealth, travel, being worshipped, and as much drink, drugs, and sex as they want: What the fuck is there not to like?*

Fans look at music stars and think they are somehow different: more complete. They see them as heroes and they think heroes are infallible. But musicians are just as prone to doubt, despair, self-hate, and suicidal thoughts as the next poor bastard.

Over the years, there have been many rock-and-roll suicides. These stars found it impossible to cope with the pressures of fame and the confusion in their heads. There was poor Kurt Cobain, shooting himself dead in 1994 despite being the singer of arguably the biggest rock band in the world. There was Chris Cornell, killing himself in his hotel room just after a Soundgarden show. Chester Bennington of Linkin Park: another one who couldn't go on.

Why the hell would they do this? Well, every case is different, and you have to respect that. But there are common factors and pressures.

Every metal and rock musician starts out yearning to be successful and famous. But sometimes they find that success and fame are not what they expected or wanted at all. The pressures of stardom and celebrity weigh them down until they crack.

Kurt Cobain didn't want celebrity. He loathed it. All he ever wanted was to write songs and play his guitar, but he had *everything else* piled on top of him. He lost all of his privacy and that is a lot to bear.

There's a line of thought that music artists are more prone to depression and mental health issues. As creative people, they wear their hearts on their sleeves and often write lyrics that lay themselves wide open. That means they're vulnerable to the world. They're *exposed*.

They're exposed, and they're living in volatile conditions. On tour, they are away from their families and friends for months at a time. They may miss seeing their children grow up. And faced with that, it's easy to put fuel on the fire and turn to drink and drugs.

That's what *I* did for years. I lived a lie by pretending I wasn't gay, and it meant I needed the escape route of oblivion every night. I was as prone to depression, which I think I got from my mom's side of the family, as I was to alcoholism and addiction. It was a potent fucking cocktail.

Looking back, I was going through extreme mental health issues, which eventually drove me to attempt suicide, yet I never talked to anybody about it. People normally confide in their partner, but I was either on my own or with somebody unsuitable. Essentially, *I was alone*.

Priest were my best mates, my band of brothers, but we'd never have talked to one another about feeling down or mental pain. We were the generation brought up to believe that men don't have feelings. And, even if they do, they certainly don't talk about them!

This lack of communication can be fatal. You hear terrible tales of rock stars killing themselves, and then their bandmates and managers saying, *"I never knew anything was wrong! He seemed fine last time I spoke to him! He was a little quiet but, you know . . ."*

Mental illness is so hard to spot. I told the terrible story in *Confess* of Brad, my lover in the eighties, shooting himself dead minutes after we had had a row. He was my partner, my soulmate, yet even I had not seen he was in such a dark place. I didn't see the danger.

Could I have done more? Saved him? It's the question that haunts any metal or rock musician when a friend or colleague kills himself. *Why didn't I call him? Why didn't I send a text?* You're eaten up by guilt and you partly blame yourself for the loss.

People talk about the 27 Club, and it's true that a lot of musicians have taken their own lives at that age. When you're young, you're intense and serious about your art, and you're not as grounded as in your later years. If you're not careful, you can believe your own hype: your own myth.

Young rock stars read that they are geniuses, they have fans screaming at them and girls throwing themselves at them every night, and they start to think they are God's gift. They can get into the stupid mindset where everything is about them:

"Hey, the limo isn't cold enough! I distinctly said it had to be at sixty-five degrees and, look, it's sixty-six degrees! I can't possibly get in there! Fire the fucking chauffeur!"

They believe they're invincible; they believe their own publicity . . . and it only takes a bad review in the music press, a wrist merchant laughing at them, to bring them crashing down into self-doubt and angst. They're in a mentally precarious position and it's a long way down.

The media can do terrible damage to famous people. I look at poor Amy Winehouse—again, only twenty-seven, struggling with drink and drugs, pursued by paparazzi*—and my heart goes out to her. She never had a chance, any more than did Marilyn Monroe or Judy Garland.

I know some rock stars struggle with fans' expectations. It's great to be applauded but some fans elevate you so high that they expect

---

*Paparazzi are scum: horrible, nasty, mean, uncaring people. I think when they chase some poor, vulnerable soul to their death, as they did Princess Diana, they should be tried as criminals. They should be in jail.

you to be some kind of role model. They expect perfection, and you're just a muddled bloke trying to make sense of your *own* life.

It's a cliché that it's lonely at the top, but, like all clichés, I think there's something in it. There's never been a support network for musicians. There are groups like MusiCares, giving both mental health and welfare help, but most troubled rockers have had to struggle on alone, in silence.

Yet things are changing. There's been a bit of a revolution in society, and I think it's a marvelous thing. In the last few years, we've finally seen everybody from musicians to movie stars, from sportspeople to even members of the British Royal Family, talking about mental health issues.

Everybody has been opening up. It's been the antidote to the attitude in my generation, especially among blokes, that it's "weak" to talk about your feelings. It's overdue, and it's necessary, because every single person on the planet has mental pressures to deal with.

I mean, I'm a down-to-earth, positive bloke from the Black Country, and even I lost my way and lost the plot back in the eighties! So, the next time a metal or rock star struggles with mental health issues, they need to be frank and talk about them. And we all need to listen.

Because it might just save lives.

THE BOOK
OF REVELATIONS

I confessed at the very start of *Biblical* that I hardly read the Bible. Well, I'll make an exception for its show-closer, its big number to round things off: the Book of Revelation. *That* crazy volume describes an apocalypse that is well worthy of a ton of SFX and pyro.

I mean, just look at its cast! An Angel of Woe, the Angel of Seven Thunders, the Beast of the Sea, the lamb-horned Beast of the Earth, the Seven-Headed Dragon, scorpion-tailed locusts, plague angels, the Whore of Babylon, and the Four Horsemen of the Apocalypse!

Whoa! Now you're talking! The Book of Revelation is certainly the most heavy metal chapter in the Bible! In fact, come to think of it, it sounds rather a lot like Priest's track listing for *Nostradamus!*

Yet, rather than predicting the end of the world, I'd prefer to close up my scriptures with a Book of Revelations that asks: What have I learned from my fifty sacred years in heavy metal? What divine wisdom have I picked up on my many pilgrimages? And has it all been worth it?

I'll answer that last one first: *fuck, yes!* Back in the mists of time, at the beginning of this book, I talked in the Book of Genesis about the need for escapism that drives kids to form a band. I remembered how, as a boy, I imagined being a rock star to be the most amazing life in the world.

Well, guess what? *It is!* I have lived such an unbelievable life in Judas Priest and I am still living it now. It's not all been easy, but it has given me the escape and the creativity and the adventure that I craved. That I *needed.* I count my blessings and I am always grateful for it.

What am I most grateful for? Firstly, that our creativity connected with people and with the world. There is nothing worse than writing a song, or writing a book, or painting a painting, and everybody sniffing and looking in the other direction. Artists need acceptance and validation.

Luckily, we got them. We started off asking ourselves questions: *Will we ever get on the radio? Or get on TV? Will we ever get in the charts? Will we ever sell out Birmingham Odeon? Get to America? Get a gold disc?* We did them all—and it has been, well, a revelation!

Although I longed to escape, I'm pleased I had the upbringing I did. Coming from a working-class background taught me that you don't get anywhere without hard work. If that slog brings you rewards, well, you deserve them. I know that Priest deserve to be where we are today.

Growing up on a Black Country council estate, the wider world seemed out of reach. We have been lucky enough to go and see those far-flung places: New York. Sydney. Jakarta. Bogota. Rio de Janeiro. Metal is our passport and it's shown us the world. I've never taken that for granted.

One revelation that fifty years in metal has taught me is that fame and celebrity can fuck you up big time. I've seen too many musicians, rock stars, and even friends get caught up in their own egos and crash and burn. Because Lead Singer Disease can be incurable.

You have to lead a double life. It's walking a thin line, but, thankfully, I have learned to do it. When I walk onstage, I am the Metal God for two hours. But off it, I am still plain old Robert John Arthur Halford, a mild-mannered bloke from Walsall who likes a nice pickled egg.

Despite that, as I said earlier, my life has followed quite a textbook rock star trajectory: obscurity, breakthrough, fame, crash, recovery. It all reminds me of Patsy and Edina in *Absolutely Fabulous,* flicking through a copy of *Hello!* magazine and pointing at the pictures:

"Look, darling! SHE had it all. SHE lost it all. Oh, and SHE has got it all again . . ."

I never lost it all, not quite, but I learned that very few people maintain an unbroken trajectory of success in metal, rock, or any branch of show business. *Everyone* has a heartbreak story to tell. It's the human condition. That which does not kill you makes you stronger.

It means that I don't have any regrets. I don't like the word *regret*: it's too brittle and negative. Life is for living and if I look back at my life, even the darkest and most painful times, I wouldn't change a thing.

Yeah, what a revelation!

I've learned: life isn't a smooth ride up and down the M1 or along the 405. It's full of potholes and bad weather, and slipping and sliding, and crashing on the A1M and getting a lift to the gig from a farmer! It's ups and downs. The big challenge is how you get through those obstacles.

If I compare myself today with the Rob who joined Judas Priest nearly fifty years ago, I think we're surprisingly similar. I'm more satisfied and content and at peace with myself than I was then. I'm grateful for that as well, because I could very easily not be here now.

The big similarity is that I still have the same drive and passion and commitment to Priest that I had then. It hasn't diminished. I count my blessings every day that I'm in a band that is still active and has profile and is still listened to. A band that is still *relevant*.

Judas Priest is at the center of my world today as it has been (apart from that accidental break) since 1973. We're still in it to win it. It's not "mission accomplished." That never comes: *it doesn't exist*. We just carry on defending the heavy metal faith.

Getting older has a few advantages. I'm more confident in how I do my job today, and I have been since I got sober. That goes for in the studio *and* playing live. I've picked up craftsmanship and musicianship as I've gone along, sometimes without even realizing it.

Aging also takes its toll, of course. It shapes how I can do my job. I have an older voice now, both speaking *and* singing, and it can be frustrating. The texture of my voice has changed, and there are certain things that I could do with it forty years ago that I can't replicate now.

It's a deterioration that's unique to singers. Most guitarists, bassists, and drummers in their seventies are still able to do what they were doing in their twenties. It's harder for vocalists. I've had to adjust my approach to singing in recent years.

The way I sing "Painkiller" now is nothing like my original performance. Well, Priest can either stop playing the song, or I can do a 2022 version of a vocal I laid down in 1990. I prefer *that* option! After all I've put my vocal cords through over fifty years, the fact that I have anything left at all is a miracle to me.

I also think there's something comforting, both for me *and* for fans, to hear more *weathered* versions of my vocals on our classic songs. It's an older voice: well, I'm an older man now! It reflects the journey of life that we're all on. It's a revelation.

The same goes for our live performances. I can't charge around the stage like a demented drag queen anymore. I know that if I tried to do that, I would be huffing and puffing too much to sing! I've had to adapt and perform it a different way.

Nowadays, I *stroll* around stage a lot. Sometimes, I finish a show and feel as if I've been running all over the place. Then I watch it back and see I was sauntering as if I was in Walsall Arboretum with Thomas on a Sunday afternoon! I'm turning into the Val Doonican of heavy metal.*

Well, I'm exaggerating. I still give our shows all the energy I can. If you watch closely, you'll see from my face that it can be hard work for me. That's OK. I grew up among grafters who put in a shift in the factories each day. I've got a working-class ethic. Your job *should* be hard work.

I see Mick Jagger gyrating and I marvel at what he can still do on a stage at nearly eighty years old, but he's unique—in fact, I'm not sure he's human! Personally, I have to take a *statelier* approach nowadays. As my early hero, the late Quentin Crisp, would say: *I'm the stately homo of heavy metal.*

---

*Val Doonican was an easy-listening Irish crooner who frequently sang his ballads from a rocking chair. Trust me: if I ever bring a rocking chair onstage with Priest, I'll *know* it's time to pack it in.

Here's one revelation that I learned very recently: I'm still as steeped in Priest and as intense about the band as I always have been, and thank God for that! And I am also still just as capable of making preposterous cock-ups.

While we were kicking our heels at the end of 2021 and the *50 Heavy Metal Years* tour was on hold as Richie recuperated, an idea took hold of me which became a fixation. It was basically this: *What would Judas Priest sound like if we went back to being a four-piece?*

When I joined the band back in 1973, we were a four-piece up until we recruited Glenn to flesh out our sound. When Glenn had been forced to dip out of playing live around the time of *Firepower*, our coproducer, Andy Sneap, stepped in to play with the live band and since then has done us, and himself, proud.

It was no reflection on Andy, who is a great guitarist and a great guy, but I began to think: Priest are nearing our final years now. There are four long-standing members: *me, Ian, Richie, and Scott. Should we go out the same way as we came in?*

I spoke to the rest of the band about my idea. They were surprised, to say the least, but they could see that I felt strongly about it. Their basic response could be summed up as: *We're not sure about this, Rob, but if it means this much to you, we'll give it a go!*

Was it asking a lot of Richie, recovering from a major heart incident, to shoulder all of the guitar work? He assured me he could do it if he had to. Tom Allom made me a recording of Priest's set at Bloodstock 2021 with just one guitar: Richie's. We still sounded colossal. *OK! It can work!*

I also wanted to bring Ian more into the spotlight. Ian Hill has spent fifty years playing bass for Judas Priest in the shadows at the back of the stage. Ian is very dramatic and powerful to watch and I wanted to put him at the front, where he belongs.

The band let me have my way and so it was time to tell Andy that Priest were going to be a foursome again, meaning he was out of the line-up. I didn't want to do it in a cowardly way, via management or an email, so I had a FaceTime call with him. I explained it was all my idea, that he was still part of the Priest family, and that I wanted him to go on coproducing our albums.

Andy, as was to be expected, was taken aback. "Rob, it's your band," he said. "You have to do what you want to do. I'm just doing the job that you offered me. Thank you for the opportunity." He let the news sink in for about three days and then he FaceTimed me again.

"Look, Rob, I've had the best three years of my life in this band," he told me. "I just hope I'm not going because I've been shit or I've caused any trouble." *What a cool guy.* I gave him the classic break-up line: "No, it's not you, it's me!"—which was true—and we went our separate ways.

Then we announced the news. And the shit absolutely hit the fan.

When we put out a statement, at the start of January 2022, that Priest would "celebrate our fiftieth anniversary as an even more powerful, relentless four-piece heavy metal band," I expected some pushback. I don't think I realized quite how much. It was a *Biblical* tsunami.

Everywhere you looked, from social media to metal websites to rock radio to music commentators, the reaction was negative. If I might be allowed to summarize the consensus view, it was:

"What?! This is madness! Judas Priest are THE classic twin-guitar, five-piece heavy metal band, and you have been for nearly fifty years! You invented the sound! You define it! Are you guys fucking crazy???"

There was not a dissenting voice to be heard. It was, not to put too fine a point on it, a PR disaster. And we quickly arranged another band conference call.

Everybody was quite shaken by the strength of the opposition. I can be a stubborn sod, and I was still sort-of saying that we should give it a go: "Come on! The fans don't even know what it will sound like yet!" But I quickly realized I was in a minority of one.

Glenn was having second thoughts. Richie was having second thoughts and argued his case very articulately. Ian said he would go along with the band's majority view. And Scott listened closely to both sides of the argument, then put his finger on the nub of the matter.

"If I can just ask," he said, "what do we *gain* from this?"

It was a bloody good question and it cut through all the chatter: *What do we gain from this?* And I realized the answer was: nothing. *Fuck-all.* It was just me, chasing a vague, nebulous idea that had appeared in my head from nowhere. Chasing it and fixating on it.

It was me maybe, just maybe, losing the plot.

I backed down and agreed with Scott. We quickly decided to forget the idea, retract the statement, and reach out to Andy to see if he'd forgive us and rejoin the band. But how should we do it?

"Let's not faff about," I said. "Let's get him on this conference call right now."

We dialed his number and Andy picked up after a few rings.

"Hello?"

"Hello, Andy," I said. "It's Rob."

"And Glenn," said Glenn.

"And Ian," said Ian.

"And Richie," said Richie.

"And Scott," said Scott.

There was a pause as Andy absorbed the situation and then, with his customary Derbyshire directness, he came straight to the point.

"I'm back in the band then, am I?" he asked.

At which point we all fell about laughing. Yes, Andy was back in the band. And thank fuck for that. We announced his return and, just to make sure nobody was in any doubt, I talked to *Loudwire* about it. I didn't mince my words.

"That all came from me. It didn't come from the band," I said. "And it blew up in my face. To go back to being just a four-piece now would have been just not right; ridiculous; crazy; insane; off my rocker . . . but I'm not the first musician to have a crazy idea!"

And that was that. Until, inevitably, Ken popped up in the press a few days later, saying he'd found our short-lived decision to return to being a four-piece "insulting" and "a slap in the face" that would have negated our entire band history. *Ah, good old Ken!*

So, one revelation is that Judas Priest are definitely meant to be a five-piece, and will remain so until we finally pull down the curtain on the band. *And when might that be?*

The first thing to say is that I don't want Priest to end. I wish we could have another fifty years! And fans never want bands to end, because they have a relationship with them, and with their music, that in some cases has lasted their entire life.

Fans love that connectivity. It's reassuring to know that there will be more music to listen to; more albums to buy; more chances to see the band live, one or two or three years down the line. Groups like us are part of their lives. *Why would they want that to end?*

I like how attitudes towards old musicians have changed over the years. In the Old Testament days of the seventies, especially when punk was around, music was seen as a young person's game. In fact, bands that hung around into their later years got laughed at.

I was guilty of it myself. I'd look at a singer who was notably getting old and lined and think, *Time you knocked it on the head, mate!* I mean, when you start playing in a band in your twenties, you can't conceive of still doing it at seventy: even *forty* sounds ancient! Yet here we are, still doing it.

We accept that we can't go on forever. Glenn, Ian, and I are all in our seventies now. Like most established metal and rock bands, Priest work in a three-year cycle of making an album, touring it around the world, and then resting. We're just starting another cycle now.

We'll finish making the album we're working on now and then tour it, which will take us to 2024 or even '25. By then, I'll be well into my mid-seventies. I guess we'll see how we all feel then—and whether we're still in good health! We certainly all know how health issues can strike us down.

I don't *feel* like we're winding down. I still have a wish list of things I'd like Priest to do and places I'd like us to go. I want to spread the metal word in countries we've never played: Iceland, India, South Africa. And I *still* want to see that opera or ballet interpretation of *Nostradamus*.

I hope we do a Las Vegas residency. People used to sneer at artists who did that, picturing the fat Elvis doing cabaret, but that stigma has long gone. Nowadays, artists like Celine Dion, Elton John, Rod Stewart, or Adele will happily plonk themselves in Vegas for a year.

That would be too long, but metal and rock bands like Mötley Crüe and Aerosmith have played Vegas for weeks or months at a time. They do Friday-Saturday-Sunday weekend residences, and I'd love Priest to do something like that.

It suits a personal vision I've long had of my exit strategy from music. I picture myself with just a pianist, crooning in an off-street dive bar. I'll tell the seated crowd: "Now, here's a Sinatra-style version of 'Living After Midnight.' You've been a lovely audience! Drive safely, and don't forget to buy a T-shirt before you go!"

So, who knows? I might well love Priest in Vegas!

☦

If I had a time machine, and could go back to the start of my time in Priest, what revelations would I give to my twenty-one-year-old self?

Well, I'd advise him that you need conviction, drive, passion, and energy to make it in metal or rock . . . but I'd be wasting my words! I instinctively knew those things already by that age, and, in any case, people in their twenties don't listen to boring seventy-year-olds!

If a bald bloke with a white beard appeared and started gabbing in my ear when I was twenty-one, I'd have thought, *Huh? What do YOU know about me and my life? You're just an old man!* And I'd have been right. That's how life works. You have to make your own mistakes.

We've made mistakes over the last fifty years, but we've got a whole lot right as well. The thing that I'll be proudest of when Priest finally pack it in is that we'll be leaving behind a treasure trail of valuable and, I think, important music. A proper musical legacy.

It may be that we'll put an end to touring but keep the band going to do one-off shows or albums: the thing we intended to do when we did the "farewell" *Epitaph* tour in 2011! Coming off the road doesn't have to mean the end of everything. *That's* one revelation I've learned.

I'm moving into my heavy metal twilight years now. When I ride off into the sunset on my Harley, like Ronald Reagan on his horse, I think I'll feel satisfied with what we've done. I won't feel sadness and regret at the end of Priest. It will be a more typical yam-yam reaction:

"That's it, then—job done!"

Metal has been good to me. It's shown me the answer to the question I used to ask myself as a lad, when I used to walk to the end of Kelvin Road and wonder: *What's out there?* Well, now I know. *A fuck of a lot!* And I've soaked it all in.

As a kid, I didn't want to live a life where I'd lie on my deathbed at the end of it and think, *Huh, that was a bit boring!* I think it's fair to say that the life I've ended up living—so far!—has put paid to that danger.

I mean, here is an incontrovertible fact:

It's estimated that well over one hundred billion humans have lived on this planet since the species began. And I am the only one—THE ONLY ONE—who became a gay Heavy Metal God.

I mean, think about it, right? What were the odds?

I feel incredibly lucky to have lived the long metal life I have. I know how quickly, and easily, it can be taken away. I had a mate called Tom Leighton who was the singer and guitarist in a Cannock band named Wolf Jaw. They were good and I followed them online.

Wolf Jaw were starting out on the long journey that Priest began fifty years ago. They might have made it or they might not—who knows?—but Tom never will, because the poor guy had a heart attack and died in his sleep next to his wife, Heather, in October 2021. So sudden. So young. RIP Tom.

I'm not afraid of death. I'm in my seventies. I know it's not so far away. But I want to die on my terms: *when I'm ready.* That's why my cancer scare freaked me out. I felt it had suddenly loomed up, from nowhere, and told me: "*Oi, mate! That's it! Time's up!*"

And I didn't like that. *Because I wasn't ready.*

I've lived a *Biblical* life and I'm happy I've taken this chance to share a few of its revelations before I'm six feet under. Writing this book has also made me wonder what epitaph I want on my grave when I'm laid to rest at St. Matthew's Church, at the top of Walsall.

I think that I'd like inscriptions on both sides of my tombstone, please. On the front, it will say:

SCREAMING MY TITS OFF
IN HEAVEN OR HELL!

Then walk round the back, and you'll read this:

TESTING . . . TESTING . . .
ONE, TWO, THREE . . .

And *there* are two great final heavy metal scriptures for you!

INDEX

SONG CREDITS